# GWYNNE'S LATIN

## ABOUT THE AUTHOR

Formerly a successful businessman, N. M. Gwynne has for many years been teaching just about every sort of subject to just about every sort of pupil in just about every sort of circumstance – English, Latin, Greek, French, German, mathematics, history, classical philosophy, natural medicine, the elements of music and 'How to start up and run your own business' – in lecture-halls, large classrooms, small classrooms and homes – to pupils aged from three years old to over seventy – of many different nationalities and in several different countries – and since 2007 'face to face' over the Internet.

His teaching methods are very much in accordance with the traditional, common-sense ones, refined over the centuries, that were used almost everywhere until they were abolished worldwide in the 1960s and subsequently. His teaching has been considered sufficiently remarkable – both in its unusualness in today's world and in its genuinely speedy effectiveness – to have featured in newspaper and magazine articles and on television and radio programmes.

*To the pupils, of all ages from youngest to oldest,
to whom I have taught Latin in many parts of the world,
and especially to those whose difficulties in learning Latin
have contributed significantly to what is in this book.*

# GWYNNE'S LATIN

THE *ULTIMATE* INTRODUCTION TO LATIN
INCLUDING THE LATIN IN EVERYDAY ENGLISH

For its own sake, to improve your English,
and to make you better at everything else.

N. M. Gwynne, M.A. (Oxon)

EBURY
PRESS

6 8 10 9 7 5

First published by Ebury Press in 2014, an imprint of Ebury Publishing
A Random House Group Company

The Random House Group Limited Reg. No. 954009

Addresses for companies within the Random House Group can be
found at www.randomhouse.co.uk

A CIP catalogue record for this book is available from the British Library

The Random House Group Limited supports the Forest Stewardship
Council® (FSC®), the leading international forest-certification
organisation. Our books carrying the FSC label are printed on FSC®-
certified paper. FSC is the only forest-certification scheme supported by
the leading environmental organisations, including Greenpeace. Our paper
procurement policy can be found at www.randomhouse.co.uk/environment

Printed and bound in Great Britain by Clays Ltd, St Ives PLC

ISBN 9780091957438

To buy books by your favourite authors and register for offers visit
www.randomhouse.co.uk

# CONTENTS

# PREFACE

W HAT CAN YOU reasonably hope to have achieved by the time you come to the end of this small volume, assuming that you use it throughout as I urge you to?

One answer is: you could know about as much Latin as a reasonably intelligent eleven- or twelve-year-old would have known in the days when I was at school. To know as much as that would have been the result of a considerable amount of exposure to Latin – for instance, at one of the best-known preparatory schools there were ninety minutes a day six days a week of Latin lessons during the eight months per annum of school time.

Another answer is: *many* times more Latin than will be known, in almost all cases, by highly intelligent scholars of today who have passed all their Latin exams and are studying Classics at any of the top universities in Britain.

A third answer, carrying the advantage of not varying according to time and circumstance, is that you will be in a position, with some help from a dictionary, to embark with pleasure on some of the greatest and in every way most remarkable works of literature ever written, starting with the traditional first Classical text for schoolboys, Julius Caesar's *Gallic Wars*. What that means is that those who use this book as methodically as I recommend will have learnt a very large amount of Latin, including all the most important grammar – word forms and sentence constructions – and plenty of vocabulary and much else.

One last answer under this heading is that you cannot fail to have improved radically – and I really do mean from the roots upwards – your grasp and mastery of English, for a number of reasons.

One is the point made by all promoters of Latin, and by me in Chapter One: that Latin is the source of more than half of the

English vocabulary, and to know the source of any word is to understand it better. For instance, 'radically', just used in the last sentence, comes from the Latin word **radix** meaning 'root'.

A second is that translating English into Latin always requires one to reorganise in one's mind, sometimes very greatly, the English sentence being translated, in order to put it into a form which will work in Latin; and this cannot be done without a clear understanding of how the English sentence was put together.

A third reason is that, when translating from Latin into English, one must first do a translation that merely makes sense, and sometimes only just, and then revise it thoroughly into what reads well in English.

Surely not to be ignored is that the English language includes hudnreds of words and idioms which are in untranslated Latin. By the end of this book you will be able to translate them, in most cases effortlessly, and this will make their meaning very much clearer than if you were to rely solely on what a dictionary says as to their meaning. This book indeed devotes exercises to the practice of dealing with everyday 'Latin–English', from **affidavit** to **e.g.** to **status quo** to **vice versa** and **vox populi**, and you cannot fail to find this a useful feature.

I T IS NOW worth making mention of what I believe to be the single gap in what this book has to offer you if used in isolation.

In one respect, this book is complete as far as it goes. It includes all the information needed in order to learn Latin up to a much more advanced level than, as just mentioned, ordinary students specialising in Classics will have reached by the time they have arrived at any of the leading universities.

In another respect, however, the book is incomplete. Nor could it be otherwise, other than at about three times its present length.

The reason is this.

If you use this book as I recommend, you can acquire a knowledge of Latin vocabulary and grammar that is so extensive that plucking out of your memory the words you want and declining or conjugating them is effortless and enjoyable. You can also gain a clear *understanding* of how to use them.

That, however, is far from the same as being able to use them accurately and reliably in sentences, whether translating from English into Latin or from Latin into English. For that you need *practice*, and much of it. Every single syntactical construction you learn must be practised – and practised and practised – until putting clauses and sentences together is, at least at this stage of reasonably elementary Latin, so easy as to be all but instinctive, virtually like a reflex action. You need to be able to see at a glance, without having to puzzle it out, that the Latin for 'The good slaves love their country's Queen' is '**Servi boni patriae reginam amant**', and vice versa if translating from Latin into English.

In this book you will find enough exercises to help you *understand* the various constructions and words, but not for the extensive practice needed for them to *become part of you*, which, as I say, is beyond the reach of a book of this convenient size. For that purpose, therefore, a website has been set up, where you will find as much practice material as you could need for developing a real mastery of what this book covers, and to give you the confidence that you are on top of the subject.

IT IS PERHAPS worth highlighting here that I believe there to be two chapters in this book that include much material which, although important, will not be found in any other Latin textbook written within the living memory of even the oldest of us, at least in the thoroughness that it is given here. These are the chapters (a) on the techniques and skills of translating Latin into English, and (b) on Latin word order and how variations in word order can dramatically change the meaning of clauses and sentences.

FINALLY, IT IS as well that, for the sake of good order, I make reference to two conventions used in this book, which had always been all but universal but recently have been largely and unsatisfactorily replaced.

The first is the now-contentious problem of how to express what for the entire history of English literature until the last few decades was the all-embracing 'he'.

Up till these last few decades, the pronoun 'he', when referring to an unnamed person, was uncontentiously used to include both sexes. It was therefore used for two separate purposes: to refer to members of the male sex in particular, and to refer to a member of the human race of either sex. In Britain at least, the second use was never considered remotely inappropriate or uncomfortable – female speakers and female authors routinely used it in this general sense without hesitation or objection. This of course has changed, the use of 'he' to embrace both 'he' and 'she' now being held by some people to be offensive.

The result has been unfortunate, to say the least. Saying 'he or she', 'him or her' and 'his or hers', when speaking about people generally, is often disagreeably clumsy. To overcome this defect, the words 'they', 'them' and 'their' are now often used in place of 'he or she' and the rest, even when referring to only one person, as in: 'Any*one* who considers this modern practice acceptable has lost *their* mind.'

There have been authoritative protests against this practice, even among highly respected authors of today – for example, by the most recent *Economist*'s authoritative *Style Guide* and by Simon Heffer, who in his *Strictly English* labels it 'abominable'.

In principle, I fully agree with the *Economist* and with Heffer. There is, however, a problem with following them completely. This is that the avoidance of the traditional, all-embracing 'he' is now so widely entrenched that this use of 'he' may be genuinely new to some readers and possibly annoying to others.

Since I wish my readers to be able to concentrate their full attention on the *information* I am putting in front of them, without being distracted by the *manner* in which I present it, I have adopted a compromise. On the one hand, I have taken trouble to avoid using 'he' to cover both sexes where I can easily do so. On the other hand, when it happens that artificially avoiding the traditional 'he' would result in awkwardness in the wording of a sentence, I have followed the traditional means of avoiding that awkwardness. Please be assured, therefore, on the few occasions that you see the all-embracing 'he' or equivalent, that it is occurring without any offence being intended.

The other convention under this heading that seems worth my making reference to is the practice, used in all the many Latin textbooks published in the last few decades that I have come across, of starting Latin sentences without a capital letter for the first word, while, however, still using capital letters at the start of proper nouns such as **Roma** and **Caesar**. I am certainly not opposed to change when change results in improvement, but in this instance I can see only very good reason for staying with tradition.

The impression given by textbooks which start Latin sentences in the modern way without initial capital letters is that the sentences are being written as the classical authors wrote them. That, however, is far from being so. Yes, in classical Latin there were no capital letters with which to start sentences. It is, however, equally true that capital letters, non-existent as they were, did not come at the beginnings of proper nouns, and also that there were no full stops at the ends of sentences, nor any punctuation inside sentences, nor spaces between words, nor even spaces to show where one sentence ended and another began.

Thus the modern convention by no means represents tradition. Rather, it creates an illusion that classical practice is being used when in fact it is not. In my view, this is scarcely an acceptable reason to adopt a practice that until recently was *never* used in *any* form of book in which any Latin was reproduced.

IT REMAINS FOR me to draw to the close of this Preface by saying that, if you would ever like further advice on how to make the best use of this book, or in any other way to further your mastery of Latin beyond where this book goes, you are very welcome to contact me direct, where indicated below. I made a similar offer in this book's immediate predecessor, *Gwynne's Grammar*, and I have had no cause to regret it. Communications from people who have contacted me as a result have often been full of interest.

Now, ALONG WITH reminding you of the claims I have made as to how the subject matter of this book cannot fail to benefit you, I bid you welcome to what follows.

N. M. Gwynne
nmgwynne@eircom.net
www.gwynneteaching.com
April 2014

# PART ONE

---

# INTRODUCTORY

## CHAPTER ONE

# About Latin

L ATIN IS, QUITE simply, the most utterly wonderful …
*thing.*

Please believe that it is not because of mental laziness that I have chosen that most all-embracing of abstract nouns, 'thing'. Rather, a more specific term – 'language', 'subject', 'element of education', 'cultural feature' – might exclude one or more valuable aspects of Latin that I should not wish excluded. Here are just some of those aspects of Latin, the ones which spring most readily to mind.

— Latin is an academic subject easy enough for the least intelligent of us to grasp all its basic elements, and yet difficult enough to be demanding for its greatest scholars.

— As an instrument for training mind and character, Latin has no parallel, as we shall be seeing in Chapter Three and elsewhere.

— For well over a thousand years, Latin was the means of communication that united the whole of Europe culturally and in every other significant way.

— Latin is the direct ancestor of, between them, the five so-called Romance languages (Italian, French, Spanish, Portuguese and Romanian) of the largest European language group, and of both of the official South American languages (Spanish and Portuguese). 'Romance' comes from the Latin word **Romanicus**, meaning 'of Roman style' or 'Roman-made'.

— Latin is the ancestor and source of the portion – well over half – of the English language which derives partly directly from Latin and partly through the Romance languages, mainly French, which for some centuries was England's official language. Not only that, but from almost the moment that English began to develop from being the spoken-only language that, in the mid-fifth century, first arrived on the shores of what was then Britain,* and to take on a written form as well, it did so with the help of Latin, which had been the written language in everyday use since the conversion to Christianity of Britain south of Scotland's border in the sixth century AD. Right from the beginning, therefore, English grammar was worked out and formalised side by side with Latin, from which our language took even the alphabet that we use today. Indeed, not least remarkably, we even owe the very word 'alphabet' to our Latin-speaking forebears, notwithstanding its not being a Latin word. It was they who adopted for the purpose the first two letters, alpha and beta, of the alphabet of the Greek language, which had been the primary influence on Latin and had helped to make it the influential language it became.

— Latin is the language of *both* of arguably the two greatest legal systems in history, Roman law and English Common Law. Even today it is still the language of forensics – technical material used in courts of law – as, for instance, in the phrase **corpus delicti**.

— Latin is the language of most family, school, university, town, city and county mottos and of the mottos of several states in the USA and most of the Canadian provinces. Even the fairly rare exception '*Honi soit qui mal y pense*', which appears on Britain's royal coat of arms and those of several military regiments and public buildings in Britain and the Commonwealth, is ultimately derived from Latin, via French.

— Latin is the language of the bi-nomial taxonomy of plants and animals invented by Linnaeus and now used universally.

— Latin is the language used for chemical elements and compounds.

* The language that Latin replaced was the Celtic language.

— Latin is the language most used in medical terminology.

— Latin has always been the main official language for the most widespread version of Christianity, the version, centred on Rome, which ruled England religiously, constitutionally, socially and in every other respect of any importance, for 900 years, and continued to rule much of Europe for several centuries after that as well.

— Latin is the language for which much of the greatest sung music of the last 1,500 years or so was written, and of even the occasional modern opera.

— Latin is the language of one of the three greatest literatures of all time (the other two being classical Greek literature and our English literature).

— Untranslated Latin is a quite significant part of present-day English, as we shall be seeing.

— Latin even features, in abbreviated form (**Fid Def** for **Fidei Defensor**), on every single one of the coins in our pockets, and can be expected to continue doing so as long as the pound sterling remains the basis of our currency.

— In the form of '**Helvetia**', the Latin word for 'Switzerland', Latin is the language which appears on all coins and stamps of that country.

— **Et cetera**. I have by no means come to the end.

In short, Latin is an intrinsic part of us. It is to some extent *even at the very heart of us*. This 'thing' that is Latin is worth a closer look, is it not?

## CHAPTER TWO

# Making the Best Use of This Book

DEAR GRACIOUS READER, as you arrive at this early part of the book that you have in your hands, I have a request to make of you, even an entreaty. It is that you throw yourself into the following pages wholeheartedly and with the utmost diligence. I ask this in the belief that there is no better way that you can spend such time as you are able to make available for this purpose – that is to say, no way you can spend the time more valuably (not merely more usefully), more satisfyingly, or even, other than in the sense of instant and swiftly come-and-gone gratification, more enjoyably.

I really am referring to your tackling Latin. I am doing so, however, to the accompaniment of a stipulation which is also one of the essential factors governing how this book has been put together. By tackling Latin, I mean setting about learning Latin in the way that it was always learnt in the past, century after century, until the revolution in all education that hit England – and indeed most of the Western world – like a bombshell in the 1960s.

Throughout the entire history of education during the last thousand years or so, up until the 1960s, what is said here would have been accepted almost universally – throughout Europe and, until a little earlier, throughout America north and south – as ordinary common sense and would have been acted upon as such. For much of that time, Latin, together with Greek but with children embarking on learning it before Greek, actually *was* education. So much was this so that, until the 1850s, Latin and Greek were *the only subjects formally taught* at all leading schools in England. Indeed, in some of those schools – as also in Harvard University in America – it was required that *even outside the classroom* only those languages could be spoken.

The reason for this exclusive concentration on Latin and Greek in schools was not, of course, that our ancestors supposed there to be no need to study the other basic subjects – English, mathematics, one or more currently spoken foreign languages, history, geography and what was commonly called Scripture. The eighteenth and nineteenth centuries, after all, were a period during which Britain shone in every single human endeavour, academic and practical, to such an extent that, 'single-handed', Britain was responsible for the Industrial Revolution and most of the scientific inventions of that period that changed the world, *and*, for better or for worse, actually ruled about a quarter of the world – and, what is more, all this while producing one of the greatest literatures of every kind of all time. No, the reason that the non-classical subjects were not taught in schools was that they were considered to be so easy by comparison with Latin and Greek, especially to people with minds and characters trained by the study of the Classics, that it was not thought worth wasting valuable schoolroom time on them. Picking them up was something that could more appropriately be done during the school holidays and in other spare time.

Even during the ten years or so of my own schooldays from the age of seven onwards, we did not have teachers of English as such. The English we learnt was taught by our Classics teachers, as it always had been. We did not suffer from that. The result, on the contrary, was that the ordinary schoolboy and schoolgirl was able to write English much better than someone of equivalent intelligence could write today.

Indeed, I believe I can safely say that the very great majority of readers who use this book as I recommend will, by the time they have finished it, have learnt a really enormous amount of valuable English which they had no idea even existed. I intend no exaggeration in saying that.

A LTHOUGH, AS I made clear in the Preface, this book covers a large amount of ground, it concentrates very much more on the early stages of Latin than it does on the more advanced ones. This is for good reason. In the first place, the size of this book dictates it. In the second place, it is making a really good *start* that matters, whether you abandon Latin at that point having even so already benefited greatly, or whether you continue on in the quest for real mastery of it.

May this book help to bring back much that was commonplace and basic in former times.

## CHAPTER THREE

# The Importance of Learning Latin, Examined in Detail

THIS IS THE most demanding of the chapters in this introductory section of the book. I believe it to be well worth your while to read it with some care; and indeed I hope you will help to propagate its message.

JEAN PAUL GETTY, an American industrialist whose interests were mainly centred on oil, and who up till the time of his death in 1976 was reckoned to be the richest man in the world, used to employ classicists to run his worldwide network of companies. Other industrialists might have considered the first necessary qualification to be a degree from Harvard or Yale Business School or some such, but not he. Once asked why he insisted on employing classicists, his reply was: 'They sell more oil.' They made him more money.

At the other social and economic extreme, an article in the *Independent* newspaper of 4 November 1987 reported that, in some parts of America, the Classics had been revived to help inner-city black youths in particular, and with extraordinary results. In Indianapolis, for example, 400 eleven-year-olds who had been receiving daily Latin teaching were significantly better, not only in reading and spelling but also in maths and science, than a group who followed the normal curriculum. This was of course despite those who followed the normal curriculum having more time for the other subjects because of the time *not* taken up with Latin.

I ask my readers to take careful note of that. Those who received daily Latin teaching were better at the *other* subjects than the other group, even though they spent significantly less time on those other subjects. We shall be coming across much more evidence to the same effect in the following pages.

Nor were these freak results, as experts on education in the higher reaches of academia have been claiming since those results were first published.* They are simply confirmations of what has been found whenever the opportunity to compare has arisen again and again in the past. Based certainly on my own experience of teaching, but based also on what has been said in the past by countless people in the best possible position to know,† it is my firm conviction that an education grounded solidly on the Classics is an education many thousands of times better – once again I intend no exaggeration there – than any education offered today, and would be even if all the subjects taught today were taught as well as they could be. Let us remind ourselves too that the long period of Classics-only education at schools which started gradually to come to an end only in the middle of the nineteenth century was the period of Britain's peak of success in most fields of human endeavour.

It is, however, all very well for me to say that, but simply setting down the facts does not necessarily carry conviction, no matter how true the facts obviously are. Exactly *why* is it and *how* is it, therefore, that Latin has this extraordinary and marvellous effect on everyone, of whatever background or intellectual inheritance?

I pluck you by the sleeve, dear reader, and beg for your closest attention to what now follows. I stress too that I am by no means

---

* Well-known experts on education in the highest reaches of academia today do indeed typically detest the experiment in Indianopolis and elsewhere in America, and maintain that it is nothing but 'anecdotal' evidence and deeply flawed. They typically assert that, for it to be a true experiment, another group of children should have been taught French or German instead of Latin, and doubtless the results would have been similar if not better. A supposition does not become fact simply because the world's leading experts state it to be fact, however. I invite readers to consider this particular supposition in the light of the evidence and reasoning that I shall be including in the rest of this chapter, and also in the knowledge that academia has been in full cry in its attacks on the Classics as part of education since much earlier than the 1960s, indeed since well over a century ago.
† Extensive quotations by some of the most impressive authors on the subject will be found on the website.

only saying this in my own name, but am also passing on the sort of thing that experienced educators have said in the past when challenged on the subject.

In summary, what a well-designed course in Latin provides is a training and development of the mind and character to a degree of excellence that no other mental or physical activity can come anywhere near to bringing about. Specifically, it trains these: the ability to concentrate and focus; the use of the memory; the capacity to analyse, deduce and problem-solve; the powers of attention to detail, of diligence and perseverance, of observation, of imagination, of judgement, of taste. In fact it trains the mind and character to the utmost extent in everything human that is valuable. It does all this as no other academic subject (other than classical Greek), or other activity of any kind at all, can come remotely close to doing.

Once again, it is all very well for me simply to state this. Do you believe it to be even possible? Does what I claim even perhaps seem absurd? It remains, therefore, to show how we can know it to be true.

There is surely no better way of demonstrating the truth of those far-reaching claims than by looking carefully at a representative example of Latin-educating in action. Here, therefore, is such an example, given in the form of showing what is necessary for the purpose of dealing adequately with a reasonably difficult Latin sentence that is part of a reasonably difficult piece of Latin prose written by a highly regarded Latin author.

First of all, you examine the words in the sentence sufficiently to break the sentence down into its various clauses (see page 29 for what a clause is). Then, taking the clauses one at a time, you start with what you had identified as the main clause or one of the main clauses, and examine more closely the individual words in it and, in the case of nouns, pronouns, adjectives and verbs, their word forms. In doing this, you are cultivating your powers of observation and of attention to detail.

Next, you need to bring your powers of reasoning more strongly into play, in order to see which words belong together and how the various words relate to each other. In Latin, this will sometimes be far from obvious, and you will have the task of weighing up various alternatives before coming up with your first solution.

Even when you have done that with all due care, your first solution, however, may well need to be only a provisional solution. You must therefore now ask yourself: is this solution correct? In the case of a clause, you must look carefully at the clause preceding it or otherwise most closely related it, to see if everything in that clause confirms your solution, or if, rather, you need to try another alternative. In the case of a complete sentence, you must check the previous sentence; and in some cases you may find even that the *subsequent* sentence will force you to change your mind.

By this stage, you have, simply by translating in accordance with the rules of grammar that you have learnt and are able to apply, already called into play your powers of observation, of reasoning, of identifying alternatives and then choosing between them, and of making judgements. You have also learnt the need to make one or more independent checks to ensure that the result at which you have arrived is indeed the correct one.

The process by no means stops there; far from it. By considering various English words available for you to use for the translation of each Latin word in the sentence, and choosing carefully the ones for your translation, you are forcing yourself to gain clearer, fuller and more knowledgeable insights into your own language. Further, you will often find yourself coming across Latin words for which there is no English equivalent; and in consequence you will be made to enlarge on what you can conceive with your mind and on the ideas you can entertain and make use of.

Next, there is the moral aspect to add to the intellectual aspect that has featured so far. In doing all that you have done so far, you are training not only your mind but your character as well. From the outset – right from when you make your very first efforts of translating either into English or into Latin – you will be running into difficulties which do not exist when you are dealing with English by itself. Addressing these difficulties will not only need a flexibility of mind that was not needed before. It will also need determination and perseverance, so that you are able to continue for as long as is needed until you have earned the deep satisfaction of having triumphed over every obstacle.

There is yet more. If you are to make a really satisfactory translation, you need to aim at reproducing, in an English way, what is there in the Latin that may not be directly translatable. This may involve putting emphasis in the right places and reproducing such features as logical coherence, persuasiveness, heart-stopping emotion, sheer literary beauty, or whatever. You will be developing mental subtlety. You will also be developing good taste.

Furthermore, with practice the stage will be reached when this whole process will have become so customary as to be often relatively effortless for you, sometimes even to the extent of being almost automatic. By then you will have gone a long way towards developing an intellect and a character which will serve you well, faithfully, efficiently and speedily, in *any* problems of *any* kind that you may find yourself faced with in *any* activity of any kind in your life that you find yourself engaging in.

Finally, differing according to whichever great Latin author, admired over many centuries, you are trying to translate, you will, as a 'side effect', have made yourself to some extent acquainted with elements of one or more of history, geography, laws, religion and culture that will have broadened your mind and widened your sympathies.

All this is the sort of thing that you can have gained from translating a single sentence in the right manner.

I should add that I have chosen this particular example – that of what needs to be applied when translating a reasonably difficult Latin sentence in a reasonably difficult piece of Latin prose – for purposes of illustration, rather than to present anything approaching a complete picture of Latin-learning in action and what is to be gained from it. What I have been outlining applies in lesser or greater degree to any other example I might have chosen, whether a translation done by beginners or a translation done by people of such competence in Latin that the kind of sentence I have selected will be undemanding for them.

That is all very well, some readers may respond. Could not, however, one of the modern languages do exactly the same job, in addition to being obviously of more practical use?

My answer, and the answer of great educators of the past, is simply: no. For the purpose of education, as opposed to merely acquiring a valuable skill, all modern languages are far inferior to Latin. First, one of the supreme advantages of Latin is, in the right sort of way, the difficulty of it – even though, by an apparent paradox, it is also easy enough at the outset for even my four-year-old pupils to find it manageable and enjoyable without my in any way compromising how it is taught. No modern language comes close to approaching Latin in difficulty.* It is the very difficulty of Latin that, however apparently off-putting, is an important part of what makes it such a valuable preparation for life. Secondly, no modern language has a literature that comes close to deserving to be revered as the writings of Latin author after Latin author have deservedly been revered throughout the centuries since they were written. And I could continue with a 'thirdly' and many more.

All in all, it is no wonder that Jean Paul Getty, who knew as much about making money as anyone in his day, insisted on classicists and only classicists being chosen to run his companies, and no wonder that experience has *consistently* shown that, with children, those who are not taught Latin in the correct manner come 'nowhere' by comparison with those who are.

I shall close this essay, on the place of Latin in education, with a claim that is most controversial of all; and, because it is so controversial, I ask my readers to make sure that they register *exactly* what I am claiming, as opposed to even the smallest exaggeration of it.

If I were to be faced with the choice – and I stress that it is not a choice that I should like to be faced with – of, on the one hand,

---

* This includes even the more demanding ones, such as present-day Polish, which, although not derived from Latin, resembles classical Latin in a remarkable number of ways – it is characterised by a high degree of inflection; it has relatively free word order; there are no articles; and there is frequent dropping of subject pronouns, with the verb endings being sufficient to make those pronouns 'understood'. Not that, in any case, Polish, or any other modern language fitting that description, is likely to be chosen for English pupils as a language useful enough to include in school syllabuses.

giving children for whom I had responsibility an education consisting of a wide variety of useful subjects, or even relatively few useful subjects as was standard in the education of my day, or, on the other hand, giving them an education consisting *only* of Latin and of no other subjects whatever, even in their spare time, I should unhesitatingly opt for the Latin-only alternative, no matter who the children were and no matter what their inborn intellectual abilities were, let alone what their stated preference would be if consulted at any point.

My reason is simply that the benefits to the child and to the future-adult of the second alternative would be so greatly superior as to be, once again, beyond the possibility of comparison, at least in percentage terms. The reality is that true education is only secondarily, and *very much* secondarily, about the amount and variety of knowledge that one picks up during the course of it. Primarily, it is about developing our mind, character and taste so that, once the education is complete, we can pick up effortlessly and quickly whatever knowledge and skills we wish to, whether for practical use or for enjoyment at any point in our lives. People's capabilities resulting from such an education will be so great by comparison with what those capabilities would have been that they would have reason to be grateful, whether their tasks were running a country on the one hand, or, to descend into bathos, picking up the skills needed to play table tennis on the other hand.

Thus the value of Latin in education and why. Let us recall too, one last time, that historically the choice I have made is *not* eccentric, and that Latin and its classical sister were the exclusive subject matter in leading schools for centuries. Moreover, not only did Britain flourish during much of that time, but complaints by the 'victims' of this education were remarkably few even though a much more varied education was standard in other European countries at the same time.

## CHAPTER FOUR

# Is *This* How to Learn Latin?

RECENTLY, MORE THAN ever before since the effective abolition of Latin in schools in and around the 1960s, Latin has been making a comeback, and some schools even mention it as an important feature of their syllabus.

What is more, this enthusiasm is also very much reflected in the publishing world and elsewhere. Both the Oxford University Press and the Cambridge University Press are selling in considerable quantity their lavish, multi-volume Latin courses that were first published in 1988 and 1977 respectively. Other titles have been pouring out: the beginners' *Minimus* books, the three-volume *So You Really Want to Learn Latin* by N. R. R. Oulton, James Morwood's *Latin Grammar*, John Taylor's *Essential GCSE Latin*, Harry Mount's *Amo Amas Amat*, Mark Walker's *Annus Horribilis* and *Annus Mirabilis*, among others. The Association for Latin Teaching, founded more than a century ago, is still flourishing. Friends of Classics, the society co-founded and headed by the wonderfully learned Dr Peter Jones, is enjoying more respect and influence than ever before; and the superb classicist Professor Mary Beard is in continual demand on radio and television as well as in print. In short, the evidence shows that the battle is well on the way to being won.

Do not believe it. Do ... not ... believe ... it.

I am certainly not saying that there are no good books among those of relatively recent publication date, or that such organisations as the Association for Latin Teaching and Friends of Classics are not doing useful work. I *am* saying that the effect in the right direction of even the best of the books available and selling well – let alone of the worst of them – at the present time appears tragically negligible, and close to being irreversibly so. My own experiences of teaching Latin, which must be at least as extensive and wide-ranging as those of any other teachers teaching today, are even by themselves fully sufficient to show that.

Over a period of many years now, I have taught Latin to people of all age groups from three years old to over seventy, in various parts of the world, in every kind of circumstance from lecture halls to school classrooms to home-schools, to individuals, in person and 'face to face' over the Internet.

I make – with due and becoming modesty! – no claim to any special gifts as a teacher. I do, however, make the most emphatic claims on behalf of my traditional, tried-and-tested-over-many-centuries teaching *methods*.

The difference in effectiveness between the traditional methods and those used by even the best schoolteachers of today is so astonishing, consistently so, that descriptions of my methods and their results have featured again and again in prominent articles in newspapers. In these articles, what tends to be singled out for special mention – not surprisingly, for it is obviously newsworthy, if only for its apparent absurdity – is my claim to be able to teach any schoolchild more Latin *in about half an hour* than the child will have learnt at school during its previous no-matter-how-many years of learning Latin.

That claim must seem ridiculous and verging on insane at first sight, and at second sight too for that matter. I assure you, though, gracious reader, that I have no interest in putting my professional credibility at risk. I stand fully behind my public and well-publicised challenge. For instance, if you visit the gwynneteaching.com website, you can see there the testimonial of a seventeen-year-old boy who had been studying Latin at school for some years, who had passed all his exams in Latin (a fact which in retrospect seems to him absurd), who was about to go to Cambridge to read Classics there, and who confirms that I did for him, in the space of about half an hour, exactly what I claimed I could. Nor is this an isolated piece of 'anecdotal' evidence. It is completely typical, as well as being what one would logically expect.

Do you find this difficult to believe even so? Perhaps you will find it less so if I devote just a small amount of space to explaining the relevant technicalities of the traditional and modern ways of teaching Latin, and to comparing them.

First, the traditional way.

In my first lesson with any new pupil or group of pupils, I open by teaching how Latin is pronounced, which is not difficult to pick up, and then move on to the easiest noun to learn, the one most usually chosen to represent the First Declension, **mēnsa** meaning 'table'. Immediately after that I teach what is called the present tense – the tense which in any verb indicates what is being done here and now – of the equivalent verb, traditionally **amō** meaning 'I love'.

Here is how **mēnsa** and **amō** 'go', set out in the traditional way.

**Mēnsa:**

|  | *Singular* | *Plural* |
|---|---|---|
| Nominative (for the subject) | **mēnsa** | **mensae** |
| Vocative (the 'addressing' case) | **mēnsa** | **mensae** |
| Accusative (for the object) | **mēnsam** | **mensās** |
| Genitive (the 'of' case) | **mēnsae** | **mensārum** |
| Dative (the case for 'to' or 'for') | **mēnsae** | **mensīs** |
| Ablative (for 'by', 'with', 'from') | **mēnsā** | **mēnsīs** |

The present tense of '**amō**':

|  |  | *Singular* |  | *Plural* |  |
|---|---|---|---|---|---|
| First person: | I love | **amō** | we love | **amāmus** |
| Second person: | you love | **amās** | you love | **amātis** |
| Third person: | he, she, it loves | **amat** | they love | **amant** |

The pupil or pupils – the more of them the better at this early stage – recite these with me at the tops of their voices until they have learnt them by heart. This does not take long. I then explain the significance of each ending: what the words mean when they end in their various different ways. Very soon we are ready to translate our first sentence into Latin, 'We love the girls', for instance.

'We love' they can read off the page they are looking at, just as you can read it a few lines higher while on this page. When they have done that, I provide the information that the Latin for 'girl' is **puella** which 'goes' exactly like – has the same endings as*

---

* On principle, I normally do not 'dumb down' technical terms, but here are two exceptions to my general rule. Latin teachers and students have always used 'goes like' to indicate that a word has the same endings as

– **mēnsa**. Perhaps with the help of my book *Gwynne's Grammar* (on *English* grammar), which I use extensively at this stage – which indeed is how it originally came to be written – the pupil works out that 'the girls' must be in the accusative case, which is the case for objects in a sentence or clause, and of course in the plural number. The answer is not difficult to arrive at: **Amāmus puellās** or preferably, because the verb tends to come at the end of a sentence in Latin, **Puellās amāmus**.

The pupil typically finds great satisfaction in achieving this. Equally typically, we reach this stage within the first half-hour of our first lesson, as was no less typical with the teaching of Latin in the past.

Note too, please, that, as was always done in the past, we start with translating English into Latin rather than Latin into English. That is the only order in which any new language can be learnt efficiently and quickly; and in Latin (and also in classical Greek) this applies much more than in most other languages, because of the multitude of different forms of the nouns, pronouns and adjectives and verbs, according to how they are being used.

Now let us turn to someone whose study of Latin has been based on the five-volume *Cambridge Latin Course*, which at the time of writing is used in about 85 per cent of schools in England and has so far sold a staggering 4 million copies.

In the course's Volume I, **mēnsa** or its equivalent is *not* set out as in the table I gave above. Not until page 32 do we learn about the cases of nouns at all, and then only the nominative and accusative cases are given. Unbelievably, not until page 119 are we given another case, the dative. Even more unbelievably (if unbelievableness admits of degrees), *that is it*, for Volume I. In the 199 pages of Volume I, no further cases are given.

During the course of the 184 pages of Volume II, a further two of the six cases are given at intervals, the vocative and the

---

one that has already been learnt, and the word 'endings' is a similarly traditional way of denoting what is technically termed the *inflexion*, i.e. usually the final part of a Latin verb or noun which changes according to how it is being used.

genitive. The ablative is yet to come. Most unbelievably of all, by the end of 207 pages of Volume IIIA the ablative is *still* to come. It finally appears in the *fourth* volume, Volume IIIB.

Verbs are treated in similarly illogical fashion, though not to such an extreme extent.

The *Oxford Latin Course* is not as extravagant as that in the number of volumes over which it spreads information that should properly be learnt on the very first day of starting to learn Latin. Otherwise, however, it is similarly illogical.

In both courses, the concentration is wholeheartedly on translating from Latin into English, with *no* English into Latin in the first volume of the *Cambridge* and perhaps 10 per cent English into Latin compared to Latin into English in the first volume of the *Oxford*, and at the end of each chapter rather than right at the beginning.

Now, I do not like to make public criticisms of the work of others. Moreover, both of these books are the result of an immense amount of hard work and, for the most part, excellent scholarship, and are beautifully presented as well as very informative, and a great pleasure to read. It is, however, impossible for me to try to persuade teachers and pupils not to use these and similar books for teaching Latin unless I name them.

Bluntly, both courses are impossible to learn Latin from (and indeed none of those who wrote them could have learnt their Latin in any such way). Not difficult; completely impossible. There is no encouragement to learn the 'endings' by heart, and plenty of discouragement from doing so. And translating either way – Latin into English or English into Latin – cannot be done without that.

Moreover, the effect of such textbooks is considerably worse than mere uselessness and wasted money. My experience with pupil after pupil who has come to me after using one or other of them has shown them to be actually *harmful* in their effects.

The reason is not difficult to understand. Very necessary for learning Latin, and of great value in every human activity once acquired, are the abilities to analyse closely and exactly, to deduce, and to problem-solve. None of these is possible in Latin without an exact knowledge of the endings and how each of them must be applied. Without them, the pupil is left with the only alternative: that of guessing.

Guessing, therefore, is what those who use the *Cambridge Latin Course* and the *Oxford Latin Course* are forced to learn to do. In the first place, however, guessing simply cannot even begin to work with a language which (a) is inflected, with its nouns pronouns, adjectives and verbs constantly changing their form according to their role in the sentence,* and (b) has no consistent word order, as almost all modern languages do but Latin does not. In the second place, as with every action that is repeated, guessing, as a substitute for making the effort of analysing, swiftly becomes a *habit*, and a habit, moreover, which, again as is characteristic with habits that are continually reinforced, soon becomes difficult if not impossible to get out of.

So it is that, routinely, I find it more difficult to teach Latin to those who have used either of those two courses for any length of time than to teach beginners. Indeed, the stage is reached when learning Latin properly has become next to impossible for the former. My experience confirms only too forcefully that the products (victims?) of modern Latin teaching are afflicted with what could be called incurable modern-teaching-induced grammatical dyslexia.

Therefore: no, the battle to restore Latin is *not* well on the way to being won.

The final problem I need urgently to bring to everyone's attention is that there are now no – or virtually no – teachers left in schools who themselves were taught Latin in the traditional, time-honoured, tried-and-tested way. If there are any left who have not yet retired, it makes no practical difference, because they will not have been allowed to teach in the traditional way, and they will almost certainly have lost whatever ability to do so that they once had.

The relevance of this stems from an important teaching principle: the principle that 'One can only teach as one was taught

---

* For instance, a single Latin verb can have well over two hundred different endings, by contrast with the four or five different endings of a normal English verb (as in 'play', 'plays', 'playing', 'played', and 'sing', 'sings', 'singing', 'sang', 'sung'). A Greek verb can have well over a thousand!

oneself'. Teaching is not something that one can learn to do by reading a book about it, though I hope this book comes as close as any book can to achieving that. Those who have not themselves *experienced* the method which teaches Latin most thoroughly, most exactly and most quickly, simply cannot *teach* it in that way, as both logic and my experience in trying to teach teachers has shown.

It is not that it is difficult in principle to learn how to teach correctly. That manner of teaching is only a matter of common sense, and I have succeeded in teaching it to willing learners within a week or so. Although not difficult in principle, it is, however, difficult in practice if one has spent a significant part of one's teaching career teaching differently from how it should be done. The main reason is, once again, the force of habit.

So much for what must be known and understood in order for there to be any chance of things being put right. Time now to be constructive!

## CHAPTER FIVE

# How *in Fact* to Learn Latin

A LMOST BY VERY definition, there can only be one *best* way to learn Latin. Happily, it is not difficult to identify it. It is the way in which I was taught; it is the way in which generations before me were taught; it is the way which has been shown to work best for people of all ages, gifts of intellect, and ability to apply themselves; and it is the way in which I teach my pupils of all ages today.

With all languages, but with Latin and Greek more than almost every other, the material that needs to be learnt in order to achieve mastery falls under three headings. One, most obviously of all, is vocabulary. The second is the subdivision of grammar technically known as 'accidence', sometimes called 'morphology', which is how some classes of words change their *form* in accordance with what role they are playing in a sentence or clause. (This happens very little in English, the main changes being singular nouns changing their form in the plural, as in 'noun' and 'nouns'; verbs changing their form according to number and tense, as in 'love', 'loves' and 'loved'; and pronouns indeed changing their form according to how they are being used in a sentence, as in 'I', 'me' and 'mine', and 'who', 'whom' and 'whose'.) The third heading is the other subdivision of grammar, 'syntax', which is how to choose the parts of the words whose accidence we have learnt as we need to, and to put them together in order to convey the sense we want.

In every human activity of any complexity without exception, there is a due order in which that activity should be learnt, step by step, in order for the learning to be both accurate and speedy. To put it in philosophical terms: (a) the *science* governing the activity in question – the part of it applicable to *everybody* who studies it

– must be thoroughly learnt first; and (b) only after that can the *art* – the personal style which varies from individual to individual according to his or her inherited talents and other circumstances – be tackled.*

In the human activity of which learning a new language consists, what follows from the principle just set out is that, side by side with learning the *vocabulary* – and I mean *really* learning it, not simply registering the meaning of a new word in our mind on a temporary basis – we first of all learn the word forms – their *accidence* – by heart; and then, and *only* then, practise using them, learning and applying the appropriate *syntax*.

As with all human activities, there is no other adequate way, in terms of effectiveness and speed, of learning a new language. To try to launch into Latin or any other academic subject by being 'creative' and by guesswork can achieve little other than the formation of bad habits which will be difficult – in fact verging on impossible – to eliminate.

Try to learn tennis by watching some first-class tennis on television and then going straight onto a court afterwards and engaging in a game, without having been told which size of racket you should use, without having been carefully taught the correct way to hold the racket, and without fairly extensive instruction in and practice of the forehand swing, the backhand swing and the serve. The chances are that, because of incorrect habits that you will have quickly acquired, you will *never* be – or come anywhere near to being – the tennis player you could have been.

It is the same with Latin. First, learn by heart the endings of the simplest nouns, and of the tenses, one by one, of the regular verbs. Then, as each set of endings is learnt, practise using them. Do not move on to the next set of endings of nouns and verbs until the one being learnt has been mastered so thoroughly that the endings have become effortless – about as effortless as reflex actions – to remember and to apply in their appropriate contexts.

---

* This all-important division of what constitutes science and art is discussed in more detail in *Gwynne's Grammar*, on page x in the Preface.

I must really stress that. In learning Latin, there are, alas, no short cuts. Attempt a short cut and you will end up either with a knowledge of Latin that is frustratingly inadequate at best, or with the need for much more time and effort for an adequate knowledge than would have been necessary if you had proceeded in the orderly, scientific way. Yes, *much* more time. A piano teacher once told me, as a morsel of traditional wisdom that had come her way, that it takes fourteen times longer to learn something having first 'learnt' it incorrectly, than it takes to learn it correctly in the first place. In my experience, I have never found any reason to doubt her.

I THINK ALL that remains under this heading of how best to learn Latin is the matter of how best to learn by heart the accidence that needs to be learnt, that is to say, the following:

— What are called the *declensions* of the nouns, pronouns, adjectives and numerals, together with the comparatives and superlatives of the adjectives and adverbs.
— The *conjugations* of verbs, of which there are basically four.
— The *principal parts* of the irregular verbs, of which there are some 200 in total, but not all of which are of immediate importance.
— A few other 'specials'.

This can be done at any age, the earlier the better. I really do mean that. Starting at three years old, when memorising is at its best and when using what is memorised is not yet possible, is ideal. Children typically *enjoy* this when it is taught in a rhythmic way, especially when more than one person can do the reciting together in the same rhythm. On the gwynneteaching.com website you can find me and others reciting declensions and conjugations in the rhythms that experience has shown to be easier for memorising. I strongly recommend going to one or other of those pages of the website and doing the reciting 'with' us, so that the rhythms are most easily mastered and remembered.

# PART TWO

# FINAL PRELIMINARIES

## CHAPTER SIX

# What You Need to Know Before Starting: General Grammar

INDISPENSABLE TO START with, in the study of Latin, are the rock-bottom basics of grammar. These basics apply to all languages, not just to Latin.

As noted earlier, grammar falls under two headings. The first is what is commonly called either **accidence** (a word of Latin origin) or **morphology** (of Greek origin). This consists of the various categories that words can be divided into, together with how words change their form, mostly their endings, in accordance with how they are being used.

The other heading is **syntax**, which is how words are used in sentences in order to make sense – that is to say, in order to think coherently, to communicate in a way that can be readily understood, and to understand what is being communicated, whether by word of mouth or in writing.

What follows in this chapter is what is needed to give an introduction, but is incomplete as to detail. This is deliberate. All the points omitted will need to be covered thoroughly when we come to use the various points of grammar for the first time; and to go into so much detail here would mean repetition without sufficient reason.

I am happy to refer those who seek a fuller understanding of English grammar to *Gwynne's Grammar*, which is of course devoted exclusively to its subject.

The definitions in bold print are worth learning by heart, and very much *ought* to be learnt by heart by children, who used to be completely familiar with them before their age had reached double figures. The rest should be studied sufficiently for an adequate understanding.

Finally, in this introductory section of the chapter, the time has come to make what is virtually a reintroduction into the English language of a word which, as far as children were concerned until recent times, was known by them all too well by the age of ten. This word is **parsing**.

**To parse** a sentence is to analyse it in every grammatical detail. If I may anticipate some technical terms that we shall be learning about in the next few pages, **to parse** is to identify the clauses including what kind of clauses they are; to identify the phrases and the words, and, with their technical terms (subject, verb, object and so on), to specify what role each phrase and word is playing in the clause. It is also to identify by name the part of speech of each word, including any details of accidence in relation to words which change their forms. In short, parsing requires us to examine the exact function of every word in a sentence, and the relations of each with the others – their syntactical relations.

Even before the 1960s, parsing was no longer playing the part in education that it had always played before; and by early in that decade it was so completely gone that the word itself, once familiar to everybody, may be completely new to many readers of this book. It is, however, an important science both in itself and, all the more especially, in the context of learning Latin. Even from the brief description which I have just given, it can be seen that parsing must help to promote the complete mastery of any language, which is bound to improve one's speaking and writing of that language. In the context of Latin, inflected as it is and with word order playing the relatively small role that it does, parsing is all but indispensable, at least at the start and for helping to avoid elementary mistakes that would otherwise be made.

I shall not be asking for the parsing of every sentence in the exercises. I shall, however, be asking for it often enough to help the reader form the habit of doing it at least mentally when tackling a translation either way.

## SECTION 1
## ACCIDENCE OR MORPHOLOGY

All complete thoughts and communications of any kind are in the form of **sentences**. Sentences are made up of **words**. Words can be conveniently divided into eight categories, according to the work they do in the sentences in which they appear. These categories are commonly known as the **parts of speech**.

There are eight parts of speech: noun, pronoun, adjective, verb, adverb, conjunction, preposition and interjection.*

### 1. Nouns
A *noun* **is the name of a person, place or thing;** that is to say, it is the name of whatever we can think about – for instance, 'person' and 'thing', 'Cicero', 'Rome', 'textbook', 'education' and 'group'.

### 2. Pronouns
A *pronoun* **is a word which stands in place of a noun** – for instance, 'I', 'me', 'mine', 'who', 'myself', 'this', 'it' and 'that'.

### 3. Adjectives
An *adjective* **is a word which describes a noun or a pronoun** – for instance, 'good', 'better', 'best', 'white' and 'inadequate'.

### 4. Verbs
A *verb* **is a doing word or a being word – a word which expresses an action or a state.** An example of a doing word is 'to love'. An example of a being word is 'to be'.

### 5. Adverbs
An *adverb* **is a word which modifies a verb, an adjective or another adverb.** For verbs and adjectives and other adverbs, adverbs are generally the equivalent of what adjectives are for nouns and pronouns – for instance, 'now', 'here', 'quickly' and 'easily'.

---

* This formal division of language into eight parts of speech dates back to at least the fourth century AD.

## 6. Conjunctions

A *conjunction* **is a word which joins together any two words of the same part of speech, or any two phrases, or clauses, or even sentences**. There are two kinds of conjunction: (1) **coordinating conjunctions**, of which there are few and which, in relation to clauses, join clauses of equal status, whether main or subsidiary, to each other (see Section 2 below) – for instance, 'and', 'but' and 'or'; (2) **subordinating conjunctions**, of which there are very many, and which join subsidiary clauses to main clauses or to other subsidiary clauses – for instance, 'if', 'although' and 'while'.

## 7. Prepositions

A *preposition* **is a word which governs a noun or a pronoun and connects it to anything else in the sentence or clause.** For instance: 'I teach grammar *from* my book *to* my pupils *in* my study *by* candlelight *with* great pleasure.'

## 8. Interjections

An *interjection* – the only part of speech of which animals are capable – **is an exclamation.** Examples: 'Phew!', 'Oooooooh!', 'How amazing!', 'Oh gracious me!' and 'His grammar, *alas!* is deplorable, but it is, *thank goodness!* gradually improving.'

## SECTION 2
## SYNTAX

1. A *sentence* **is a word or group of words expressing a complete statement, wish, command or question, whether as a thought, or in speech, or in writing.** Examples: 'I *love* learning about grammar.' 'Long live the Queen!' 'Do this homework for tomorrow.' 'May I please have some more homework to do?'

2. A *clause* **is a group of words with a verb in it**. Example: 'If you study hard . . .'

3. Less important in the context of Latin, **a *phrase* is a group of words *without* a verb in it**. Examples of phrases are 'group of words', 'without a verb' and 'in it'.

4. The *subject* of a sentence or clause is who or what the sentence or clause is all about. In Latin, a word which is the subject of a sentence or clause is always in the nominative case.

5. The *predicate* of a sentence or clause is the rest of the sentence, apart from the subject. That is to say, the *predicate* of a sentence or clause is whatever is said about the subject. Predicates normally include a verb, at least understood.

6. A *doing* verb is either a transitive verb or an intransitive verb.

7. A *transitive* verb is a doing verb that needs a direct object.

8. The *direct object* is perhaps the most difficult of all grammatical terms to define really clearly, so here are no fewer than *three* definitions. Choose which one you prefer to learn by heart. As can be seen from the examples given above:

   (i) **The direct object is that which undergoes what the subject of the sentence or the clause does.**
   (ii) **The direct object is the person or thing to which an action or feeling is directed.**
   (iii) **The direct object is the person or thing directly acted on by the subject of a sentence or clause** – for instance, 'I study *Latin*.'

9. An *intransitive* verb is a doing verb that does not take a direct object, as in the sentence 'I come and I go', where neither verb can have a direct object. With intransitive verbs the doer's action stops with the doer, and involves no one and nothing else.

10. Some verbs can be **either transitive or intransitive**. For instance, we can *grow* food and *grow* in height.

11. In addition to a **direct object**, some verbs (such as 'give', 'show' and 'teach') can be followed also by an **indirect object**. An *indirect object* is a noun or pronoun only *indirectly* affected by the verb it follows. That is to say, whereas a *direct* object is the

person or thing that the action of the verb is *directed at* (as in 'He teaches *grammar*'), the *indirect* object is the person or thing *to whom* or *for whom* the action is done (as in 'He teaches grammar *to me*' and 'He bought some grammar books *for me*').

12. **After a being word, what follows is *not* an object in the accusative case, but a complement in the same case as the subject, the nominative case**. This is much more important in Latin than in English. It does occasionally apply in English as well, though. Thus it is grammatically correct to say 'It is *I*' rather than the colloquial 'It's *me*.'

To explain the *complement* further, and to contrast it more clearly with the *object*, a collection of words such as 'Grammar is' is usually incomplete. The *complement* is the part of the sentence or clause that is added to the being word to complete the sense, as in 'Grammar *is a science*'. Yet another way of looking at it is that, in the case of a *complement*, the complement and the subject refer to the *same* person or thing, whereas, in the case of an *object*, the object and the subject refer to *different* people or things.

## SECTION 3
## THE ADDITIONAL GRAMMAR EXPRESSLY NEEDED FOR LEARNING LATIN

### Nouns

As should be remembered from the last chapter, in English almost all nouns – the word 'sheep' is a rare exception – change their form according to whether they are in the singular or plural, which is their **number**. In Latin, they also change their form according to what they are *doing* in the sentence. These different forms are called **cases**, of which in Latin there are six.

### Cases

The **six cases**, which apply also to pronouns and adjectives, are as follows:

1. **Nominative Case**, used when a noun or pronoun is the **subject** or **complement** in the **sentence** or **clause** in which it appears,

or, in the case of adjectives, when it **agrees**\* with a noun or pronoun which is the subject or complement. Examples: 'I am a teacher', where 'I' is the subject and 'a teacher' is the complement following the being word 'am'; 'I am a good teacher', where the adjective 'good' agrees with the complement 'teacher' (if we may assume for this purpose that 'agree' can apply to a word that does not change its form, as English adjectives do not).

2. **Vocative Case**, when the person represented by the noun or pronoun is being directly addressed, as in 'Yes, *sir*.'

3. **Accusative Case**, when the person, place or thing represented by the noun or pronoun or described by the adjective *either* (a) is the **object** in the sentence or clause *or* (b) depends on a **preposition** which governs or 'takes' the accusative. Examples: 'I teach him' and 'I look at him', 'him' being the direct object in the first case and governed by the preposition 'at' in the second case.

4. **Genitive Case**, conveniently known as the '*of* case', as in 'the importance *of Latin*' and '*Latin's* importance'.

5. **Dative Case**, the '*to* or *for* case' as in 'He gives something *to* her and does something *for* her.' In English, though not in Latin, the dative is often concealed, as in 'He gives *her* something.'

6. **Ablative Case**, often referred to, somewhat incompletely, as the '*by*, *with* or *from*' case, as in 'It was made *by* him and done *with* him and taken *from* him.'

A rare survival from pre-classical Latin is the **Locative Case**, which continued to exist in classical Latin, but only in very few nouns, most of them place names. It is used by itself in a noun rather than in the form of a preposition together with the case it takes. (An equivalent in English is 'I am going home' rather than '. . . to home', although dictionaries call 'home' an adverb in that construction – understandably because its use there is as adverbial as the adverb-phrase 'from home'.)

---

\* An adjective qualifies a given noun and must 'agree' with that noun by matching its case, number and gender.

## Gender

In Latin, as in every European language other than English, a complicating factor in nouns is that they have genders which are often independent of the sex of what they refer to. There are very occasional examples of this in English, such as 'ship', usually referred to under the feminine gender, for instance by the pronoun 'she'. The genders used in Latin are masculine, feminine, neuter; and, for instance, **mēnsa**, the Latin for 'table', is feminine; **flōs**, meaning 'flower', is masculine; and **bellum**, meaning 'war', is neuter. A few Latin words are said to be of *common* gender. Common, in the context of gender, means either masculine or feminine according to the sex of the particular person involved. Thus **iudex** meaning 'judge' would be masculine if the judge were of the male sex and feminine if of the female sex.

## Number

Nouns and pronouns are either singular, when there is a single one of the person or thing involved, or plural, when there is more than one. In both instances, the nouns and pronouns change their form according to both their case and their number. Thus in theory there are twelve different endings for each noun (only ten in the case of pronouns, which have no vocative case), though in practice the endings often overlap.

## Pronouns

Latin pronouns must grammatically match ('agree with') the noun they stand for – that is, they must be in the same case, number and gender. Personal pronouns are often omitted. Thus, for instance, the word **amat** can mean 'he loves', 'she loves' or 'it loves', or can have a noun as its subject, to be found somewhere in the sentence.

## Adjectives

Adjectives too must 'agree' in every respect – case, gender and number – with the noun or adjective that they are describing. That is, they must have, in their form, the same case and the same gender and the same number as the noun or pronoun in question.

## Articles

The English articles consist solely of 'the', 'a', 'an' and 'some'. Latin has no articles whatever, which makes it different from almost all other European languages and even from classical Greek.

## Adverbs

Most adverbs are, with very few exceptions (known as *irregular*), formed directly from adjectives. They do not change their form other than when they are comparative and superlative.

## Conjunctions

As already mentioned, there are two main types of conjunction: *coordinating conjunctions* and *subordinating conjunctions*. The main coordinating conjunctions, which we shall meet in our first chapter devoted specifically to Latin, Chapter Nine, are 'and', 'but' and 'or'. Typical subordinating conjunctions are 'if', 'unless' and 'when'.

## Prepositions

Prepositions, as will be remembered, govern nouns and pronouns. They 'take' cases, which is to say that a noun or pronoun governed by them has to be in the particular case appropriate to the preposition in question. As we have seen, there are instances of this in English. For example, 'between him and me' rather than 'between he and I'.

## Interjections

The rules for interjections are the same as those for interjections in English. They belong outside any clause that they relate to, rather as a noun or pronoun in the vocative case does. Example: 'My goodness, I am pleased to be learning Latin.'

## Verbs

Relative to any of the other parts of speech, the complexities of verbs are so great and so many that it is appropriate to give them a full chapter of their own, the next one.

## CHAPTER SEVEN

# What You Need to Know Before Starting: All About Verbs

EACH VERB HAS many forms. Thus the basic verb 'to be' in English has forms as varied as 'am', 'are', 'being', 'shall have been', 'was being', 'would have been', etc. This chapter summarises the changes in meaning conveyed by all the various forms of a verb. It teaches no Latin but ensures that you will understand the basic vocabulary used in the rest of the book to identify different verbal forms and their meanings. You already know all the English verb forms discussed here; what you may not yet know are their technical names.

We shall be using the verb 'to love' as our model.

Take the following table:

| Person | Number | |
|--------|--------|--------|
| | Singular | Plural |
| First | I love | we love |
| Second | you love | you love |
| Third | he, she or it loves | they love |

What this table shows might casually be called the Present Tense of the verb 'to love', but it is technically called the Present Tense, Active Voice, Indicative Mood of the verb 'to love'.

## Number and person

As you see, the verb has six forms, three for the singular and three for the plural. The first person is 'I' or 'we' – that is, the speaker is doing the loving. The second person is 'you' singular or plural – the person being addressed is doing it. The third person is anyone else – that is, the person or persons doing the loving include neither the speaker nor the person being spoken to, but someone else.

## Active and Passive Voices

The above table is said to represent the *Active* Voice to distinguish it from the Present Tense, *Passive* Voice, Indicative Mood of the same verb, which is given in the following table.

| Person | Number | |
| --- | --- | --- |
| | Singular | Plural |
| First | I am loved | we are loved |
| Second | you are loved | you are loved |
| Third | he, she or it is loved | they are loved |

By comparing the two tables, you see that in the *Active Voice* the subject of the verb loves while in the *Passive Voice* the subject is being loved by someone else. Reminder: only transitive verbs have passives. You can be loved but you cannot, for instance, be 'sleeped' or 'slept'.

## Indicative, Subjunctive and Imperative Moods

We do not always make statements about *facts*, such as that someone is loving or being loved. We sometimes use language to express wishes, doubts, conditions, consequences and commands. Statements and questions belong to the Indicative Mood. The Subjunctive Mood is used much less in English than in Latin but we find it in: 'Be that as it may', 'Be it so', 'So be it', 'If I were you', 'If only that were mine', 'Would that it were so', 'God save the Queen', 'Rule Britannia!', 'Come Christmas', and many other familiar expressions. Commands (such as 'Love thy neighbour') belong to the Imperative Mood.

## The six tenses

The table below sets out the six tenses that are found in Latin as they occur in the Indicative Mood, Active Voice. The meanings given are the English equivalents of each Latin tense. Only the first person singular is given, to show the meaning of the tense, though in fact all six persons occur in each tense, and in Latin each person has a distinct form in both numbers.

| Tense | Meaning |
|-------|---------|
| Present | I love, I am loving, I do love |
| Future Simple | I shall love, I shall be loving |
| Imperfect | I was loving, I loved, I used to love |
| Perfect | I have loved, I loved |
| Future Perfect | I shall have loved, I shall have been loving |
| Pluperfect | I had loved |

The above six tenses are found in the Active and Passive Voices of the indicative. Four of them (not the future simple or future perfect) are also found in the subjunctive, both Active and Passive Voices. Hence a Latin verb can be conjugated (matched to any 'person' and 'number') in six tenses multiplied by two voices for the indicative, and again in four tenses multiplied by two voices for the subjunctive.

We must not confuse Present Indicative Active (e.g. 'she loves') with Present Indicative Passive (e.g. 'she is loved'), nor with Present Subjunctive Active (e.g. 'may she love!'), nor indeed with the Present Subjunctive Passive (e.g. 'may she be loved!'). It is essential to know what each of these tenses, voices and moods mean.

Finally under this heading, it is worth mentioning that, in effect, English has two tenses which do not exist as separate tenses in Latin. One is commonly called Present Continuous Tense, as in 'I am loving' and 'I am being loved'. The other is known either as the Preterite or as the Aorist Tense, when the Perfect Tense in Latin is translated as 'I loved it' or 'I was loved' rather than 'I have loved' or 'I have been loved.'

## Other verbal forms

In addition to the forms we have just learnt, verbs also have other forms that do not 'conjugate' to match each person.

## The Infinitive

'To love' is the Present Infinitive Active. The Present Infinitive Passive is 'to be loved' and Latin also has a Perfect Infinitive, 'to have loved' – or, in the passive 'to have been loved' – and a Future Infinitive 'to be about to love' or 'to be going to love'.

## Participles

Our English participles include 'loving' and 'loved'. They are forms of the verb that have turned into adjectives. Latin also has a Future Participle, meaning 'about to love' and 'going to love'.

## Gerundive

Latin has another verbal adjective, the Gerundive, which corresponds in meaning to 'worthy to be loved', 'who or which ought to be loved', and sometimes almost to 'going to be loved'.

The few other verbal forms, such as the Gerund and the Supine, will be explained when we meet them in practice.

## CHAPTER EIGHT

# What You Need to Know Before Starting: How to Pronounce Latin

THE PRONUNCIATION OF Latin is a genuinely interesting subject in its own right, as well as being one of obvious practical importance.

Until about a hundred years ago, there were two main pronunciations of Latin.

One was the pronunciation used throughout the English-speaking world. This was simply that of pronouncing Latin words exactly as though they were English words (though with each vowel being part of a separate syllable, so that **domine** would be pronounced like 'domminnay' rather than as it would be pronounced if rhymed with 'refine'). This is still the pronunciation of Latin when it is used in everyday English expressions, such as **et cetera** and **modus vivendi**.

The other was the pronunciation used in Italy and, with small variations, in the other Catholic European countries, as it had been for many centuries. Primarily this was for the singing of Church music, but it was used in ordinary speaking as well. In this pronunciation, most of the vowels and diphthongs are of equal length, and most of them long, and some of the consonants were and are pronounced differently from ours.

So it had been for many centuries.

There came a time, at around the end of the nineteenth century, when there was an urge to find out and restore the pronunciation which had been used in classical times, and on which, after all, some of the greatest literature of all time was based. Interestingly, this urge originated in England. Prior to that, the pronunciation here was so far from the original as to be absurd, and of course this very fact provided a good motive for correcting it. It would, after all, not occur to us as adequate to pronounce, for instance, French or German according to the English pronunciation when speaking, even if we were not speaking to native speakers, other than in the case of place names such as Paris. There is an intrinsic rightness about getting things right.

To UNEARTH THE pronunciation of Latin's so-called Golden Age, the period in which the greatest Latin poetry and prose of all were written, needed such a depth of scholarship, ingenuity, wide reading and resourcefulness that it makes one shudder to think of the effort involved. Work after work of classical Roman times, of both poetry and prose, must have been painstakingly examined in every tiny detail, in the search for clues in the detective work – and often without even knowing which kinds of clues might be helpful. Nothing as simple as looking for rhymes could be part of the research, for instance, because rhyming was never part of the poetry of *any* nation until Ireland invented it well after the end of the classical era, and in due course – by the early Middle Ages – 'conquered' the whole of Europe with it.

Fortunately, heroes were at hand in England who were equal to the task. The several different types of evidence that they identified as helpful, cumulatively, for each word and its syllables included:

— the occasional specific statement in the classical period made by Latin grammarians and other Latin authors as to the pronunciation of their language;

— the representation of the same word in classical Greek (Greek and Latin were living side by side during that period, because Greek was then the *lingua franca* – the common language – used throughout the entire Roman Empire);

— puns and other plays on words;

— imitations of natural sounds, such as those made by animals, birds, and different kinds of weather;

— written variations of words, where one spelling evidently had much the same sound as a different one;

— and of course developments into the five Romance languages that are the descendants of classical Latin.

Analysing these with the greatest care, and avoiding, where possible, relying on only a single piece of evidence in relation to any combination of letters, the researchers ended up between them putting together a pronunciation that was so obviously well argued, indeed compellingly argued, that it was accepted as correct throughout Europe. For some time, indeed, it has been not uncommon for children at school in Europe, even in Italy, to be taught two separate pronunciations of Latin: one for singing in church and one for use in the schoolroom.

This unearthing of essentially the correct pronunciation of classical Latin was an important development worldwide, since classical poetry, based very much on the difference between short and long vowels, cannot be properly recited other than when pronounced as it was originally written.

As of today, there are no fewer than four different pronunciations of Latin traditionally used by those who learn it, all of which I teach according to whatever the context is. Perhaps as good an example as any to illustrate differences between them is the common Latin and English word **circus**, all four different pronunciations of which are clearly distinguishable.

One is the Latin that we speak when we are speaking English, a language which, as we learnt back in Chapter One, includes a considerable amount of Latin in its original form. Here the pronunciation of **circus** is of course as you know it to be – it could be written 'serkuss'. That is also how it was pronounced in the Latin that was taught in schools throughout England until well into the twentieth century, and is still used in the law courts (much less in recent years but still very much so in, for instance, South Africa); in mottos of families, towns and other institutions; and in botany and medicine.

In Church, or Italianate, Latin, **circus** is pronounced

'cheercoose', reflecting amongst other things the fact that the letter 'c' is pronounced differently after 'e', 'i' and 'ae' from how it is pronounced after 'a', 'o' and 'u', as indeed it usually is in English.

In the Latin used by Julius Caesar, Virgil, Cicero and Horace, **circus** is pronounced 'keerkuss', with the stress on the first syllable and the last syllable rhyming with 'puss', as in 'pussycat'. This is the so-called Restored Classical Pronunciation.

Finally, there is the pronunciation of **circus** that is unquestionably wrong but is the pronunciation I normally teach, along with countless other wrong pronunciations. This, I hasten to add, is not eccentricity on my part. From the time, starting in the early part of the twentieth century, that the Restored Classical Pronunciation was established as the basic pronunciation that ought to be taught in schools in place of English-pronounced Latin pronunciation, it has been the way that Latin has been taught for the purpose of learning by heart declensions and conjugations throughout the English-speaking world

This fourth pronunciation is again as though the word were pronounced 'keerkuss', but this time with the stress on the second syllable.

The reason is simple. There is a vast quantity of Latin words to learn by heart in which the *stem* – the first part of the word – stays the same and the *ending* changes, and it is *very* much easier to learn such material by heart if the stress is kept on the part of the word which changes.

Take the word **amō** as an example. In the correct pronunciation it is pronounced as if it were '*am*mō'. If what we needed to learn were '*am*ō', '*ba*mō', '*ca*mō', and so on, it would be easiest for us to learn it if the stress were on the *first* syllable in each case, pronouncing them '*am*mō', '*bam*mō', '*cam*mō'. Since, however, the *first* syllable stays the same and what changes is the syllable (or syllables) that comes *after* it, conjugating it is much easier to learn if the stress is on one or other of those latter syllables – so much easier that the imperfection has traditionally been considered worth putting up with.

Specifically, then, when learning by heart we stress the syllable that is most subject to change in the conjugation or declension, which will be the last syllable in many forms and the last but one in some others. In our 'wrong' pronunciation, therefore, **amo** is wrongly pronounced as though it were 'a mow', as in 'It is time to give the lawn a mow' and **amat** as in our 'a mat'.

The pronunciation of the individual letters is not difficult, since it resembles English pronunciation reasonably closely. This is not surprising given that, along with most other European countries, we use the Latin alphabet. The most important thing to concentrate on getting right is the difference in pronunciation between vowels when they are short and the same vowels when they are long.

One other English tradition that we shall be adopting is to pronounce Latin as though with a *regional* Latin accent. In other words, we shall happily assume, as is certainly correct, that Latin, although in principle pronounced the same everywhere in the Roman Empire, in practice was pronounced differently in different parts of that empire, just as English is today in different parts of what used to be the British Empire. Thus although in Rome the letter 'a' in **amo** would almost certainly have been pronounced 'ummo', we shall assume that, for instance, St Helen (*c.* AD 250–330), mother of the first Christian emperor, Constantine, and herself from Britannia, would have pronounced **amat** as 'a mat' rather than as 'ummutt', though unlike us (see below) she would have put the stress in the right place.

## Correct stress

While we deliberately mis-stress words in order to learn them by heart, we must know the correct stress-rules to use at all other times. The summary that now follows is highly simplified but in practice is almost invariably correct.

In every Latin word of more than one syllable there is a stressed or accented syllable; that is, one that is pronounced more emphatically than the others. In words of two syllables it is always the first syllable that is stressed. In words of more than two, the stressed syllable is the last but one (penultimate) if it is long and the last but two (antepenultimate) if the penultimate syllable is short. A syllable is long if its vowel is long (see below for the use of the horizontal line to mark this) or if it ends with a double consonant.

It would appear that in antiquity and even well into the early Middle Ages the stress was in fact more a matter of pitch than loudness. I do not recommend trying to recapture that usage, however; nor was this done in schools in England in my schooldays or before. Just raise your voice on the accented syllable as we do in English.

## Vowels

The convention followed in this book is to mark long vowels with a horizontal line – called a macron – above them, and not to mark short vowels at all. These macrons should *not* be confused with accents used to indicate stress. They are there to help beginners choose between two possible vowel lengths. They are not usually used in Latin texts aimed at those who have already learnt their basics, though they appear in dictionaries because even the most erudite do not know them all by heart. Normally I use them (a) when introducing you to a new word and (b) in the Reference Grammar and the vocabularies. Here are the vowels with an example of a word in English in each case to show how they should be pronounced.

Ā ā, pronounced as in 'f*a*ther'. A a pronounced as in 'c*a*t'.
Ē ē pronounced as in 'gr*ey*'.* E e pronounced as in 'g*e*t'.
Ī ī pronounced as in 'mach*i*ne', not as in 'm*i*ne'. I i pronounced as in 'p*i*n'.
I i is also used as a consonant (see below under Consonants).
Ō ō pronounced as in 'm*o*te'. O o pronounced as in 'g*o*t'.
Ū ū pronounced as in 'r*oo*t'. U u pronounced as in 'p*u*t' (or the English 'f*oo*t'), *not* as in 'p*u*tt'. In my experience, these two pronunciations of 'u' are the only ones that are at all difficult for beginners to remember.

---

* If the long ē is followed by two or more consonants the need to pronounce it long is seldom respected; and, frankly, I do not respect it myself. Thus the noun **mēnsa** is usually pronounced as '*mensa*', almost rhyming with 'denser', even though it should strictly be '*mainsa*'. While I *incline* to recommend the correct rather than the traditional pronunciation, do not adopt it if you find that it makes learning by heart more difficult.

## Diphthongs

Diphthongs are two letters pronounced as one letter. Semi-diphthongs are two letters run so closely together as to amount *almost* to one letter. There are in total five diphthongs or semi-diphthongs. The only ones we shall be using in this book are:

**Ae ae** pronounced as in the English word '*I'll*', or indeed '*ai*sle', or indeed '*i*sle'.
**Au au** pronounced as in the English word 'm*ou*se'.
**Ei ei** as in 'f*ai*nt' or indeed 'f*ei*nt'.
**Eu eu** pronounced as in the English word 'f*ew*', or possibly as in the sound '*ee-oo*' said very quickly.
**Oe oe** pronounced as in the English word 'b*oy*'. In Church Latin it is pronounced as **ē** (see page 44).

Occasionally there are instances where it is impossible to tell whether two vowels in succession are a diphthong or not. For instance, the 'eu' of **deus** is not a diphthong whereas in **eheu** it is, and the same applies to the 'oe' of **poeta** and **poena** respectively. Indeed, the word **aere** completely changes its meaning, from 'with the air', if the 'ae' is not a diphthong, to 'with the brass', if it is. Although which is which can often be worked out, as in **deus** because it declines, sometimes it cannot – regrettably, a book has occasional limitations in its capacity as teacher which a human being has not!

Here is an important point. Other than in the case of those diphthongs or semi-diphthongs, with one possible exception all vowels should be pronounced separately. The possible exception: some authorities say that **Ui ui** should be pronounced quickly enough to make the sound effectively one syllable. The French '*oui*' is perhaps the best equivalent, provided that it is completely distinct from our 'we'.

## Consonants

The Latin alphabet had no **j** or **v**. In the place of our **j** and **v**, the letters **i** and **u** respectively were used, which meant that those two letters were used as both vowels and consonants.

Latin consonants are mostly pronounced like English consonants. The only difference of any importance is that the letter **c**
and the letter **g** are always hard. The word **cēnsor** is pronounced
as if it were spelt '*k*ensor' and in the word **gens** the **g** is pronounced as in the English '*g*et' rather than as in the English
'*g*entle'.

The **h** is always sounded.

In theory, the **s** should always be as in the first **s** in '*s*eason' and
not as in the second **s** in that word. In practice, we shall take no
notice of that, because it is important to distinguish between
words with only one **s**, such as **mīsī** ('I sent') and **missī** ('people
who have been sent').

Once the writing of Latin verse is embarked on, one other
refinement that needs to be known is the pronunciation of **gn**,
as in **magnus**. Rather than its being correctly pronounced
exactly as it is spelt, as we shall be pronouncing it, the real pronunciation is more like '*ngn*', as in 'stro*ngn*ess' if there were such
a word.

The letter **i** as a consonant is pronounced '*y*' as in '*y*es', so that
the Latin word **iūdex** (originally in English spelt **judex**), meaning
'judge', was pronounced '*yoo*dex'.

As already mentioned, the Latin alphabet did not include a
letter **j** or the letter **v**. For our purpose they need to be looked at
separately.

From the time of the adoption of the more-or-less correct
classical pronunciation of Latin back in the first half of the
twentieth century, the **j** was indeed dropped and replaced by **i**, as
in the Latin word **iūdex**. We shall be using that pronunciation
because there is no good reason not to.

In the case of **v**, however, this was the one respect in which
until recently the modern grammars kept the non-classical pronunciation. Most of the more modern grammars have moved on
from there, however, and pronounce the **u**, when it is a consonant rather than a vowel, as '*w*'. This means that the Latin for
slave, **servus**, is written as **seruus** and pronounced '*serwoos*'.

Though that is strictly correct, and taught in many schools
today, I strictly object!

There is no problem with adopting the correct pronunciation

of **i** when it is a consonant, because there is never any problem in deciding whether that letter is a consonant when it comes before another vowel, as in **iūdex**, or a vowel when it comes before the same vowel as in **filius** (meaning 'son').

This is *not* the case with the letter **u**, which, for instance, can sometimes come before another **u**, as in **tuus**, meaning 'your' (singular). Therefore, if you were to see the word **seruus**, which previously could be written **servus**, you would have no way of knowing whether it had *two* syllables or *three* syllables. To save myself from having to tell you how any word using **u** before another vowel is pronounced every time it appears, therefore, I am going to stay with the tradition of right up to very recent times – the tradition of writing and pronouncing **u** as a **v** when it is being used as a consonant.* So there!

WITH THAT OUTLINE in place, the easiest and most convenient next step for most people, of any age, would be to take advantage of modern technology and visit gwynneteaching. com. There you will find me and others going through all the main nouns, pronouns, adjectives and verbs, showing how they should be pronounced. We take pains also to show the easiest way to learn them by heart, which means using the rhythm that is best for exact and quick memorising. We even give examples of very small children reciting them, well before they can understand them, yet obviously enjoying what they are doing.

My recommendation is to visit this website, with whatever is the relevant part of this book open. First of all listen to us reciting, so as to get an idea of the rhythm. Then join in, reciting it all in unison with us.

---

* The most used grammars of all by far up till the 1960s, *Kennedy's Revised Latin Primer* and *Kennedy's Shorter Latin Primer*, used **v** as the consonant rather than **u**, and the editions in print still do. So also do the classic, long-used exercise books by Hillard and Botting, *Elementary Latin Exercises* and *Elementary Latin Translation*, and even the standard Latin–English dictionaries in print, such as those published by Cassell's and Collins.

# PART THREE

# INTO BATTLE

## CHAPTER NINE

**Mēnsa** and **annus** in full; present and future simple
tenses of **amō** and **sum**; the theory of Principal
Parts; the principal coordinating conjunctions; our
first adverbs; and basic Latin word order

## ACCIDENCE – WHAT MUST BE
### *LEARNT BY HEART*

### Our first two nouns

This chapter is almost certainly going to need more time and
effort on your part than any of its successors. The reason is that in
the next few pages I am introducing you to a fair number of different concepts all at the same time, and these concepts are likely
to be new to you. This is so to such an extent that getting hold of
them really adequately will involve your setting about forming
genuinely new *mental habits*.

I should make it clear that bringing in so many different topics
at the same time at the very outset is unusual in Latin textbooks,
which on the whole try to minimise the difficulty of Latin at the
start, by introducing new topics one at a time. I need make no
apology for this different approach, however. On the one hand, each
concept individually is easy enough to be grasped by anyone who
has reached the age of reason; and, all things being equal, the more
complete a 'picture' is, the more satisfying and satisfactory it must be.
On the other hand, you have the relief to look forward to, that the
remaining chapters in this book will be not *quite* so demanding!

I start with an introductory piece of information which applies
from now on throughout this book. In the previous chapter, on
pronunciation, I amongst other things gave the pronunciations of
vowels, all of which vary according to whether the vowel in question is a long vowel – indicated there by a short line immediately
above the letter – or a short vowel, indicated there by having no

additional mark. The difference in pronunciation between long and short vowels is important, because in very many cases the meaning can be affected, as we shall see. In ordinary prose- and verse-writing, however, no such clarification is made, as indeed it was never made in either classical or medieval Latin. It is yet another difficulty of Latin that, in normal circumstances, the length of a vowel in any new word is something additional that the reader of Latin has to work out when that is possible, and look up when it is not; and it very often is not.

The practice that I have adopted in this book is: (a) always to show the vowel-lengths in the parts devoted expressly to setting out the grammatical details of words – specifically where the grammar is given and in the vocabularies; (b) in this chapter only, to show the vowel-lengths in every Latin word that appears, other than in the exercises. In subsequent chapters I do this less and less, and eventually only when some special reason seems to call for it. Such vowel-length indications were unknown to the classical authors and readers, and usually do not appear in modern textbooks giving exercises.

Once again, I recommend that learning by heart should be done by reciting out-loud where possible. This, moreover, does not mean doing the reciting *once or twice*, but doing it as often as is necessary – perhaps hundreds of times – until every declension and conjugation is known as well as one's telephone number and can never be forgotten. The need to remember the lengths of vowels, because of their often being important to the meaning of words, is as good a reason for this recommendation as any, but it is a good tip anyway, and a traditional one. 'Let it be emphasised that for maximum value you must say *aloud* all the Latin words, phrases and sentences,' says the American best-selling *Wheelock's Latin Grammar*\* uncompromisingly, and, as you can see, emphasising the word '*aloud*'. So say I.

## Accidence

We now turn to our very first Latin words and their grammar.

In this chapter, I shall make everything easy and obvious, to

---

\* Fourth Edition, 1992, page 270.

make sure that the reader can be in no doubt as to how the learning is to be done. In future chapters, I shall be gradually abandoning the spoon-feeding, until, quite soon, I shall be limiting what I say to:

— instructing what should be learnt by heart next;
— explaining new points of syntax;
— and sometimes giving advice that seems immediately relevant on the generality of how best to learn and to teach Latin.

In almost all the traditional grammars, the first Latin learnt is the noun **mēnsa**, which means 'table'. On the face of it, it is a strange choice. Much more commonly used nouns which change their endings in exactly the same way include **fēmina**, meaning 'woman', and **puella**, meaning 'girl'. These also have the advantage that for them the vocative case can be used in practice, especially in the plural, whereas no one is likely to address a table. We cannot, however, go wrong by staying with tradition except when there is compelling reason not to; and **mēnsa** does have the advantage of showing at the outset that words with neuter *meanings* can have non-neuter *genders*. Furthermore, it could even be argued that the 'nonsense' of a vocative for a non-personal noun helps to make a useful start in developing abstract thinking generally.

Nouns fall into five categories, or groups, called **declensions**, according to how the endings change from case to case. **Mēnsa** is a **First Declension noun**, and declines as hereunder. Immediately after it, I am giving the declension of what is traditionally the first of four model **Second Declension nouns**. This noun is **annus**, meaning 'year'.

Please go no further until you have learnt these two nouns, **mēnsa** and **annus**, by heart, making sure that both your pronunciation and the rhythm are correct. Although I have already made clear what the cases are for, I am repeating this point of grammar just this once, in the interest of being as 'spoon-feedingly' helpful as I can at this early stage to get you off to a good start.

| mēnsa, -ae, f., table | | |
|---|---|---|
| | Singular | Plural |
| Nominative (for the subject) | mēnsa | mēnsae |
| Vocative (the 'addressing' case) | mēnsa | mēnsae |
| Accusative (for the object) | mēnsam | mēnsas |
| Genitive (the 'of' case) | mēnsae | mēnsarum |
| Dative (the case for 'to' or 'for') | mēnsae | mēnsīs |
| Ablative (for 'by', 'with', 'from') | mēnsā | mēnsīs |

Remember to recite reading down the singular column first: **mēnsa, mēnsa, mēnsam, mēnsae, mēnsae, mēnsā;** then the plural: **mēnsae, mēnsae, mēnsas, mēnsarum, mēnsīs, mēnsīs.**

Then you must move on immediately to **annus**, for the Second Declension, which you learn in exactly the same way until you can repeat all twelve forms of both nouns without risk of error or hesitation.

| annus, -ī, m., year | | |
|---|---|---|
| | Singular | Plural |
| Nom. | annus | annī |
| Voc. | anne | annī |
| Acc. | annum | annōs |
| Gen. | annī | annōrum |
| Dat. | annō | annīs |
| Abl. | annō | annīs |

One last thing to mention before we leave our first two nouns is that, whenever you learn the meaning of a new noun (or indeed any other word of variable endings), you should learn its **Principal Parts** or main forms.

## What exactly are **Principal Parts**?

They are the minimum needed to make clear how any noun or adjective declines and how any verb conjugates. For nouns, it is enough to give the nominative singular and the genitive singular for all the other endings to be knowable. We shall be coming to what is needed for verbs and adjectives shortly.

Back to nouns: as just noted, their **Principal Parts** are: the nominative singular, the genitive singular, the gender, and the meaning. Thus if you were to look up **mēnsa** as a new word, you would see that its **Principal Parts** are 'mēnsa, -ae, f., table'. You should say to yourself, therefore, not simply **mēnsa**, but 'mēnsa-mēnsae-feminine-table'. Similarly, with **annus**, when you see 'annus, -ī, m., year' you should say 'annus-annī-masculine-year'. You must continue repeating these forms until they are comfortably in your memory – as much in your memory as the nominative singulars. Do this conscientiously from the start, and you will save yourself much time and from countless errors in the long run. With all the parts of speech for which they are needed, **Principal Parts** are wonderfully convenient.

## Our first verb

Most usually, verbs have four of the **Principal Parts** just referred to. These are: the first person singular of the present indicative active (**amō** in the case of **amō**); the present infinitive active (**amare**); the first person singular of the perfect indicative active (**amāvi**); and the supine (**amātum**). Some verbs do not have what is called the Passive Voice (which we shall be coming to in due course). And others, called Deponent Verbs, have in their forms only the Passive Voice. These too we shall be coming to later. One other exception is the being word **sum**, which we shall be coming to immediately after **amō**.

Just as Latin nouns are divided into five different **declensions**, verbs are divided into four different **conjugations**. Traditionally the first verb to be learnt is the 'doing-word' verb **amō**, which belongs to the **First Conjugation** and therefore serves as a model for all other verbs of the same conjugation. Here I shall give first of all the **Principal Parts**, as I shall be doing with all verbs when I introduce them, and then the first two **tenses**: the **present tense** and the **future simple tense** of the **indicative mood** of the **Active Voice**.

Refer back to Chapter Seven if necessary for what those technical terms mean.

The present indicative active is the Latin which corresponds to the English 'I love' or 'I am loving' or 'I do love'.

**Principal Parts**: **amō, amāre, amāvī, amātum,** I love.

| The **present tense** of **amō** | | | | |
|---|---|---|---|---|
| | Singular | | Plural | |
| First person | I love | **amō** | we love | **amāmus** |
| Second person | you love | **amās** | you love | **amātis** |
| Third person | he, she, it loves | **amāt** | they love | **amant** |

| The **future simple tense** of **amō** | | | | |
|---|---|---|---|---|
| | Singular | | Plural | |
| First person | I shall love | **amābō** | we shall love | **amābimus** |
| Second person | you will love | **amābis** | you will love | **amābitis** |
| Third person | he, she, it will love | **amābit** | they will love | **amābunt** |

Please now go no further until you have learnt the present and future simple tenses of **amō** by heart. You should do this thoroughly enough to be able to use what you will have learnt by heart for three different purposes.

One is to be able to recite them in Latin beginning to end – that is, from the first person singular to the third person plural. For this purpose, it is sufficient in the third person singular to say only the Latin for 'he loves' (representing the Latin for 'she loves' and 'it loves' as well), in order to save time and to preserve the rhythm.

The second is to be able to identify *in both directions* the case and number of any of the words. By 'in both directions' I mean that, if challenged to give the first person plural of **amō**, you will unhesitatingly reply **amāmus**, or if asked to identify **amāmus** you will at once say that it is the first person plural.

The third is to be able to identify the meanings in both

directions. By this I mean that you can, again without hesitation, identify 'we shall love' as **amābimus** or identify **amābimus** as 'we shall love'.

Only when you have reached that stage of having mastered this part of **amō** in those three ways will you have adequately learnt the present and future simple tenses of **amō** by heart.

This principle of thoroughness applies to everything in this book that you need to learn by heart.

As in the case of nouns, you must learn the **Principal Parts** of every new verb you meet before all else. You will find them in the Reference Grammar or in the vocabularies. As you will see there, in most cases there are four **Principal Parts** and in some cases there are only three.

Do not at this stage concern yourself with what each **Principle Part** *means* in any verb. The meaning of each one is of minor importance compared to the importance of the **Principle Parts** as a whole, which is simply that, if you know the **Principal Parts** of a verb, you have, against the background of the knowledge of how the conjugations work that you will soon have, enough information to know the accidence of that particular verb in every detail.

## Our second verb

Having learnt our first 'doing-word' verb, we shall next look at the main 'being-word' verb, which is **sum**, meaning 'I am'. Doubtless because it is so much used, **sum** is one of the most irregular verbs in the whole of Latin, as indeed is its equivalent, 'I am', in English. It is therefore rather more difficult to learn by heart than is the one we started with, **amō**, which is completely regular. (It does, however, have the advantage, shared with all 'being verbs', that it has no Passive Voice.) As with **amō**, we shall tackle the **present** and **future simple tenses** of the **indicative mood**.

The **Principal Parts** of **sum** are: **sum, esse, fuī, futūrus**,* I am.

---

* **Futurus** is the future participle, there being no past participle of this verb.

| The **present tense** of **sum** | | | | |
|---|---|---|---|---|
| | Singular | | Plural | |
| First person | I am | **sum** | we are | **sumus** |
| Second person | you are | **es** | you are | **estis** |
| Third person | he, she, it is | **est** | they are | **sunt** |

| The **future simple tense** of **sum** | | | | |
|---|---|---|---|---|
| | Singular | | Plural | |
| First person | I shall be | **erō** | we shall be | **erimus** |
| Second person | you will be | **eris** | you will be | **eritis** |
| Third person | he, she, it will be | **erit** | they will be | **erunt** |

## Our first conjunctions

**Reminder.** There are two kinds of conjunction: **coordinating conjunctions**, which join clauses of equal status together, and **subordinating conjunctions** which join *subsidiary* clauses either to main clauses or to subsidiary clauses of superior status. Here we shall look at the principal **coordinating conjunctions**, of which there are just three.

The first one in English is 'and', for which there are in fact no fewer than four different Latin conjunctions. The commonest one is **et**. The next most common is the three letters **-que** tacked on to the end of the word which would have 'and' in front of it in English. Thus 'and the table' in English can be **mēnsaque** in Latin if 'table' is the subject or the complement in the relevant clause. The other two, less common (and we shall not be using them at this stage) are **atque** and **ac**.

Next is the English for 'but', which is **sed**.

Our third is the English for 'or', which is **aut**; and 'either ... or' is **aut ... aut**. Incidentally, conjunctions used in pairs in that way – 'neither ... nor' is of course another example – are technically called **correlative conjunctions**.

Finally we must learn **neque**, used to mean 'and ... not'.

## Our first adverbs

| **nōn** (note the **ō**: **nōn** rhymes with known) | not |
|---|---|
| **numquam** | never |
| **semper** | always |
| **umquam** | ever |
| **saepe** | often |
| **mox** | soon |
| **nunc** | now |
| **tunc** | then |
| **tum** | then (freely exchangeable with **tunc**) |

**Important rule.** Never put **et** before a negative word such as **nōn** or **numquam**; e.g. do not say '**et nōn amō**' for 'and I do not love', but '**neque amō**'; do not say '**et numquam**' for 'and never', but '**neque umquam**' ('and not ever').

## SYNTAX – WHAT MUST BE *UNDERSTOOD*

## Our first syntax points

It is now time to mention some important differences between the English and the Latin construction of sentences.

## Cases and numbers

### *Sum and the complement*

As **sum** is a being verb rather than a doing verb, it is *not* followed by a direct object, as transitive doing verbs are. Instead it is followed by a **complement**. It cannot be followed by a direct object, because the definition of an object, as we have seen, is 'that which undergoes what the subject of the sentence or the clause does', and the subject of a being verb is not *doing* anything. It is only in a certain *state*. Another way of saying the same thing is to call **sum** a 'coupling verb', as opposed to a verb of action.

What a being verb and the complement that follows it are doing, therefore, is saying more about the subject, just as they would be if the being verb were followed by an adjective describing the subject. Indeed, the complement that follows a being verb often *is* an adjective describing the subject. There is no essential difference in construction between 'Latin *is a language*' and 'Latin *is easy*'.

The result is that, just as with adjectives, what follows a being verb must be in the same case, gender and number as the subject. For the time being, that will always be the nominative.

**Example.** In the sentence 'Amanda loves the queen', the queen is undergoing the act of being loved by the subject Amanda. 'Queen' is therefore the object of the verb and in Latin must take the accusative case. In the sentence 'Amanda *is* the queen', however, the queen is not undergoing any act and cannot be the object of the verb. 'Queen' will be in the same case as 'Amanda' – the nominative case used for subjects and their complements.

## Adverbs

An adverb should go immediately in front of the word it relates to, which at this point in our studies will always be a verb. Thus: 'He does *not* like the girl' is **Puellam *non* amat**.

## Word order: the basics

**Reminder.** In English, word order is normally essential to the sense of a clause. The word order is *enough* to distinguish 'Caesar has defeated Pompey' from 'Pompey has defeated Caesar', and it is also absolutely *necessary* in order to distinguish them. In Latin, it is much less essential, because the same information is already conveyed by the *endings*. Hence word order is *not* a sufficient guide to meaning. (If you try to guess the meaning of a Latin sentence using word order instead of the endings, you will only ever be right by chance and you will develop bad habits that will make it much harder to learn Latin properly.) This is not to say that word order does not matter in Latin, but rather that different rules apply.

For our present purposes, there are just four principles to learn.

1. The usual place for any verb is *at the end* of its clause.

2. Adjectives – which we have not yet met – usually go *after* the noun or pronoun they describe, rather than before as is usual in English.

3. Adverbs usually go *in front of* the verb that they modify.

4. When a possessive pronoun can be safely inferred from the context, it is usually left out in Latin. Thus the English 'The Queen loves her friend' would normally be translated into Latin simply as '[The] Queen loves [the] friend' in the English word order or 'Queen friend loves' in the most usual Latin word order.

## Vocabulary

### Our first vocabulary

Any words you encounter in the exercises or explanations that are not met in these vocabulary lists you will need to look up in the vocabularies at the end of the book.

### Nouns

The following nouns are declined like the First Declension **mēnsa:**

| amīca, -ae, f. | female friend |
| patria, - ae, f. | country (fatherland) |
| puella, -ae, f. | girl |
| pugna, -ae, f. | battle |
| rēgīna, -ae, f. | queen |
| epistula, -ae, f. | letter |
| curia, -ae, f. | court |
| Anglia, -ae, f. | England |

The following nouns are declined like the Second Declension **annus:**

| amīcus, -ī, m. | friend (male or of unspecified sex) |
| dominus, -ī, m. | lord |
| captivus, -ī, m. | prisoner |
| servus, -ī, m. | slave |

| filius, -ī, m. | son |
| Iūlius, -ī, m. | the first name of Julius Caesar |
| Pompeius, -iī, m. | Pompey |

**Note.** Second Declension words ending in **-ius** often have the vocative ending **-ī**, not, **-ie**. Thus to address my son I must say '**filī**', and if his name is Julius I must say '**Iūlī**'.

We shall also be using the name **Caesar**. Because, however, it is a Third Declension word (**Caesar, Caesaris,** m., Caesar), we shall be using it only in the nominative case until we have learnt the Third Declension.

## Verbs

The **Principal Parts** of **cantō** (I sing) have the same endings as **amō**: **cantō, cantāre, cantāvī, cantātum**. This is usually presented in a shortened form: **cantō, -āre, -āvī, -ātum**. This is how you will find verbs presented in the vocabulary lists. When you see **cantō, -āre, -āvī, -ātum** you say aloud: '**cantō, cantāre, cantāvī, cantātum**', and you repeat it until you know it by heart.

The following verbs also conjugate like **amō**:

| cantō, -āre, -āvī, -ātum | I sing |
| laudō, -āre, -āvī, -ātum | I praise |
| pugnō, -āre, -āvī, -ātum | I fight |
| rogō, -āre, -āvī, -ātum | I ask (for) |
| superō, -āre, -āvī, -ātum | I overcome, outdo |
| vocō, -āre, -āvī, -ātum | I call |
| liberō, -āre, -āvī, -ātum | I free, deliver |
| parō, -āre, -āvī, -ātum | I prepare |

After the next chapter, in which the spoon-feeding will continue but less so, the new vocabulary to be learnt for each chapter will usually be found only in the vocabularies at the back of this book, as is usual in textbooks. This gives additional incentive to learn new vocabulary by heart as soon as you meet it.

When everything in this chapter has been learnt, which includes being able effortlessly to decline and conjugate the nouns and verbs which go like **mēnsa** and **amō** respectively, you will be ready to move on to the exercises for this chapter. If you translate these sentences correctly you will already have done better than most present-day Latin students who have already passed GCSEs or equivalent exams in Latin.

Please do not go on to the exercises until everything so far in this chapter has been *thoroughly* learnt by heart – so thoroughly that you can effortlessly rattle out the conjugations and declensions, find the Latin for any phrase such as 'we shall love' and 'of the tables', and identify by its technical name any person, number and tense of a verb and any case, number and gender of a noun.

Do not worry about how long this takes, which must vary widely from person to person. It could take a day or so; it could take a week or longer; it could take a month. If you yield to the temptation of starting the exercises *before* this preliminary labour is properly done, you will not be using this book in the way best calculated to teach you Latin most thoroughly, most quickly and to your greatest benefit.

## EXERCISES ON WHAT HAS BEEN LEARNT SO FAR

The exercises in this book have been put together strictly for the purpose of conveniently testing and practising what has been learnt, rather than for any interest in their content, which indeed may verge on the nonsensical. For the same reason, some of the early exercises include sentences which, although grammatically correct, are not idiomatic classical Latin.

### Instructions

1. Remind yourself what the word 'parse' means, and what parsing involves.
2. When translating *from* Latin *into* English, *two* translations should be made of each sentence, however short it is: (a) one that is completely literal down to the tiniest detail, with no attention paid to its awkwardness, or even idiotic appearance, in English. This ensures that no guessing takes place, even half-consciously or less; (b) a re-translation of that first trans-

lation into the best and most natural English you can manage.

3. *Do not hurry.* What you should be aiming at is to complete the exercises without having made a single mistake, though experience suggests that only the very strongest learners will achieve this at once.

4. Have your blank sheet of paper or open exercise book ready, look at your watch and note down the time that you are starting, and . . . start. Translate the English into Latin and the Latin into English and do anything else you are asked to do. You are not expected to include the sign marking long vowels.

## A. Easy

| |
|---|
| 1. I love the queen. |
| 2. You are not the queen of England. |
| 3. The son outdoes his friend. |
| 4. We shall soon fight. |
| 5. You will be lords. |
| 6. The friends of the queen praise Julius. |
| 7. **Reginae patria Anglia est.** |
| 8. **Dominum saepe laudabimus.** |
| 9. **Captivi numquam cantant.** |
| 10. **Epistulam rogabitis.** |

## B. Harder

| |
|---|
| 1. The girls love the queen, but the queen does not love the girls. |
| 2. I love the friend of the girl, and we shall love the friends of the girls. |
| 3. Never will queens praise girls, and girls either love queens now or will never love queens. |
| 4. The queen loves her friends and her friends are girls. (In this sentence you do not know what sex the friends are in the first clause.) |
| 5. The girl will never be queen but she will always love the queen. The sons are outdoing their friends but will soon often be singing. |

| 6. Friends never outdo friends and sons never outdo girls, but the queen often praises her sons. |
| 7. Julius Caesar will never be a friend of Pompey's, and Pompey is not calling his son Julius. |
| 8. **Claudius captivos liberat et captivi Claudium laudant.** |
| 9. **Epistulas reginae parabimus sed pecuniam puellis non dabimus.** |
| 10. **Aut amicam curiae amamus aut amicam curiae non amamus.** |

C. Parse and then translate, looking up any words you need to in the vocabularies, the following words and idioms which, in their untranslated Latin forms, are part of the English language and included in English dictionaries:

1. **Aegrotat; concordat; extant; ignoramus; aqua vitae.** (All these words are also to be found in a good English dictionary. Compare their meaning there with your Latin translation.)
2. Julius Caesar loves his son and his son's friend. His son's friend does not love Pompey's daughter but does love the queen. (Use **-que** for 'and' whenever the word 'and' appears.)

When you have completed this task to your satisfaction, note down the time, so that you can compare the amount of time taken over this exercise with the amount of time taken over future ones. You will find the answers to the above exercises in the form of the exercises for translating in the opposite direction at the end of the next chapter.

Please do not turn to these now, however. Rather, wait until you have studied and mastered the contents of Chapter Ten and are ready to embark on its exercises. By then, you will probably have sufficiently forgotten the original English for them to be genuinely useful for you. When you have completed your translation of those sentences of Chapter Ten back into English, return to these exercises here and make the comparison.

## CHAPTER TEN

Second Declension in full; remaining active
indicative tenses of **amō** and **sum**; some more
adverbs; and our first prepositions

## ACCIDENCE – WHAT MUST BE
### *LEARNT BY HEART*

Now the learning-by-heart which is such an essential part of Latin at this stage must really get under way.

### Nouns

First, turn to page 162 and learn the remaining nouns of the **Second Declension**. These are **puer**, meaning 'boy', **magister**, meaning 'master', and **bellum**, meaning 'war'. Note that nearly all First Declension nouns are feminine in gender while most Second Declension nouns tend to be masculine if they end in **-us** or **-er** and are neuter if they end in **-um**.

That done . . .

### Verbs

Turn to pages 181–2 and learn the remaining four tenses of the **indicative active** of **amō**, and the remaining four tenses of the **indicative** of **sum**.

Learn the nouns before the verbs, or after, or at the same time, as you prefer, but have all the learning done before going on to the exercises. Do remember that reciting all the declensions and conjugations with the recommended pronunciation and in the recommended rhythms is very important for maximum efficiency and speed in the learning process.

## Adverbs

| iterum | again, for a second time |
|---|---|
| ōlim | formerly, once upon a time |
| hodiē (short for hōc diē) | today |
| herī | yesterday (compare the French 'hier') |
| crās (compare English 'procrastinate') | tomorrow |
| hīc | here |
| ibi | there |
| hinc | from here, hence |
| inde | from there, thence |
| alibī (compare same word in English) | elsewhere |
| aliās (compare same word in English) | at another time |
| nūper | recently, lately |
| nōnnumquam | sometimes |

That is a considerable amount of new vocabulary. I am not in fact firmly recommending that these adverbs are learnt by heart at once, as I do insist that the burdensome declining of nouns and conjugating of verbs must be. The adverbs can be gradually committed to memory with practice.

## Prepositions

Prepositions (such as 'in', 'on', 'between'), as I trust you remember, introduce nouns and pronouns, which they are said to 'govern'. In English, nouns or pronouns introduced by prepositions always take the objective case when they can, which is only in pronouns – that is why we say 'between him and me', rather than 'between he and I' or any other variation.

In Latin, they take one or other of two cases.

Most take the **accusative case**. Examples are **ad**, meaning 'towards' or 'at', **post** meaning 'after', **per** meaning 'through' and **trans** meaning 'across'.

Others take the **ablative case**. Examples are **ā** (and **ab** before a vowel) meaning 'by', **ē** (and **ex** before a vowel), **cum** meaning 'with' and **sine** meaning 'without'.

Just four prepositions take *either* the **accusative case** *or* the **ablative case**, according to whether the preposition in question indicates motion or a state of rest. These four are: **in**, according to whether it means 'into' or 'in'; **sub**, according to whether it means 'going under' or 'situated under'; **subter**, also according to whether it means 'going under' or 'situated under'; and **super**, according to whether it means (a) 'going over' or 'going on to' or (b) 'situated over' or 'situated upon'.

All the most important prepositions, together with the cases they take, will be found on page 175. It is not necessary to learn them all by heart at this stage. At present you can simply look them up as needed for the exercises, gradually getting them into your memory with continued use. What *is* important, each time you look at a preposition, is to try to remember which case it governs. Thus, as soon as you meet **ē** or **ex**, meaning: 'out of', you should try at the same time to commit to your memory '**ē** or **ex** *plus the ablative*'.

As indicated above, the Latin for 'by' is **ā** if the word immediately following it starts with a consonant, and **ab** if the word immediately following it starts with a vowel. The Latin for 'out of' is **ē** if the next word starts with a consonant, and **ex** if it starts with a vowel. They are the only Latin prepositions which vary in their forms in this way.

## EXERCISES ON WHAT HAS BEEN LEARNT SO FAR

### Instructions

1. As before, translate all Latin sentences into English and all English into Latin.
2. You are always welcome to use the Reference Grammar and the vocabularies, unless instructed otherwise.

3. Every time you look up a word, do take time to learn its **Principal Parts**, all of which you will find in the vocabulary.

## A. Easy

| |
|---|
| 1. **Reginam amo.** |
| 2. **Angliae regina non es.** |
| 3. **Filius amicum superat.** |
| 4. **Mox pugnabimus.** |
| 5. **Domini eritis.** |
| 6. **Reginae amici Iulium laudant.** |
| 7. England is the country of the queen. |
| 8. We shall often praise the lord. |
| 9. (The) prisoners never sing. |
| 10. You will ask for a letter. |

## B. Harder

| |
|---|
| 1. **Puellae reginam amant sed regina puellas non amat.** |
| 2. **Amicum puellae amo et amicos puellarum amabimus.** |
| 3. **Reginae puellas numquam laudabunt, puellaeque aut reginas nunc amant aut reginas numquam amabunt.** |
| 4. **Regina amicos amat et amici reginae puellae sunt.** |
| 5. **Puella regina numquam erit sed reginam semper amabit. Filii amicos superant sed mox saepe cantabunt.** |
| 6. **Amici amicos numquam superant neque filii umquam puellas superant, sed regina saepe filios laudat.** |
| 7. **Iulius Caesar amicus Pompeii numquam erit, neque Pompeius filium Iulium vocat.** |
| 8. Claudius frees captives and the captives praise Claudius. |
| 9. We shall prepare letters to the queen but we shall not give money to the girls. |
| 10. Either we love the (female) friend of the court or we do not love the (female) friend of the court. |

C. Parse and then translate into English the following, which feature, untranslated, in the English language: **adsum; advocatus diaboli**.

**Reminder.** Minor variations in the order of words in sentences you have translated into Latin are acceptable.

## Answers

You will recall that the above exercises comprise the answers to the exercises at the end of Chapter Nine. Needless to say, the same also applies in reverse: you can check your answers to this set of exercises against those in Chapter Nine to gauge your progress.

## CHAPTER ELEVEN

Starting on **moneō**, **regō** and **audiō**; and the
adjectives of the first two declensions in full

## ACCIDENCE – WHAT MUST BE
### *LEARNT BY HEART*

### Verbs

Now turn to pages 181–2, and learn first the **Principal Parts** and
then the six **tenses** of the **Indicative Mood** in the **Active Voice**
of **moneō** by heart. **Moneō** is our model for the Second
Conjugation and means 'I warn'. This will be much less time-
consuming than learning the same for **amō** was, because there is
a considerable amount of overlap. All the tenses are basically the
same, except that the *stem*-changes are different. Thus, for
instance, the perfect **amāvī**, **amāvistī** and so on for **amō** resembles in its endings **monuī**, **monuistī** and so on for **moneō**.

Once that is done, and not before, go back to the same pages
and do the same for **regō**, our model for the Third Conjugation.
It means 'I rule' or 'I govern'. Learn the six **tenses** of the **Indicative
Mood** in the **Active Voice** by heart. **Regō** is significantly different from **amō** and **moneō** in the future simple, but still similar in
the very ends of each word. The perfect is the same in every
respect once you have learnt the stem. Overall, you will by now be
seeing a clear pattern for these regular verbs in their various
tenses.

That done, and not before, go back to the same pages and learn
by heart **audiō** – our model for the Fourth Conjugation. You
should find this much quicker than when you were starting on
**amō** two chapters back in Chapter Nine. The endings are the
same as those of **regō**, while the stem of the perfect, future perfect
and pluperfect tenses is formed similarly to the stem of those
tenses of **amō**.

I shall not be expecting you to return here for the next step until tomorrow at the earliest; and, once again, if it is a week before you are able to return, so be it. Everyone's learning speed is different, and it is much more important to have material thoroughly grasped than to have tried to respect some arbitrary time limit.

## Adjectives

Adjectives change their form to agree with (a) the **case**, (b) the **gender** and (c) the **number** of the word they are describing. Thus if an adjective is describing a masculine noun that is in the nominative case and singular number, its ending must be that of its nominative masculine singular form.

Once the learning of the **Principal Parts** and indicative tenses of those three verbs has been completed, turn to pages 166–7 and learn the adjectives representing the **Adjectives** of the **First** and **Second Declensions**.

They are called **First** and **Second Declension Adjectives** for good reason. The masculine gender of **bonus**, meaning 'good', goes exactly like the masculine noun **annus** of the Second Declension; the feminine gender goes exactly like **mēnsa** of the First Declension; and the neuter goes exactly like **bellum** of the Second Declension. The same applies to the other two, **tener** meaning 'tender' and **niger** meaning 'black', except that **tener** goes like **puer**, not dropping the **e** before the **r**, whereas **niger**, like **magister**, *does* drop the **e** before the **r**.

Although, on the face of it, learning these adjective declensions *downwards* (that is, first the masculine column and then the feminine and then the neuter columns) would appear to be the easier way of doing it, I ask you to resist the temptation, and rather to learn them *across* – starting with the masculine, feminine and neuter in the *nominative*, continuing with the masculine, feminine and neuter in the *vocative*, and so on – **bonus, bona, bonum; bone, bona, bonum** ... You will find that it works better in the long run if you do this, and also that the rhythm is more satisfying and therefore easier to commit to memory.

## Vocabulary

**Advice.** Make a habit of trying to identify as many English words derived from each Latin word as you can. This is where some of the most important advantages of learning Latin are most evident. Examples of such advantages include:

1. It improves our powers of observation and analysis.
2. It improves our understanding of English, for instance by indicating more exactly the present or original meaning of an English word.
3. It increases our vocabulary and helps us to use the words we know correctly.
4. It also often explains the reason why words are spelt as they are, and makes it easier to remember those spellings. For instance, their derivations show why 'vulnerable' is not spelt 'vulnerible' (it is because **vulnerō** is a First Conjugation verb), and why 'irresistible' cannot be spelt 'irresistable' (because **resistō**, as we shall be seeing later on, is a Third Conjugation verb).
5. It helps us to remember the Latin words that we are learning.

Back, now, to the specific subject of vocabulary.

Some **nouns** which go like **mēnsa** are:

| **lingua** | tongue, language |
|---|---|
| **lūna** | moon |
| **poena** | punishment, penalty |
| **terra** | land |
| **victōria** | victory |
| **sapientia** | wisdom |
| **ianua** | door |

Some **nouns** which go like **annus** are:

| **equus** | horse |
|---|---|
| **mūrus** | wall |
| **servus** | slave |

A new **noun** which goes like **puer** is **līberī** (which exists only in the plural), meaning 'children'.

There are more nouns which go like **magister**, the next one in the vocabulary, dropping the **e** before the **r**, than that go like **puer**; but there are not even *very* many **magister** ones.

Two **nouns** which go like **magister** are: **ager**, 'field' and **liber**, 'book'.

Some **nouns** which go like **bellum** are: **castrum**, which, confusingly, means 'fort' in the singular but 'camp' when **castra** is in the plural, and the following:

| concilium | meeting, council |
| cōnsilium | advice, plan, stratagem |
| oppidum | town |
| tēlum | weapon |

**Castra**, incidentally, is responsible for a large number of names of English towns (and counties), which were founded as fortresses during the period of the Roman occupation which ended in AD 410. Examples: Bicester, Colchester, Gloucester, Lancaster, Leicester, Worcester.

Note that **cōnsilium** denotes a single piece of advice. You will need the plural where the English word 'advice' (which has no plural) denotes more than a single piece.

Some **verbs** which go like **moneō** are:

| habeō | I have |
| terreō | I frighten |
| timeō | I fear, I am afraid of |

Also worth noting at once is the verb meaning 'I see', **videō,** as we shall need it soon. It follows **moneō** in the present, future simple and imperfect of the indicative active, after which it diverges. We shall for the time being use only its regular tenses.

Some more **verbs** which go like **amō** are:

| errō | I wander |
| **nūntiō** | I announce |
| **oppugnō** | I attack |
| **servō** | I save, I preserve |
| **vītō** | I avoid |
| **vulnerō** | I wound |

Verbs that go like **regō** include:

| **dūco** | I lead |
| **dīcō** | I say |
| **iūngō** | I join |

Verbs that go like **audiō** include:

| **aperiō** | I open |
| **impediō** | I hinder |
| **sciō** | I know, I know *how to* |

Some **adjectives** which go like **bonus** are:

| **dūrus** | hard |
| **longus** | long |
| **malus** | bad |
| **Latīnus** | Latin |
| **multus** | much (singular), many (plural) |
| **nullus** | no (in quantity) or none |
| **meus** | my |
| **tuus** | your (or 'thy' in old-fashioned English) |

**Meus** and **tuus** are called **adjectival pronouns** – or alternatively **possessive adjectives**. Another one of these worth learning at once is **suus**, which also declines exactly like **bonus** and **tuus**, though we shall not be discussing its use until the next chapter, Chapter Twelve. **Meus**, incidentally, has a single irregularity in its declension, which must be carefully noted because it occurs quite often. The vocative masculine singular is **mī** (in other words, *not* the original and obviously more-awkward-to-pronounce **mee**, in two syllables of course).

To refer to Latin as a noun – the language – use **lingua Latina**. For 'in Latin', or to convey the idea of knowing Latin, use the adverb **Latine**.

Some **adjectives** which go like **tener** are: **līber**, 'free'; **miser**, 'wretched'; **prōsper**, 'prosperous'.

Some **adjectives** which go like **niger** are: **pulcher**, beautiful; **noster**, the adjectival pronoun 'our'; and **vester**, the adjectival pronoun 'your', when there is more than one of you.

From now on, I shall normally give no vocabulary in these chapters other than the words I ask you to learn by heart. I shall be leaving it to you to look up and learn words in the vocabularies as they become needed.

## EXERCISES ON WHAT HAS BEEN LEARNT SO FAR

### A. Easy

| |
|---|
| 1. We know how to attack the camp of Pompey. |
| 2. The bad children will see their friends. |
| 3. Yesterday the slave had led the horse. |
| 4. Tomorrow the horse will have led the slave. |
| 5. The towns of our good country are beautiful. |

### B. Harder

| |
|---|
| 1. The queen will never say many Latin words. She has always ruled her country, and has sometimes saved it. |
| 2. My master has opened the door, and he sees many good slaves. |
| 3. Soon I shall have much wisdom, and I shall have heard many Latin words. |

> 4. The bad children wander across the long wall under the
> beautiful moon. There they see many black horses but have no
> weapons.
>
> 5. Our prosperous friends are now in the big camp with your
> children, Julius. They fear the plans of the slaves but have
> always loved the wisdom of the masters.

C. Parse and then translate into English the following, which, again
and as almost always in the C exercises, are, untranslated, part of
English : **ab initio**; **terra firma**; **persona non grata**; **et cetera**.

D. Your first test on etymology.

## Instructions

Please remember, for all tests on etymology in this and future
chapters, the following strict rules, which do not necessarily apply
to etymology as such but are always to be strictly applied in these
exercises. (a) Words with prefixes and suffixes can be included as
being derived from the relevant Latin word. Thus, for words
derived from **canto**, answers could legitimately include 'descant'
and 'recantation'. (b) On the other hand, your answers should
include *only* words which are *directly* derived from their Latin
word. Thus, for instance, again taking the Latin word **canto** as an
example, the word 'chant', although ultimately derived from
**canto**, only reached English via the French language, and therefore does not count for this purpose.

Now write down one word derived from each of **liber** (meaning
'book'), **līber** (meaning 'free'), **mūrus** and **equus**; two words
derived from **magister**; and three words derived from **servō**.

## CHAPTER TWELVE

The personal and reflexive pronouns; the
possessive adjectives; the demonstrative, definitive
and emphatic pronouns; the pronominal
adjectives; the numbers; and the most
straightforward questions

FROM NOW ON we are progressively increasing the pace. This should not be worrying, however. Although there is more to learn in quantity, you should be finding the learning easier, both because the general patterns of how the declensions and conjugations go are by now becoming familiar to you and because learning itself is now becoming easier for you, both as a science and as an art.

Please do not be tempted at *any* point to rush on. However long it takes you to get the learning done, do not move on from any item to be learnt until you have properly learnt it.

Not all new material need be learnt by heart. Sometimes, gradually acquired familiarity is enough. I shall always make it clear which is required.

## ACCIDENCE – WHAT MUST BE
### *LEARNT BY HEART*

### Pronouns

**Reminder.** The personal pronouns are used in Latin only when they cannot be inferred from the context. Thus, for instance, the word **amat** can mean 'he loves', 'she loves' or 'it loves', or can have a noun as its subject.

I am giving the **personal** and **reflexive pronouns, the posses-sive adjectives, the demonstrative** and **emphatic pronouns** and the **pronominal adjectives** a considerable part of a chapter to themselves because, although they are not genuinely difficult, it is my experience that they can cause more trouble to beginners than any of the rest of beginners' Latin. We shall be coming to that a little later in this chapter, however. First of all, please turn to pages 171–2 and learn the declensions of the following **personal pronouns** by heart: **ego, tū, nōs, vōs**, and the single pronoun, **sē** or **sēsē**. Learn them in the usual way, including their meanings, but do not try to understand the meanings of **sē** or **sēsē** at this stage – just learn them blindly, so to speak.

To make the learning easier – which, as usual, means using a good rhythm – do not bother to include in your recitation the alternative genitive plurals, **nostrum** and **vestrum**, in addition to **nostrī** and **vestrī**. You need only be *aware* of them in case you come across them when translating from Latin, since both are very much used and in different circumstances.*

That done too, turn to page 74 and revise the declensions of all the possessive adjectives learnt in the last chapter, Chapter Eleven.

That done as well, turn to pages 172–3 and learn the **demonstrative pronouns** by heart. They are **is, ea, id; hic, haec, hoc; ille, illa, illud** and **iste, ista, istud**.

Finally, turn to pages 172–74 and learn by heart the emphatic or intensive pronoun **ipse** ('-self'), the definitive pronoun **īdem** ('the same'), the pronominal adjectives **alter** ('one of two', 'the other of two') and **alius** ('another'). Once the pronouns we have already looked at in this chapter are learnt, these will not be difficult to learn by heart, because they all decline very similarly. What you should take some trouble over is to learn their meanings; once that has been done, they are not difficult to use.

The use of the pronouns is covered later in this chapter.

## The numbers

There are four categories of numbers, of which, however, for practical purposes, we need to concern ourselves with only three in the third and fourth categories. These four categories are: the cardinal numbers (which answer the question 'how many?'), such as 'one',

---

* These different uses are explained in the Reference Grammar, page 171.

'two' and 'three'; the ordinal numbers ('in which number order?'), such as 'first', 'second' and 'third'; the distributive numbers ('how many each?'), such as 'one each' and 'two each'; and the numeral adverbs ('how many times?'), such as 'once', 'twice' and 'three times' or 'thrice'.

We start with the cardinal numbers. Other than the first three, these do not decline. The first three, however, are the ones most often used. 'One' is **ūnus.** Although it declines like **bonus** in principle, it does so very irregularly; but, as it closely resembles **alius,** which you have just learnt, you will not find it very difficult. 'Two' is **duo,** which declines partly like **bonus** and partly as though it were a Third Declension adjective (we meet the Third Declension in the next chapter, Chapter Thirteen). 'Three' is **trēs,** which declines only like a Third Declension adjective.

Since these are the most used numbers, please turn to page 177 and learn them by heart, before returning here. As usual, you should learn them so that you can not only rattle them off in your sleep, but also answer the usual questions about them in relation to their meaning and how they are parsed. Note that, remarkably on the face of it, **ūnus** declines in the plural as well as in the singular. There is a good reason for that, as we shall see.

Next, turn to page 176 and learn the ordinal numbers by heart up to twenty. You will see that there is a complication in that the numbers eighteen and nineteen are represented by the Latin for two-from-twenty and one-from-twenty.

That done, learn the first ten ordinals – 'first' to 'tenth' – by heart. I dare say to your relief, these all decline regularly like **bonus.**

Finally, learn by heart the first three numeral adverbs on page 177.

## SYNTAX – WHAT MUST BE *UNDERSTOOD*

### The personal and reflexive pronouns, other than sē or sēsē.

These are used as might be expected by now. The nominative cases are little used, because they are usually unnecessary. When they are used it is to indicate emphasis. The other cases are used as they are needed, in the same way as the cases of nouns are used.

A first complication is the **Third Person Pronoun**. While Latin has a single pronoun meaning 'I' (**ego**) and another meaning 'you' in the singular (**tu**), it has no equivalent for the third person pronoun, i.e. the English 'he', 'she' and 'it' (and, in the plural, 'they'). Instead it uses for this purpose the demonstrative, **is, ea, id**, which, unlike **ego** and **tu**, declines like an adjective. Thus it has three gender forms and both the singular and the plural numbers.

## The possessive adjectives, other than suus

Like personal pronouns, possessive adjectives are used very much less in Latin than in English. When possible, they are omitted, other than for emphasis, and this includes their being omitted where they never would be omitted in English. If in English 'I scratch my head' were reworded as 'I scratch the head', that would automatically provoke the question: 'Whose head?' In Latin, it would be just as automatically assumed that '*my* head' was the object in question, unless the previous sentence had made it clear that a different head was being referred to.

The rule, therefore, is that possessive adjectives are included only when necessary for clarity. This principle is especially important when translating from Latin into English. Again and again, it is necessary to supply a missing possessive adjective in a clause or sentence to make sense, and this is something that beginners often take some time to become accustomed to.

## The demonstrative pronouns

Please play close attention at this point, to minimise chances of confusion.

The demonstrative pronouns that you have learnt by heart are **is, ea, id; hic, haec, hoc; ille, illa, illud** and **iste, ista, istud**.

**Is, ille** and **iste** all mean 'that', but in different senses. **Is, ea, id** means 'that' (and of course 'those') as opposed to 'this'. **Ille, illa, illud** means 'that yonder', or 'that over there' in less old-fashioned English. **Iste, ista, istud** means 'that near you'. **Hic, haec, hoc** means 'this' (and 'these'). **Hic** and **ille** are often used in contrast, with **hic** meaning 'the latter' and **ille** meaning 'the former'.

Where confusion can arise, especially when translating from

Latin into English, is that all of them can be used either as genuine pronouns, by themselves, or as demonstrative adjectives qualifying nouns. In other words, **is** by itself means 'he' but can also be part of the phrase **is puer** meaning 'that boy'; and the same applies to the other three demonstrative pronouns.

Now we come to the biggest problem relating to pronouns, and one which causes as much trouble to beginners as any of the early Latin. It is in fact a twofold problem.

The first part of this twofold problem is this.

If we wish to say 'I see my mother', the translation is straightforward: **Meam matrem video.** 'I see our mother' and 'I see your mother', whether singular or plural, are no less straightforward – **nostram, tuam** and **vestram** respectively in place of **meam**.

With 'I see his mother' or 'her mother' or 'their mother', however, we run into difficulties. We cannot say **eam matrem video**, for that means 'I see *that* mother'.

The problem is solved by using the genitive singular or genitive plural of **is**, according to whether the person whose mother is seen is a single person or many people. What, in effect, we must do, therefore, is mentally to translate 'his' and 'her' into 'of him' and 'of her', and 'their' into 'of them' and then put that into Latin. Therefore, 'I see his mother' would be **eius matrem video** which could also mean 'I see her mother'. And for 'I have seen their mother' we say **eorum matrem video** if 'they' are masculine (or mixed) and **earum matrem video** if 'they' are feminine.

At first sight it may seem unsatisfactory that **eius** is both masculine and feminine, i.e. can mean either 'his' or 'her', or indeed neuter ('its'). How, when we see that word without knowing its gender, can we always be certain who or what is being indicated? The same applies in French and many other languages, however, and in reality there is scarcely ever any doubt as to who or what is represented by the pronoun. The reason is that it is made clear by the previous sentence or clause, and, wherever there could be doubt, a competent writer of Latin will reorganise the wording so as to eliminate the ambiguity.

Now we come to the second problem. How can we discern what is meant in the sentence 'The boy who saw *his* friend yesterday saw *his* mother today'? Whose mother was it that the boy saw?

To answer this question we must learn about **sē** (or **sēsē**) and **suus**, which until now have been no more than sounds to you. This is where your concentration is perhaps most needed; it is where, in my experience, mistakes are most often made by beginners who allow their attention to wander.

**Sē** or **sēsē** is what is called a **Reflexive Pronoun**. This means that the pronoun, as also its possessive adjective or pronoun **suus**, 'bends back' at the subject of the clause or sentence, and cannot be used otherwise.

Therefore **Sē in suō speculō vīdit** means 'He saw *himself* in *his own* mirror', whereas **Eum in speculō ēius vīdit** means 'He saw him [someone else] in his mirror [the mirror of that person whom he saw]'.

For this reason very special care is needed in the early stages when confronted with translating a clause or sentence which has in it a third person personal pronoun or possessive pronoun.

The other reflexive pronouns are exactly the same as the personal pronouns, so that 'I love myself' is simply **mē amō** or possibly **ego mē amō**. The only difference is that they have no nominative forms because no nominative forms are needed. For the same reason **sē** and **sēsē** have no corresponding nominative. Furthermore, because it is always going to be clear from the subject of the sentence and from the verb whether the third person pronoun is singular or plural, **sē** and **sēsē** – again as with their equivalents in French – have no need for separate plural forms and have none. They are the singular *and* plural third person reflexive pronouns.

## The definitive and emphatic pronouns and the pronominal adjectives

As already mentioned, these are not difficult to use either, once their meanings have been learnt.

## Straightforward questions

In English, there are two ways of asking questions. One is by using an interrogative word such as the interrogative adverbs, 'where', 'when' and 'why' or the interrogative pronouns 'who' or 'which'. The other is by changing the order of the words of a sentence, as when 'You are learning' is changed to 'Are you learning?'

In Latin, the first is straightforward, the same system as in English. The second is inevitably less so, because of Latin's always flexible word order. At a more advanced stage, the rules are quite complex and difficult to remember, but for the simplest questions, which is all that we shall consider here, the rule is simple. The letters **ne** are joined on to the end of the first word of the sentence or clause, whichever it is. 'Have you always liked Latin?' can be **Linguam*ne* Latīnam semper amāvistī?** or **Latīnam*ne* linguam semper amāvistī?** or **Amāvistī*ne* semper linguam Latīnam?** or … I leave the other variations to you.

When everything in this chapter has been thoroughly mastered, and please not before, turn to the exercises.

## EXERCISES ON WHAT HAS BEEN LEARNT SO FAR

### A. Easy

| |
|---|
| 1. You see this man. |
| 2. The queen will love this country. |
| 3. Does that boy praise a slave? |
| 4. We have conquered the friends of Pompey and laid waste their camps. |
| 5. Those camps were big and beautiful. |
| 6. These girls love no camp. |
| 7. No Roman has two fatherlands. |
| 8. **Contra tria oppida pugnaveritis.** |
| 9. **Suumne gladium perdidit Pompeius?** |
| 10. **Latinamne linguam laudat ille magister?** |

### B. Harder

| |
|---|
| 1. The beautiful queens will soon be advising the bad boys. |

| |
|---|
| 2. One thousand and fifty men have fought for a long time against three thousand men. |
| 3. One fort is not one camp in the Latin language. |
| 4. I am present now. Will he be present soon, and will they be present also? |
| 5. The 'Devil's Advocate' is never a bad man. |
| 6. Two forts are not two camps in the Latin language. |
| 7. He attacked the town and they defended themselves and their town. The women themselves were also defending the same town. |
| 8. The barber holds his (own) mirror and the master sees his (own) beard in his [the barber's] mirror. |
| 9. **Si me videbis iam te videro.** |
| 10. **Heri servi Caesarem viderunt et hodie Pompeium; hunc laudaverunt sed illum amaverunt.** |

Sentences 3 and 6 are of special interest. In sentence 3, the plural of **ūnus** is justified. If there were no plural, there would be an instance of its being impossible for an adjective to agree with its noun. In sentence 6, translation looks impossible. How could one distinguish between two camps and two forts since the word for a camp is the plural of the word for a fort? The Romans solved such problems by substituting for the word 'two' the words 'two each'. Thus the translation of that sentence is: **Duo castra bina castra in lingua Latina non sunt.**

In sentence 10, note the economy of Latin. A word is not repeated if it can be understood. Thus in the clause before the semicolon both accusatives are objects of the same verb, but in English the verb must be repeated.

C. Put into the accusative singular and genitive plural cases of the English idioms: **terra firma; persona non grata; et cetera.**

D. Write down two words derived from **contrā.**

## CHAPTER THIRTEEN

The passive indicatives; the Third Declension nouns; the Third Declension adjectives; adverbs of all the declensions; and participles and gerundives

## ACCIDENCE – WHAT MUST BE
### *LEARNT BY HEART*

ALTHOUGH NOT VERY long, this chapter contains a considerable amount to be learnt by heart. The learning by heart should not be daunting, because some of it – the verbs – is much like what we have already done, and the rest of it – the Third Declension nouns and the Third Declension adjectives – is more a matter of learning **Principal Parts** than of learning different endings.

### Verbs

#### *Passive Voice*

You will find the Passive Voice dealt with extensively from pages 180 onwards in the Reference Grammar. Here I am setting you the task of learning all six Indicative tenses of the Passive Voice of all four conjugations by heart, because this should be relatively easy now that you know – as I hope you do – all the active indicatives of those four conjugations by heart. Granted, the endings are very different from those of the same tenses of the Active Voice, but by now you should have a 'picture' of how verbs go which you could never have had four chapters ago and which makes learning much easier. Furthermore, there is sufficient similarity between the conjugations to make it much easier, once you have fully mastered the First Conjugation, to learn the remaining three.

It is also time to introduce a new verb form, the non-finite

**Participle**. Two things about participles are to be specially noted here:

1. Latin has three participles: the **Present Participle**, the **Future Participle** and the **Past** or **Perfect Participle**. Present and future participles occur only in the Active Voice, while the Past or Perfect Participle occurs only in the Passive Voice. The Past Participle is much used in Latin; indeed it is the most used of the participles. **Amātus**, which goes like **bonus**, means 'having been loved' or simply 'loved' in the adjectival sense.

2. The perfect tense passive of most verbs makes use of the Past Participle in order to form them, and this is potentially confusing. The reason is that, because the Past Participle of **amō**, which is **amātus**, means 'having been loved' or simply 'loved', one could legitimately expect **amātus sum** to mean 'I *am* loved'. It does not, however. It is the form of the *Perfect* Passive Indicative, and means 'I *have been* loved' or 'I *was* loved', while 'I *am* loved' is expressed by the straightforward Present Tense Passive, **amor**.

## Nouns

Then turn to pages 162–4 and learn the three **Third-Declension Nouns** which are given there, and the **Principal Parts** of the other nouns listed on those pages, and the rules showing why one noun declines in one way and another noun declines in another. There is a considerable amount of work involved in mastering that part of this chapter. I urge you to tackle it patiently.

## Adjectives

Once those nouns are mastered, and not before, turn to pages 167–8 and learn by heart the five **Third Declension Adjectives** shown there. This will not be difficult if the Third Declension nouns have been well learnt. They are set out there for the best-for-learning rhythms. If you would like to pay special attention to any particular one of them, the one to select for this purpose is **ingēns**. This is because the **Present Participle** of every single verb that has a **Present Participle** declines like **ingēns**, as we shall shortly be learning.

## Adverbs

It is time to learn how to form adverbs from the corresponding adjectives. There are rules governing most of them, and exceptions to the rules for those that tend to be most used. These will be found on pages 170–1, to which I now ask you to turn, and from which I ask you not to return until you have obtained a clear understanding of everything set out there and learnt much of it.

## Adverbs and conjunctions

Teachers who set their pupils the task of learning by heart the following cleverly put-together list of common adverbs and the occasional conjunction could earn the pupils' gratitude in the long run, giving them a store of very useful knowledge while training their memories at the same time.

AT FIRST I did not know **prīmō** – and ALMOST despaired of **paene**; – BUT I knew **sed**; – and WHILE I was studying **dum**, – I SUDDENLY recognized **subitō** – and IMMEDIATELY **statim** became familiar. – AT THAT TIME **tum** seemed hard – and I wrestled IN VAIN with **frustrā**, – but I ALREADY knew **iam** – and EVEN **etiam**; – and I SOON acquired **mox**. – I NEVER recognise **numquam** – and FORMERLY I found **quondam** difficult – while FOR A LONG TIME **diū** puzzled me, – and I studied **nēquīquam** TO NO PURPOSE, – but I have ALWAYS known **semper** – and NOW I am sure of **nunc**; – I can, THEREFORE, conquer **igitur**. – I am NOT YET familiar with **nōndum**; – I know **tamen**, HOWEVER; – MOREOVER **autem** is an old friend, – while **tam** is SO simple – THAT **ut** will be easy. – I hope to learn **simul** at THE SAME TIME – FOR I do know **nam** – and have OFTEN met **saepe**. – THUS I was learning **sic** – and had SCARCELY made sure of **vix**, – when ONCE UPON A TIME I found I knew **ōlim**; – THEN I learnt **inde**, – THEN **deinde**, – and FINALLY I shall master **dēnique**. – MEANWHILE I am struggling with **intereā**, – and AS SOON AS I learn

simul atque – I shall AT LENGTH know **tandem**, – and
PERHAPS **forsitan**. – AFTERWARDS I mean to learn
**posteā**, – and when I have met **iterum** a SECOND TIME
and yet AGAIN – I hope to know **quoque** ALSO.

## Verbs

### *Passive Voice*

The use of the Passive Voice is completely straightforward and
problem-free until we need to deal with the preposition 'by' when
it follows a passive verb. We shall be looking at special uses of all
the cases in the next chapter, Chapter Fourteen, and therefore, in
this chapter, I am asking the reader simply to make sure that
tenses in the passive are thoroughly known, partly with the help
of the exercises, in preparation for what will be coming next.

## Participles, introduction

If you turn to page 179, you will find, after the *active tenses* of
**amō**, two participles given and translated: the **Present Participle
amāns** meaning 'loving', and the **Future Participle amātūrus,**
meaning about to love. These decline like straightforward adjectives, **amāns** exactly like **ingēns** and **amātūrus** exactly like **bonus**.
Under the *passive tenses* of **amō**, you will find only one participle
given and translated: the **Past Participle amātus**, meaning 'loved'
and 'having been loved'. It too goes like **bonus**.

Study and understand the formation of these participles
and their meanings. They are basically the same for all verbs,
other than deponent verbs, which we shall be coming to in the
next chapter. Even though the formation of the **Past Participle**
is irregular in irregular verbs and can vary widely from verb to
verb, they all have this in common: that **Present Participles**
decline like **ingēns** and **Future** and **Past Participles** decline
like **bonus**.

As we shall be seeing in the rest of this book, participles play
a much greater role in Latin than they do in English, so do make
sure that you fully understand everything in the last two para-
graphs before moving on to . . .

## Gerundives

While the verbal adjectives called participles are fresh in our minds, let us look at the other verbal adjective too: the **Gerundive**. It is formed by adding **-andus** or **-endus**, according to the conjugation, on the end of the verb stem; it declines like **bonus** and means 'fit to be ——', 'worthy to be ——', 'that ought to be ——' as explained below.

## Supines

The **Supine** is a verbal noun which does not decline. It has two forms: the form ending in **-um** and the form ending in **-ū**. Both are in the Active Voice. Its meaning will be discussed immediately below, in the section on syntax.

## SYNTAX – WHAT MUST BE *UNDERSTOOD*

## Participles, introduction

As noted above, participles decline like straightforward adjectives, **amāns** exactly like **ingēns** and **amātūrus** exactly like **bonus**. To some extent adjectives is what they are, because their function is to describe nouns and pronouns, as in '*dangling* participle' and 'Watch me *learning*'. They are not always only adjectives, however; they can perform part of the function of verbs as well, in that they can govern objects. An example: 'You are a person (who is) perhaps about to love Latin' translates into **Homo linguam Latinam forsitan amaturus es**.

As also already noted, these two participles occur only in the Active Voice, while the only other participle, the **Past Participle**, occurs only in the Passive Voice. We shall be becoming more thoroughly acquainted with them all in the next chapter, Chapter Fourteen.

## Gerundives

The gerundive has two meanings.

The commoner of the two indicates obligation. Example: the famous **Carthago delenda est**, meaning 'Carthage ought to be destroyed', was uttered so frequently and persistently by the Roman senator Cato the Elder (234–149 BC) in his speeches that it is a wonder it is not still ringing in our ears. Persistence paid on that occasion, incidentally: Carthage, the second-greatest city of the world at that time, *was* completely destroyed by Rome, razed by the Roman general Scipio, and its surviving citizens sold into slavery, after which the Roman Empire was effectively unchallengeable.

The other is perhaps best described negatively, as *not* carrying any meaning of obligation. Examples: **consilium urbis vincendae**, 'a plan for conquering the city'; and **operam damus liberis docendis** (dative), 'we pay attention to teaching our children'.

## Supines

The supine is used only rarely, except, of course, when we are reciting the great majority of the **Principal Parts** of verbs. If I leave it out, though, you will probably come across it, and this is the obvious place to include it, because it is the only other verbal adjective.

It does not decline, but has two forms.

The form ending in **-um** expresses *purpose* and is *only* used together with a verb of motion. It is an alternative to the constructions **ut** or **qui** with the subjunctive and **ad** with either the gerund, which we shall be coming to in a later chapter, Chapter Fifteen, or the gerundive. Example: 'They have come in order to see.' **Venerunt visum.**

The supine form ending in -**ū** is used with adjectives. It is the equivalent of the ablative of respect. What is the ablative of respect? It is when the part of speech and the ablative *limits* or *specifies* the verb or adjective that it is attached to. Thus if a particular book is perhaps not necessarily difficult in *every* respect, but it is difficult *to read* – **Liber difficilis lectu est**.

Now you know, unless you forget – which would not much matter.

## EXERCISES ON WHAT HAS BEEN
## LEARNT SO FAR

### A. Easy

| |
|---|
| 1. The queen is loved. |
| 2. Good books are often read. |
| 3. This book is easy to read. (Use a supine.) |
| 4. The name of the general was long unknown. |
| 5. The camp of the barbarians will at length be destroyed. |
| 6. Scarcely any citizens are found in the huge mountains. |
| 7. If the courageous general was once praised he will be praised again. |
| 8. **Olim Anglia bene regebatur.** |
| 9. **Visum veni.** |
| 10. **Pulchrae puellae hodie laudamini.** |

### B. Harder

| |
|---|
| 1. He is unhappy because he is ill. |
| 2. There are many things that ought to be done today. |
| 3. The suggestion of something false by bad people has never been difficult and never will be. Have you yourself, whose opinions I always want to know, heard suggestions of false things by dishonest people? |
| 4. The beautiful little girls were frightened by the fierce citizens and by the soldiers' weapons. |
| 5. A healthy mind in a healthy body: this motto can usefully be said and is fit to be heard often by everyone. |

C. Parse and then translate into English the following, all of which are English idioms – some of them fairly common ones – in English untranslated from the Latin: **alma mater, annus mirabilis, rara avis, suggestio falsi, suppressio veri, tempus fugit, corpus delicti, repetitio mater memoriae (est), rigor mortis, sui generis, eiusdem generis, dramatis personae, fons et origo**.

D. Put into the accusative singular and genitive plural cases: **fons et origo, alma mater, annus mirabilis, rara avis, suggestio, suppressio, rigor**.

E. Write down in alphabetical order no fewer than fifty words derived from **duco**, doubtless starting with 'abduct', including 'introduce' on the way through, and probably ending with 'viaduct'. Remember our derivation rule that only words directly derived from **duco** are admissible, to which I shall add a further rule that only moods and voices of **duco** that you have already learnt are admissible (which excludes the subjunctive mood that we shall be coming to in Chapter Seventeen – English words are never derived from Latin subjunctives).

F. (a) Write down two words derived from **audio** and two words from **video**, in each case one of them derived from the Latin original in the Active Voice and the other derived from the Latin original in the Passive Voice.

(b) Write down two words derived from **transfero** which have not one letter of the alphabet in common with each other except the five letters of the prefix.

## CHAPTER FOURTEEN

The deponent verbs, regular and irregular, and
the semi-deponent verbs; the Fourth and Fifth
Declension nouns; some important information
about prepositions; more on the participles; and
special uses of the vocative, accusative, genitive,
dative and ablative cases, including when time
and space are dealt with

DEPONENT VERBS *look* like passives but are in fact active in
meaning. Thus **ūtor** means 'I use' and not 'I am used'.
Precisely because they are passive *in form*, deponent verbs have
no *actual* passive, and in most cases their meaning is not such as
to call for a passive. Semi-deponent verbs have some of the
forms of active verbs and some of deponent verbs.

Turn to page 186 and learn by heart the Principal Parts of
**ūtor**, and then its six indicative tenses. You will see that it is a
Third Conjugation verb. For some reason – perhaps because
there are more verbs of the Third Conjugation than of any of the
other conjugations – this Third Conjugation **ūtor** is traditionally
used as the main model for deponent verbs rather than a First
Conjugation verb as one would expect. Anyway, we shall stay
with tradition on this matter.

Once **ūtor** has been learnt, learn by heart the same in respect of
the three verbs used for the other three conjugations, **cōnor, polliceor** and **orior**. You will have no difficulty with them if you have
diligently learnt the passive conjugations as instructed at the beginning of the last chapter, Chapter Thirteen, because the deponent
conjugations are identical to the passives of ordinary verbs.

I do not think you will have found this chapter difficult so far;
but be sure to have mastered what is explained in the Reference
Grammar about the meaning of the participles of deponent verbs.

## ACCIDENCE – WHAT MUST BE
### *LEARNT BY HEART*

## Verbs

### *Deponent and semi-deponent*

My recommendation is that you learn the four deponent conjugations by heart, and, at this stage, only make yourself sufficiently aware of all the others, including semi-deponent ones, to know that you will need to look them up when you come across them. You will want to improve on that before long though. Some of them, such as **cōnor**, **hortor**, **loquor**, **mereor**, **morior**, **nāscor**, **patior**, **sequor** and **videor**, are in frequent use, and others by no means infrequent.

## Nouns

### *Fourth and Fifth Declensions*

Learning the Fourth and Fifth Declension nouns will need little effort compared to what was involved in learning the previous first three declensions.

There are only two forms of the Fourth Declension, that of masculine and feminine and that of neuter; and the neuter is in fact agreeably easy and genuine fun to learn, as you will see.

There is but one form of the Fifth Declension. The only thing about it worth drawing attention to is that many who find no difficulty in mastering **rēs** then do experience difficulty in reciting the others, such as **diēs**, **faciēs** and **speciēs**. The difficulty, such as it is, is caused by the **i** in front of the **ē**, and especially in the Genitive and Dative Singular, where the three vowels in succession are pronounced separately. What is needed in order to get it right is nothing more than to apply straightforward logic, perhaps allied with patience; but some find this surprisingly difficult even so. If necessary, you can get help in the pronunciation from gwynneteaching.com as usual; but in this case I strongly recommend that you put yourself to the toil of getting it consistently right without that assistance.

## SYNTAX – WHAT MUST BE *UNDERSTOOD*

### Prepositions or no prepositions

The time has come for a closer look at the **Locative Case**, which was briefly mentioned in Chapter Six, especially in the context of the Passive Voice, to which we addressed ourselves in the last chapter.

Although its use is limited, it is important to remember that, wherever the **Locative Case** is found, there is no need for the prepositions that we should expect to use, because the work done by them is already done by the case itself. To use a preposition in addition to the **Locative Case** would be in effect to use that preposition twice over.

Here are the rules.

In classical Latin, the ablative of place, for expressing where something is happening, normally has in front of it a preposition governing the ablative case. 'In the city' and 'in Britain' are therefore **in urbe** and **in Britanniā** respectively. In the names of towns and small islands, however, mainly of the first two declensions, but very occasionally of the Third Declension as well, the old-fashioned Locative Case is still used. Therefore 'in Rome' is not **in Rōmā** but **Rōmae**. It is also used for a very few other words: 'at home' is **domī**; 'on the ground' is **humī**; and 'in the country' is **rūrī**, from **rūs**, a neuter Third Declension noun.

Special care is needed, therefore, with place names. When any appear for translation, you need to notice whether they are towns as opposed to any other groups of buildings and whether they are small islands as opposed to large islands and countries in any other geographical situation.

We turn now to the **Instrumental Case**, still very much in existence although now always in the form of the Ablative Case, and indeed always referred to as the Ablative Case.

When you see in English the preposition 'by' or 'with', you must always be alert to distinguish whether what is being done is being done by *someone* or by *something*. Technically, when it is done by *someone*, it is being done by *an agent*, a word derived from the Latin **agō**, meaning, among countless other things, 'I do' and

'I act'. When it is done by *something*, it is done by *an instrument*, a word derived from the neuter Second Declension noun **instrūmentum**, meaning 'a tool' or 'an implement'. When the thing is done by an agent, it needs a preposition as well as the ablative, because there is no 'agent case'. When it is done by an instrument, a preposition would not make sense because it would amount to a doubling up, and the ablative only is therefore used.

Therefore 'He is killed by a soldier' is in Latin **Ā milite occiditur**, whereas 'He is killed by an arrow' is **Sagittā occiditur** and 'He kills him with an arrow' is **Eum sagittā occidit** – no **cum**.

May you be one of the few beginners who never include or exclude a preposition when they should not!

## Participles, their use

1. Since a participle is a verbal adjective, it always agrees with a noun or pronoun, or possibly a noun or pronoun phrase or even clause, at least understood. Thus: 'The weeping mother has a loved daughter' is **Flens mater filiam amatam habet**.

2. An important thing to remember when translating both into and out of Latin is that, in Latin, a participle is often used where we would use a subordinate clause. Thus: 'He was wounded while he was fighting' would be best translated into Latin as **Pugnans vulneratus est**, and 'I fear my master when he is blaming me' translates as **Me culpantem meum magistrum timeo**.

3. Now we come to a piece of syntax which beginners often relish when they master it, and delight to use in English even though it seldom sounds natural in our language. This is the **Ablative Absolute**.

   When a participle can agree with the subject or the object in a clause, then make it do so, as in the examples above. Sometimes, however, it cannot. Take the sentence, 'When we heard our teacher's voice, we wanted at once to laugh.' Someone thinking about how best to translate this into Latin would first revise the English as follows: '*Having heard our teacher's voice*, we wanted at once to laugh.' This achieves the first goal of replacing a clause with a participle, *but* runs into the problem that Latin has no active past participle corresponding to 'having done something'. It is therefore necessary to reconstruct the sentence a second time, into one that, although it would not be used in English, we can understand clearly enough: 'Our teacher's voice *having been heard*, we wanted at once to laugh.' The 'detached' participle in that clause, having nothing to do with either the subject or any object, there being no object, goes into the ablative case, a construction – the **Ablative Absolute** – especially invented for this purpose. Thus: **Voce nostri doctoris audītā, ridere statim voluimus.**

4. There cannot be a past participle of intransitive verbs. 'Italy having been arrived at' is as impossible in Latin as it would be in English without the preposition at the end, and although 'Italy having been reached' would be an acceptable way of solving the problem in English, there is no suitable transitive verb for 'reach' in Latin. Instead we need to say 'When we arrived in Italy' and translate that, which we shall learn how to do in Chapter Seventeen.

## More on the subject of adverbial time and place

These are the general rules. They fall into the category of rules that can be picked up gradually with practice rather than needing to be learnt by heart.

### Place *where*

**In** is used together with the ablative case, but remember that the names of towns and small islands and a few common nouns such as **domus**, **humus** and **rūs** go into the locative case – **domī**, **humī** and **rūrī**. Example: 'Not in Rome but in Gaul' translates into **Non Romae sed in Gallia**.

### Place *from which* or *whence*

**Ā/ab**, **ē/ex** and **dē** are used together with the ablative case, but the ablative case alone is used for names of towns and small islands and for **domus**, **humus** and **rūs** (**domō**, **rūre**, **humō**). Example: 'Not only out of London but even out of Britain' translates into **Non solum Londinio sed etiam e Britannia**.

## Place *to which* or *whither*

To express where one is going, use **ad**, or **in**, together with the accusative case, but the accusative is used alone for names of towns and small islands and **domus** and **rūs** (**domum, rūs**). Example: 'Into Britain and into London' translates into **In Britanniam et Londinium**.

## Time *how long*

The accusative is used without any preposition to express the length of time an action takes. Example: 'They read this book for two hours' translates into **Duas horas hoc librum legerunt**.

## Time *when*

The ablative is used without any preposition to specify a point in time. Example: 'He departed on the third day' translates into **Tertio die discessit**.

## Time *within which*

The ablative is used without any preposition. Example: 'We shall see him in three days' time' translates into **Eum tribus diebus videbimus**.

## Time *how long ago*

**Abhinc** is used together with the accusative case. Example: 'Ten years ago' translates into **Abhinc annos duos**. In the context of that example, this is as good a place as any to include either **multis ante annis** or **ante multos annos**, 'many years before' and either **multis post annis** or **post multos annos**, 'many years after'.

## Time *how long before* and *how long after*

*Either* use the ablative by itself *or* use the prepositions **ante** or **post** together with the accusative case. Examples: 'Many months after his death' translates into **Multis mensibus post mortem eius**; 'After many months' translates into **Post multos menses**; and 'Shortly before his departure' translates into **Paulo ante discessum eius**.

## Special uses of the different cases

We have already learnt the basic uses of the different cases in Chapter Six. It is now time to learn some more advanced uses, as needed by the more advanced constructions we are beginning to meet. There now follows a summary of what the various cases can be used for in addition to their obvious uses.

The **Nominative Case**, as we know very well by now, is for the subject of a sentence or clause and for the complement if there is one. In addition to that, a noun can be put *in apposition* to another noun, as in **Caesar imperator Romam rediit**, 'Caesar, the general, returned to Rome'. A noun 'in apposition' is in the same case as the noun it is in apposition to, and this is often, but not necessarily, the nominative case.

The **Vocative Case** has only the peculiarity that, if it is used at the beginning of a sentence, **O** is used with it, and otherwise **O** is omitted – **O Iuli, veni huc** for 'Julius come here' and **Veni huc, Iuli** for 'Come here, Julius'. (We have not yet met the imperative **veni** used here, but it will be coming shortly.)

The **Accusative Case** (a) expresses the direct object of an intransitive verb; (b) expresses what in English would be the indirect object of one or two transitive verbs, such as **doceō** and **rogō** (for what follows other intransitive verbs, see **Dative Case** (b) below); (c) as we have seen, expresses motion to, with or without the prepositions **ad** and **in**; and (d) as we have also seen, when used without any preposition expresses time how long – **unum diem duasque horas**, 'for one day and two hours' – and distance how far – **duo milia passuum**, 'for two miles', literally 'for two thousands of steps *or* strides'.

The **Genitive Case** has a number of different uses.

(a) In many cases of course its use is the same as that in English, as in **amor linguae Latinae**, though also, not so obviously, **cupīdo praemii**, 'desire for a reward'.

(b) The so-called **Partitive Genitive** is used when only a *part* is involved of something that can be measured or counted. Examples: **pauci eorum**, 'few of them'; **multi militum**, 'many of the soldiers', which of course differs in its meaning from **multi milites**, 'many soldiers'; **plus pecuniae et satis pecuniae**, 'more money and enough money'. It is, however, *not* used in many cases where it *would* be used in English. Examples: **omnes vos**, 'all of you'; **tota Anglia**, 'the whole of England'; **ceteri liberi**, 'the rest of the children'.

(c) It indicates ownership, as in **liber pueri**, 'the boy's book'.

(d) It indicates quality, as in **lingua multae pulchritudinis**, 'a language of much beauty' (Latin, of course).

(e) It follows – or is 'taken by' – a number of adjectives including the following: **plēnus**, 'full of'; **memor** and **immemor**, 'mindful of' and 'unmindful of' *or* 'forgetful of'; **similis** and **dissimilis**, 'similar to' *or* 'like' and 'dissimilar to' *or* 'unlike'; **perītus**, 'experienced in' *or* 'expert in'; **cupidus**, 'eager for'.

(f) It follows, or is 'taken by', a number of verbs summed up by the following aesthetically painful, but easily memorised, doggerel couplet:

> With pity, remember, forget – a genitive mostly is set.

The **Dative Case** also has a number of different uses.

(a) Its most frequent use, of course, is to indicate the person to whom or for whom an action is done. Grammatically speaking, it indicates the indirect object, as in **Hic liber multa utilia tibi dat**, 'This book gives you many useful things.'

(b) It is 'taken by' a number of intransitive verbs which can be memorised with the help of another piece of doggerel:

> A dative put, remember pray, – with **imperāre** and obey,
> **studēre, nūbere, nocēre**, – **placēre, parcere, favēre**
> to these add envy, trust, forgive, – resist, indulge, persuade, believe.

I am leaving it to you to look up the verbs given in English in the above.

(c) The **Possessive Dative**, as it is sometimes called, is used with **sum** as another way of indicating the person who has or owns something, as in **Mihi sunt filius et filia,** 'I have a son and a daughter.'

(d) It can also be used with **sum**, in this case sometimes called the **Predicative Dative** or **Dative of Purpose,** for a category of words which include the following: **bono,** 'an advantage', as in 'This is an advantage to me'; **oneri,** 'burden'; **curae,** 'care'; **auxilio,** 'help'; **impedimento,** 'hindrance'; **honori,** 'honour'; **odio,** 'object of hatred'; **argumento,** 'proof'; **usui,** 'use'.

(e) It is used with adjectives including the following: **par,** 'equal'; again, **similis** and **dissimilis,** 'like' and 'unlike'; **aptus,** 'fit'; **grātus,** 'pleasing'; **idōneus,** 'suitable'; **ūtilis,** 'useful'; **cārus,** 'dear'. Examples: **Linguam Latinam discere liberis aptum et utile et gratum est,** 'The learning of Latin is suitable, useful and pleasant for children.'

The **Ablative Case** has more uses than any other case, partly because it has absorbed the **Locative Case.** Amongst other things, it represents the English prepositions 'by', 'with', 'from', 'at', 'on' and 'in'. Sometimes it is used *with* prepositions; sometimes, as when it is replacing the locative case, it is used *without* prepositions. Here is a by-no-means complete list of uses of the ablative.

(a) It is used without prepositions when it is showing the *instrument* responsible for an action, and the *cause* on account of which an action or event takes place. Examples: **Sagitta vulneratus est et fame moritur,** 'He has been wounded *by an arrow* and is dying *of hunger.*'

(b) Together with a preposition (**a, ab**) it is used to show the agent, either human or animal, by whom an action is done. I trust that no example of this need be given.

(c) Always with the preposition **cum,** it indicates a person with whom one is doing something. Example: **Linguam Latinam**

**tecum discit sed cum amico tuo cantare non vult**, 'He is learning Latin together with you but does not wish to sing with your friend.' In the following cases, it is joined to the end of the pronouns that it governs, all of which I hope you remember the meanings of by now: **mecum**, **tecum**, **secum** (*do* be careful about when you use **secum**), **nobiscum**, **vobiscum**, **quocum** and **quibuscum** ('with whom' in the singular and the plural).

(d) Sometimes with **cum**, but not of necessity, it indicates the *manner* in which something is done. Example: **(Cum) honore patriam defendunt**, 'They are defending their country with honour.' Included under this heading are **hoc consilio**, 'with this intention', and the useful **hoc modo**, 'in this way'. If there is an adjective with an abstract noun, the ablative only is used, as in **Summa fortitudine pugnat**, 'He fights with the greatest courage', but if there is no adjective **cum** is used, as in **Cum dignitate dixit**, 'He spoke with dignity.'

(e) It can indicate quality when describing the noun, in which case, however, the noun in question must always have an adjective with it. Example: **miles summa virtute**, 'a soldier of great courage'.

(f) As we know, it expresses motion 'away from', always needing one of the prepositions **a** or **ab** and **e** or **ex** (according to whether the first letter of the next word is or is not a vowel) except in the case of the names of towns and small islands, **domus** and **rus**. Examples: **ab oppido**, 'from the town'; **Londinio**, 'from London'; **rure**, 'from the country'; **domo**, 'from home'.

(g) As we also know, it expresses the concept of 'in' and 'at' in relation to place. Once again, the preposition **in** is needed other than with towns, small islands, **domus** and **rus**.

(h) As yet again we already know, without any preposition it expresses time 'when' and 'within which'. Examples: **media nocte**, 'in the middle of the night'; **prima luce**, 'at first light', meaning 'at dawn'; **eo die**, 'on that day'; **duobus diebus**, 'in two days' time'.

(i) To anticipate what is taught on pages 112 and 113, it can act as an alternative to the conjunction **quam** when expressing a comparison, but only when someone or something in the nominative or accusative case is being compared. Example: **Tu eis linguam Latin celerius discis**, 'You are learning Latin more quickly than they are.'

(j) With very few adjectives, it expresses separation, as in **timore et odio liber**, 'free from fear and hatred'.

(k) It expresses *in what respect* something is so. Examples: **par sapientia**, 'equal in wisdom'; **dignus honore et laude**, 'worthy of honour and praise'.

(l) It is used with certain verbs, a fact which I shall record with our last bit of doggerel:

> *With use, perform, lack, need, enjoy, – an ablative you must employ.*

Once again, I am leaving it to you to look those verbs up.

## Exercises on what has been learnt so far

### A. Easy

| |
|---|
| 1. Caesar fought with great courage and spoke with dignity. |
| 2. He defeated the fleet without delay. |
| 3. The barber will come on the fourth day and will remain for two days. |
| 4. Within two days he will have shaved the long beards of all the soldiers. |
| 5. This barber shaves faster than his brother. |
| 6. Julius, your love of wisdom is equal to your desire for honour. |
| 7. The captives will be freed by the queen. |
| 8. **Audientibus militibus Caesar loquitur.** |
| 9. **Male hoc libro uteris si non omnia memoriae mandas.** |
| 10. **Sapiens in horto ambulans discipulos hortatur.** |

## B. Harder

(Note: any insertion in brackets is an instruction, rather than something to be translated.)

1. Caesar had attacked the enemy at the beginning of the year, and within a month he had defeated them.

2. Last year, Cicero sometimes spoke for two hours, and in the same year he was elected consul.

3. My mother left Britain and went to Rome in order to see Caesar and Cicero and to hear them speaking; many years afterwards, she left Rome.

4. Hello, Julius! Is your father at home? Does he want to see me? I do not live in Italy but in London. Tomorrow I shall set out for Rome.

5. If the boys were idle they were always punished by the wise master.

6. My name is Marcus, and I have three horses but only two dogs. Next year however I shall get possession of another dog. (Do not use the subject–verb–complement construction in the first clause of the first sentence, and do not use **habeo** anwhere.)

7. Caesar was not killed by spears while fighting in a battle against Rome's enemies but by Brutus.

8. While the soldiers were all asleep, the enemy approached very slowly and attacked their camp without delay. (Translate 'While the soldiers were all asleep' in two different ways.)

9. Tomorrow I am going into the city, after two days I shall be going out of the same city, and then I shall be making a journey across the mountain.

10. My old father is now at home in Rome. When did your mother arrive home?

C. Parse and then translate the following into English. All of them either are or include Latin idioms used untranslated in English. **Non sequitur, res ipsa loquitur, dei gratia, bona fides, bona fide, viva voce, casus belli, tabula rasa, Deo volente, ipso facto, locum tenens. Mutatis mutandis cives feliciores fiebant. Mens sana in corpore sano.**

D. Put into the accusative singular and genitive plural cases: **bona fides, casus, tabula rasa**.

E. Translate into Latin, taking special care with your translation: 'There are many causes of war.'

F. Write down one word each derived from **culpo** and **timeo**, and two words derived from **odium**.

**Post Script.** In the exercises at the end of Chapter Thirteen you were asked to produce a list of words derived from the Latin **duco**. If by any chance you included 'educate' in your list, you fell into the trap! This is because 'educate' demands for its source a word whose stem is **ducu-**, and **duco**, being a Third Conjugation verb, has no such stem. 'Educate' is derived from **educare**, meaning ' to educate' or 'to bring up', and only indirectly from **duco**, which of course has no First Conjugation form other than in the subjunctive.

## CHAPTER FIFTEEN

To be able, to want, not to want, to prefer; to
go, to bear, to become, and even to eat; also
to begin, to remember, to hate, and to say;
the impersonal verbs; infinitives and gerunds;
comparatives and superlatives of adjectives
and adverbs

## ACCIDENCE – WHAT MUST BE
### *LEARNT BY HEART*

### Verbs

*Commonly used verbs that are very irregular*

Turn to page 188 onwards in the Reference Grammar. There you
will find a collection of, as to their forms, the strangest verbs in
Latin. They became strange because they were much used and
being much used often results in words becoming corrupted in
their form. They do need to be learnt, in order both to use them
and to recognise them. In this chapter I shall usually mark the
long vowels because it is important to become familiar with the
sounds of the verbs before any habit of pronouncing any of them
incorrectly takes hold.

**Possum** ('I can' or 'I am able') is based on **sum** in the way it
conjugates – it is a corruption of **potēns**, able, and **sum** – and is
therefore easy to learn. Other useful verbs conjugated like **sum**
are: **absum**, 'I am absent'; **adsum**, 'I am present'; **dēsum**, 'I am
failing (in my duty)'; **praesum**, 'I am in charge of'; **prōsum**, 'I am
of use'. **Volō**, 'I wish' or 'I want' or 'I am willing'; **nōlō**, 'I do not
wish' or 'I am unwilling'; and **mālō**, 'I prefer' or 'I wish rather', are
highly irregular until the tenses which use the perfect stems
(**voluī**, and so on), after which they are completely regular. **Eō**, 'I

go', is again highly irregular, but important inasmuch as it is used in a large number of compound forms, such as **adeō, exeō, ineō**, and **trānseō** meaning respectively 'I approach', 'I leave', 'I enter', 'I cross'. **Ferō**, 'I bear', may be the most irregular verb in Latin in the remarkable change in its forms – be ready to gape as you stare at its **Principal Parts**, and then to gape further as you look at some of its tenses. **Fīō**, 'I become' or 'I am made', is mainly remarkable for its use – for some reason, **faciō**, 'I do' or 'I make', has no passive form of its own and **fīō** takes its place. **Ēdō**, 'I eat', is extraordinary because very much of how it conjugates in some of its tenses resembles exactly the conjugation of **sum**, other than that the **e** at the beginning of the **sum** forms is short and at the beginning of the **ēdō** forms is long; for instance, **sum, es, est** as opposed to **ēdō, ēs, ēst**.

The following actually have no present, future simple or imperfect tense forms at all but only perfect stems: **coepī**, 'I have begun' – a completely different word **incipiō** is needed for the other tenses; **meminī**, 'I remember' (which takes the genitive); and **ōdī**, 'I hate'; and, while **coepī** at least means what it appears to mean, the last two do not even do that, being *perfect in form*, but *present in meaning*. While I am about it, I may as well include **nōscō** as well. Although not especially irregular in its forms, it is strange in the meaning of some of its tenses. The perfect, **nōvī**, means either 'I have come to know' or 'I know'; while the future perfect, **nōverō**, only means 'I shall know'; the pluperfect, **nōveram** or **nōram**, means 'I knew'; and the perfect infinitive (we shall be coming to perfect infinitives shortly), **nōvisse** or **nōsse**, means 'to know'.

What shall I ask you to do with all this? Unquestionably, **possum, volō, nōlō, mālō, eō, ferō** and **fīō** must be learnt by heart, and thoroughly. They are much used. Pay attention to the frequently different pronunciations of the first letter **o** in **volō** and in **nōlō**. If you do not, you will form the habit of pronouncing incorrectly some of the forms of **nōlō**, which, as you will see, often has **ō** where **volō** has **o**, the reason being that **nōlō** is a corruption of **nōn volō** (as indeed is obvious in that some of its forms, such as **nōn vis**, are not even corrupted).

As to the remainder of these verbs, I suggest that you gradually learn them as you meet them, and that meanwhile you make

sure that you are at least *aware of* them so that you are on the alert
to look them up when they cross your path. Alternatively, as there
are not so very many of them, you may like to treat a few extra
minutes spent on learning them now as a piece of constructive
entertainment.

## Impersonal verbs

On page 193 you will find fourteen impersonal verbs – thus called
because their subject is always the mysterious 'it' we use in English
in expressions such as 'It is raining' or 'It beats me'. They have
only third person singular, an infinitive, and a gerund so although
the **Principal Parts** are of necessity unusual, there is little to
learn.

## Infinitives

We must delay dealing with the infinitive no longer, because
**possum**, **volō**, **nōlō** and **mālō** are much more often used with the
infinitive of a second verb than used on their own. The infinitives
of other verbs are used as their *direct objects*. This construction is
called the 'prolative' infinitive and we also use it in English when
we say, for example, 'I want to learn Latin.' 'To learn' in that
sentence is a prolative infinitive.

As may be remembered from Chapter Seven, ordinary verbs
have six infinitives, the present, perfect and future infinitives in
the Active Voice, and the present, perfect and future infinitives in
the Passive Voice. They correspond to the English 'to love', 'to
have loved', 'to be going to love', 'to be loved', 'to have been loved'
and 'to be going to be loved'. Off you go, please, to pages 180 and
185, and learn first of all the infinitives of **amō** and then the infinitives of the rest.

Note that, for the future infinitive active and the perfect infinitive passive, participles are used which decline like **bonus**. The
future infinitive passive is complicated because it is always used in
conjunction with the infinitive **īrī** (the passive present infinitive of
**eō**, 'I go', if you can believe that such a thing exists), rather than
with **esse**, and is therefore always used impersonally, and therefore
is in the neuter form even with a feminine subject. Thus 'We think

that the Latin language will never be loved by everybody' translates best into **Putamus linguam Latinam numquam ab omnibus amatum iri** – a sentence that will make better sense to you when you have studied indirect statements in Chapter Eighteen.

## Gerunds

Just as is the infinitive, the **gerund** is a verbal noun. It is formed by adding either **-andum** to the stem of a First Conjugation verb or **-endum** to the stem of a verb of the other three conjugations. It is a neuter noun, and it declines, as one would expect, like **bellum**.

In pre-classical times the gerund did not exist. What then happened was that certain parts of the adjectival gerundive, a *passive* participle which we met in Chapter Thirteen, began to feature by themselves, rather than only when attached to a noun, and gradually this new usage took on a life – an *active* life, in both senses – and a name of its own.

Remarkably, Caesar on one occasion used both constructions *in the very same sentence*, **Germanis neque consilii habendi neque arma capiendi spatium datum est** (*Gallic Wars*, IV, 14). I shall repeat it as one of the exercises at the end of this chapter, and after you have tried to parse and translate it, we shall, just this once, look at it together.

## Adjectives – positives, comparatives and superlatives

The forms of the comparatives and superlatives of positive adjectives (as adjectives which are neither comparatives nor superlatives are called) are not difficult to pick up. All comparatives but one, the comparative of **multus** which is **plūs** (see page 169), end in **-ior** (in the masculine–feminine nominative singular) and decline like **trīstior**, which will be found on page 170 following the other information needed on comparatives and superlatives. All superlatives without exception decline like **bonus**.

What you need now is to learn the rules for forming the comparatives and superlatives, and also the exceptions, as usual applicable to those most commonly used. You will find this information on page 169.

## Adverbs – positives, comparatives and superlatives

By the nature of things, none of these decline – they have no nouns or pronouns to agree with. You will find information on them on page 170, immediately after the treatment of adjectives.

### SYNTAX – WHAT MUST BE *UNDERSTOOD*

## Verbs

### *Infinitives as straightforward nouns*

The infinitive 'to love' is a verbal noun, exactly as is the gerund, 'loving', which we shall be coming to shortly. Indeed, the infinitive and the gerund are interchangeable as to their meaning, both in English and in Latin. Thus in theory (we shall see shortly why I say 'in theory'), 'to see is to believe' is interchangeable with 'seeing is believing', identical in meaning. The same applies to 'to be'. I have no need to translate for you **Esse aut non esse, illa est quaestio,** possibly the single most famous sentence in the English language, but surely not the wisest.

In the use of the infinitive in conjunction with **possum, volō, nolō, mālō,** only three things need to be pointed out.

1. After those verbs the infinitive that follows them is in effect, being a noun, the *direct object* of those verbs – an object consisting of a noun which does not decline, of course.

2. In Latin, where two verbs are used together in a clause, it is the verb which changes its form that usually goes at the end. Thus 'I am unwilling to teach you now' normally translates into **Te nunc docere nolo**.

3. There is a distinct and even drastic difference in meaning between **Te nunc docere nolo** and **Te nunc non docere volo** – 'I do not wish to teach you now' as opposed to 'I am willing not to teach you now.'

In addition to **possum, volo, nolo** and **malo,** other verbs which also take a prolative infinitive include: (a) verbs of duty and habit, such as **debeo**, 'I ought', and **soleo**, 'I am accustomed'; (b) verbs of deciding and daring, such as **constituo**, 'I decide', and **audeo**, 'I dare'; (c) verbs of starting, stopping, trying and hastening, such as **coepi** and **incipio**, both meaning 'I begin'; **desisto**, 'I cease'; **conor**, ' I try'; and **festino**, 'I hurry'; and (d) verbs of learning, teaching and knowing how to, such as three that we by now know well: **disco**, **doceo** and **scio**.

## Gerund

Gerunds are perhaps most commonly dealt with at the same time as gerundives in textbooks, but it is more logical to deal with them here, because they are nouns rather than adjectives and also play a very similar role to infinitives.

In theory, 'seeing is believing' could be translated into *either* **videre est credere** *or* **videndum est credendum**. In practice, it would never be translated into the second of those alternatives, and they are *not* in fact interchangeable. If the verb-noun that could be either in the infinitive or in the gerund is syntactically in the nominative or the vocative or the accusative case by itself (no preposition in front of it), then the infinitive is exclusively used. If, however, the verb-noun belongs to the genitive, dative or ablative case, then the gerund is used – for the evidently good reason that infinitives cannot have cases. The same applies if there is a preposition before the verb-noun, even if that preposition does in fact take the accusative – the gerund is used rather than the infinitive.

Some examples will help fix all this in the memory: **Discere difficile est**, 'Learning is difficult.' **Discere incipio**, 'I am beginning to learn.' **Sum hic ad discendum**, 'I am here for the purpose of learning.' **Amor meus discendi magnus est**, 'My love of learning is great.' **Discendo** (in the dative) **operam do**, 'I am paying attention to learning.' **Legendo** (ablative) **disco**, 'I am learning by reading.'

One final complication is that a gerund cannot govern an object in the accusative case. When that appears necessary, the gerundive, which we met in Chapter Thirteen, is used instead. Therefore 'He learns by reading books' cannot be translated as **Libros legendo discit**, but must be retranslated into English as

'He learns by books being-read', whence it can be rendered in Latin as **Libris legendis discit**.

We now turn to something a little easier.

## Impersonal verbs

Some of these, such as **licet**, are frequently used. What gives rise to difficulty is that, by their nature, they are followed by constructions different from those which follow ordinary verbs. More difficult still, different impersonal verbs are followed by different constructions. What their syntactical constructions are will be found in each case with each verb in the Reference Grammar, and my recommendation is that, for the time being, whenever an impersonal verb is needed, how it should be used – as opposed to how it conjugates, which should be thoroughly known – should be looked up until everything becomes familiar.

The most important of them are **licet**, 'it is lawful *or* allowed', with the dative and infinitive; **placet**, 'it pleases', with the dative and infinitive; and **oportet**, 'it behoves', with accusative and infinitive. The English meanings I have just given help one to understand the Latin construction, but should often be changed to a more natural variant in translation. For example, instead of 'it is allowed to me', 'it is pleasing to me' or 'it behoves me', it will generally be better to say, 'I may', 'I am resolved' and 'I ought' respectively. Thus: 'You may not stay here', **Non licet tibi hic manere**; 'I am resolved to stay here', **Mihi hic manere placet**; and 'Why ought I to stay here?', **Quare me hic manere oportet?**

## Adjectives – positives, comparatives and superlatives

For the most part the use of comparatives and superlatives is straightforward, exactly the same as the use of positive adjectives. They simply agree with their noun or pronoun, whether expressed in the clause or understood, in number, case and gender.

The only new feature is when one person or thing is being compared with another. Always, this can be done by using the conjunction **quam**, meaning 'than', when comparing one with the other. In that case, the two things being compared are always in the same case. Thus 'This man is wiser than that man' is (with a word not strictly necessary included in brackets) **Hic vir quam is (vir) sapientior est**.

There is, however, another comparative construction, which applies only when the person or thing that is subject to the comparison is in either the nominative case or the accusative case. In such an instance, **quam** can be omitted and the second person or thing can go into the ablative case instead, to indicate the comparison. The sentence above could therefore read: **Hic vir eo (viro) sapientior est**. It is never wrong to use the **quam** construction, but of course you need to be familiar with the other construction, as you can expect to meet it frequently when translating from Latin.

## Adverbs – positives, comparatives and superlatives

All that needs to be said under this heading is that the construction of comparisons is in all important respects the same. It is worth noting that **quam** can join clauses as well as parts of speech. Thus 'He can learn more quickly than I can learn' translates into **Is celerius discere potest quam ego (discere possum)**.

With either a superlative adjective or a superlative adverb, **quam** means 'as ... as possible'. **Quam celerrime** therefore means 'as quickly as possible'.

### EXERCISES ON WHAT HAS BEEN LEARNT SO FAR

## A. Easy

| |
|---|
| 1. Can you see me already, Julius? |
| 2. Julius, can you hear me now? |
| 3. Do you prefer to come with me or to go with them? |
| 4. Our towns are larger than Caesar's two camps. |
| 5. I have borne great burdens because long ago I became a slave. |
| 6. Slaves are not allowed to speak in the Senate. (Translate as 'It is not lawful for slaves ...'.) |
| 7. Caesar has resolved to go to Rome as quickly as possible. (Translate as 'It has pleased Caesar to ...'.) |

8. Rome did not begin to rule Britain while Caesar was alive. (Use an ablative absolute.)

9. **Linguam Latinam a sapientioribus disci oportet.**

10. **O matre pulchra filia pulchrior.** (This phrase is taken from a poem of Horace's.)

## B. Harder

1. From the beginning, reading this book has been easy.

2. I myself did not wish to see myself in a mirror, but I have often not been able to avoid this.

3. The Roman soldiers are said to have fought very bravely and very fiercely and to be about to attack the other city that is near Rome.

4. The old man often cannot remember the things that were to be done.

5. I wish to go away and I am trying to go away but I have never been able to go away because I am not allowed [it is not lawful for me] to go away.

6. I fear that the old men will never learn Latin well.

7. The very old ambassadors have said many useless things about the Romans and about the city of Rome.

8. The happy slaves have been building a broad, high wall in the middle of Britain for many months. This wall is being built with large stones.

9. I want to know much about the Latin language that you have taught for many years before I can start to like learning it.

10. Some like Latin and some do not like it but everyone ought to learn Latin. It is lawful to teach it to everyone. I pity those who do not wish to learn it and are wearied or vexed by having to learn it.

C. Parse and translate this sentence, almost straight from the pen of Julius Caesar: **[Eis] Germanis neque consilii habendi neque arma capiendi spatium datum est** (*Gallic Wars*, IV, 14). When you have done your best for this, turn to the end of these exercises for some help.

D. (a) Of the following English-but-in-the-form-of-untranslated-Latin idioms, say which is gerund and which gerundive, and then translate each idiom into literal English: **agenda, corrigendum, modus operandi, modus vivendi, nil desperandum**. (b) Parse and then translate this sentence: **Hoc telum pugnando utile est.**

E. Translate the following short passage of continuous prose into English.

**Reminder.** First stage: translate it with word-for-word exactness. Second stage: 'translate' your first translation into English that you can be proud of.

**Caesar, ubi iam totam fere Galliam vicerat, quod Britanni auxilium ad Gallos saepe miserant, in Britanniam proficisci constituit. Itaque primum cum omnibus copiis in Morinorum** [of the Morini] **fines proficiscitur, quod inde erat brevissimus in Britanniam traiectus. Huc naves undique e finitimis civitatibus, et classem quam ad Venetorum bellum aedificaverat, convenire iussit.**

F. Parse and then translate into English these untranslated-Latin English idioms: **nolle prosequi, prima facie, reductio ad absurdum, Deus ex machina, in vino veritas**.

G. Write down one word derived from each of **do, incipio** and **possum**.

We return now to C, after you have done your best to translate that sentence into English.

Completely literally, and parsing some of it in square brackets as we go along, it can be translated as: 'Time was given to those Germans neither for a plan being adopted [gerundive and therefore *passive*, with the noun and gerundive agreeing with each other in the genitive case] nor for taking up arms [with **capiendi** *this* time a verb-noun – a gerund – in the genitive singular, with **arma** its direct object in the accusative].'

I hope you arrived at this answer before you arrived at *my* answer!

## CHAPTER SIXTEEN

Introduction to translating from Latin into
English; also, the relative and interrogative
pronouns and their use

## ACCIDENCE – WHAT MUST BE
## *LEARNT BY HEART*

### Relative and interrogative pronouns

Please turn now to page 174 and learn the **Relative Pronoun
qui**, **quae**, **quod** by heart. You will not find it difficult because,
except at the end with the alternative datives and ablatives plural, it
declines almost exactly like **hic, haec, hoc**. Learn by heart also
the **Interrogative Pronoun**, which you will find even less difficult, because most of it, other than in the nominatives and voca-
tives singular, goes exactly like the Relative Pronoun. Indeed an
alternative declension of it is *exactly* the declension of the Relative
Pronoun and the English equivalents 'who' and 'which' are indif-
ferently used with relative or interrogative meaning.

## SYNTAX – WHAT MUST BE *UNDERSTOOD*

### Translating from Latin into English

Now at last we are fully ready, if you have been using this book as
I hope you have, to tackle properly the techniques and skills
needed to translate from Latin into English.

We have of course done a certain amount of this right from
the beginning. That, however, has been more for the purpose of
becoming more familiar with Latin, and with the idea of translating both ways, than in order to make a really good translation.

Let us now set forth then. Please make sure you have a reasonable amount of time when you start this chapter, because we are

going to go into painstaking detail. You will find it worth the effort because nothing approaching what follows will be found in any other textbook likely to be available today, and indeed, to the best of my knowledge, you will find nothing as detailed and thorough in *any* other textbook. Without doubt, you will need to come back to this chapter again and again, especially just before embarking on some reading of Latin, until its contents have become, obviously not learnt by heart, but built solidly into your mental make-up.

## The golden rules for translating Latin into English

1. Be sure you know the basics of accidence and syntax such as: the eight parts of speech; what exactly a sentence, a clause and a phrase are; and how to identify, in any clause, the subject, the verb, the object or the complement, and any indirect object.

2. This point is of primary importance. When working out the translation of a passage, *never* guess.

   It would be difficult to exaggerate how important this is. In the relatively uninflected languages that most modern languages are, it can sometimes be reasonably easy to work out the meanings of sentences with the help of guessing. Indeed, this even applies in inflected languages, such as German, where word order is subject to clear rules. It cannot, however, possibly be done – cannot even remotely begin to be done – in a language such as Latin, which is not only inflected but has much looser word-order rules, and not even an article such as the equivalent of 'the' or 'a' to provide any assistance.

   Not only is there not the slightest reasonable hope of getting the translation right by guessing, but there is a further problem as well, which my experience with even the most intelligent pupils has shown to be a very real one. This is that it does not take long before guessing becomes a *habit*, and a habit so solidly and irreversibly entrenched that it completely takes over from what is really necessary in translating Latin, which is to concentrate, analyse, and persist until the solution is arrived at.

The only occasion when guessing might be legitimate is in a formal examination, once the stage has been reached that, if a guess is *not* made, the passage will be left blank on the examination paper.

3.  In translating from Latin, possibly more than in any other academic subject, close attention to every tiny detail is indispensable. You must *analyse closely* in order to *understand*.

4.  To help you do this, you are about to be shown:

    (a) how to locate the most important essentials of a sentence: the subject, the verb, and the object or complement (if any);

    (b) once those are found, how to fit in adjectives, adverbs, prepositional phrases; and

    (c) how to recognise and then analyse subordinate clauses in much the same way, since they follow the same basic rules.

5.  *Two* translations should be made of each sentence, however short it is:

    (a) First, a translation that is completely literal down to the tiniest detail, with no attention paid to its awkwardness in English. This ensures that no guessing takes place, even half-consciously or less.

    (b) Secondly, re-translate that first translation into the best and most natural English that you can.

    It is worth mentioning that at least half the value of the exercise of translating from Latin into English is in the practice it gives in *handling one's own language*. Especially because Latin is as different from English as any European language could be, translating from good Latin into good English via doggerel – if there is such a thing as doggerel in prose – is as valuable a mental exercise in accurate and useful thinking at any level as can be imagined.

6.  A sentence may consist of a single clause, or of two or more main clauses, or of main clauses and one or more subsidiary clauses. Identify the clauses in the sentence under examination. First of all, identify the main clause or clauses. Then identify the subsidiary clauses if any, including, in very

complicated sentences, clauses which are subsidiary to subsidiary clauses. (Beware of subsidiary clauses hidden in the
middle of main clauses, as in, to give an example in English:
'He found the book *he was looking* for under another book.')
Subsidiary clauses will usually be introduced by a relative
pronoun or a conjunction, as for instance, 'who' or 'whom',
'which', 'where', 'if', 'unless', 'before'.

7. Take each clause one by one, in order of importance or apparent importance. Thus, take the first main clause first, if there is
more than one. If there are any subsidiary clauses belonging to
that main clause, move straight on to them before going on to
the second main clause (if there is a second main clause). Only
when everything in that first main clause is completed, move
on to the next clause in what you have deduced to be its order
of importance. And so on. In the case of each group of clauses,
in a clause followed by subsidiary and possibly sub-subsidiary
clauses, take the main clause first, and only when everything in
it is solved, go on to what is the next most important clause.

8. We now come to the clauses themselves. We find out everything that is inside them, which means first thorough analysis and then translating.

9. Inside the main clause or first main clause that we are starting
with, the first thing we need to identify is the subject. This is
because the subject is what the clause is about. The subject
will always be in the form of a noun, or pronoun, or noun
phrase or noun clause, but it can be difficult to locate in
Latin. Indeed it may be and quite often is, in effect, invisible,
'concealed' inside the verb.

10. Although the subject is the first thing we need to identify,
this does *not* mean that the first thing we look for is a noun,
pronoun or adjective in the nominative case. Because of the
absence in Latin of various means of assistance in finding the
subject that other languages have, the only sure way to locate
the subject is by first finding *the main verb*, and examining it
for clues. The main verb can help us in our quest in a number
of ways. First, the number of the verb will tell us whether the

number of the subject is singular or plural, which will often eliminate otherwise possible candidates as the subject. Secondly, the verb will tell you the person of the subject, and if the person is first or second person, you normally need look no further, for there will be no noun and seldom a pronoun that is the subject. Thirdly, the meaning of the verb will often make it easy to deduce what the subject is. In the sentence **Opera difficilia pueri non amant**, it is immediately obvious from the meaning of the verb that it cannot be the difficult labours that are doing the disliking, but must be the boys.

11. Having deduced as much information as possible about the subject by looking at the verb, the next step is to look for the subject itself. It may be implied in the verb, as the subject 'I' is implied in '**amo**', or it may be separately expressed. It may be more than a single word, for instance a noun together with one or more adjectives describing that noun. Assuming that it is not a whole clause or phrase, the subject can be pared down until it is reduced to a single word at most. This word will be either:

(a) a noun; or

(b) pronoun; or

(c) an adjective or participle doing the work of a noun or a pronoun (as in **bonus/boni** which can mean 'the good man/men' as well as simply 'good'; **bona/bonae**, which can mean 'a good woman/women' as well as simply 'good' in the feminine; and **bonum/bona**, which can mean 'the good thing/things' as well as 'good' in the neuter); or

(d) an infinitive, as in **Linguam Latinam discere dulce est**, 'To learn Latin is delightful'; or

(e) a relative clause, as in **Qui linguam Latinam discunt vere felices sunt**, 'Those who are learning Latin are lucky indeed'; or

(f) none of those, but 'hidden' in the verb, with the pronoun 'understood'.

If the subject is a noun, a pronoun or an adjective functioning as a pronoun, it will be in the nominative case. There may of course be two or more subjects in any clause.

12. It can happen that it is impossible to identify from the grammar alone whether the subject is a noun or is contained in the verb. For instance, **Vir bonus est** can mean *either* 'The man is good' *or* 'He is a good man.' In such cases it is necessary to infer what the writer intends from the context.

13. **Reminder.** Never, never look for the subject until you have found and examined the verb first. Until you have located the verb, it can be impossible to identify the subject, if only because the *same* endings sometimes correspond to *different* cases and numbers and genders. For instance:

    (a) The noun **mensae** can either be nominative plural and therefore a subject, or genitive singular or dative singular and therefore of course *not* a subject.

    (b) The adjective '**bona**' can be *either* nominative feminine singular (meaning 'a good woman' *or* nominative neuter plural (meaning 'good things') and thus a subject, *or* ablative feminine singular or accusative neuter plural and thus *not* a subject.

14. If the subject is a noun or pronoun, and especially if it is a noun, it may well have an adjective with it in the same case and number, which should be translated with its noun at this stage. There should be no problem in identifying which noun an adjective is describing, but many mistakes are made on this because of carelessness, not taking the trouble to identify all three elements of the ending.

15. Now, using the subject and the verb that you have identified, translate them both, normally putting the subject *first* in the English sentence.

16. **Reminder.** Postpone any attempt at good style and concentrate at this stage *only* on translating with word-for-word accuracy.

17. Now go back to the verb you have just translated, to see whether it is:

    (a) a being verb, in which case it will have a complement in the nominative case, or

(b) a transitive doing verb, in which case there will be a direct object somewhere in the accusative case, or

(c) an intransitive doing verb, in which case there will be no direct object but there may be an indirect object, normally in the dative case, or an even more indirect object with a preposition in front of it (as in 'We are going to Italy').

18. If there is a complement or object to be found, find it. Remember that there are verbs which, although they govern direct objects when translated into English, in Latin govern different cases: some, such as **memini**, 'I remember', take the genitive; some, such as of course **pareo**, 'I obey', take the dative; and some, such as **fruor**, 'I enjoy', **fungor**, 'I perform' and **utor**, 'I use', take the ablative. Remember also that there are expressions of direction, extent and time which use the accusative, which means that an accusative case does not necessarily indicate a direct object.

19. Some verbs may take an indirect object as well as a direct object. Verbs of giving, promising, showing, telling and taking away often have two objects: a direct object in the accusative, and an indirect object in the dative, completing the sense of the verb, as in **Id tibi dico**, 'I am saying it to you.' Remember, however, that there are also a very few verbs which have both a direct object in the accusative and what in English would be the indirect object in the accusative case also. Examples are **doceo** and **rogo** (see Chapter Fourteen).

20. When things are most straightforward, the verb will be in the indicative mood. When it is not, it will be almost as straightforward if it is in the imperative mood, but less so if it is in the subjunctive mood. This is because there are a number of different uses of the subjunctive mood. We shall learn about them in outline in the next chapter, Chapter Seventeen.

21. One last thing about verbs. Although they are usually in the same tense in English as in Latin, Latin writers often use the present tense where we should use the aorist or preterite tense (as in 'he loved') in a narrative piece. If you see that

happening, you will need to put the verb into the present tense in your first translation, and then convert it into the more 'English' tense in your second translation.

22. Next, look around to see whether there are any nouns or pronouns in the genitive case, and, if there are any, to identify whether they 'belong' to the subject, or to an object of the verb, or to an indirect object of the verb. If the context leaves any doubt as to where a noun in the genitive case belongs, it will normally relate to the closest noun or pronoun.

23. Remember that further nouns can be added to a noun, in the same case, in order to say more about the first noun, and, that such nouns are said to be *in apposition* to the first one. The first noun or pronoun can be in any case, and a noun in apposition always agrees with the noun or pronoun to which it refers, as in **Ciceronis consulis memini**, 'I remember Cicero *as* consul', *or*, '*when he was* consul'. (It may be remembered that **memini** takes the genitive case.)

24. Next look around at all the other words and phrases in the sentence and work out where they belong. For instance, adverbs will most often modify a verb in the sentence, but they can also modify adjectives and other adverbs.

25. If the sentence was a complex one, now go on to the next clause in order of importance and do the same thing. First identify whether it is a main clause or a subsidiary clause, and, if it is a subsidiary clause, whether or not it is a relative clause. The importance of whether or not a subsidiary clause is a relative clause is that, if it is, it will be introduced by a Relative Pronoun (see below).

## Relative Pronouns

In number 25 above, I mentioned the **Relative Pronoun**, which you have just learnt. This is as good a time as any to explain its use properly, along with that of the Interrogative Pronoun.

Attention is needed with theRelative Pronoun, because:

either (a) the Relative Pronoun will be in the nominative case, in which case it will be the subject of its clause,

or (b) it will be in the accusative case, in which case it will be the object in the clause, and the subject must be sought elsewhere,

or (c) it will be in one of the other cases, in which case again the subject must be sought elsewhere.

This point is perhaps most easily explained by examples in English. An example of (a) is: 'You are boys and girls who are learning Latin.' An example of (b) is: 'You are the boy whom this book is greatly helping.' Examples of (c) include: 'You are the girl whose Latin is better' and 'You are girls to whom this book is giving much help' and 'This is a book by which you have been greatly helped.'

Once all this has been accomplished, let us make sure that you understand what is involved in relative clauses by translating together the examples given, very slightly adjusted. After that you should be ready to try the exercises without further explanation.

'Who are you? You are boys and girls who are learning Latin.' **Qui estis? Pueri puellaeque estis qui linguam Latinam discitis.**

'Who are you? You are the boy whom this book is greatly helping.' **Quis es? Puer es quem hic liber magnopere iuvat.**

'Who are you? You are the girl whose Latin is getting better.' **Quis es? Puella es cuius Latinitas fit melior.**

'Who are you? You are girls for whom this book is very useful.' **Quae estis? Puellae estis quibus hic liber utilissimus est.**

'What is this book? This is a book by which you have been greatly helped.' **Quid hic liber est? Hic liber est a quo magnopere iuvatus es.**

## EXERCISES ON WHAT HAS BEEN
## LEARNT SO FAR

### A. Easy

| |
|---|
| 1. The queen who reigns in Britain is courageous. |
| 2. The burden which the slaves bore was heavy. |
| 3. The army of which Caesar was general was feared by all. |
| 4. We shall never forget the good things which we have learnt. |
| 5. He whom all men obey is powerful. |
| 6. **Quae tibi Romae videndae causa fuit?** |
| 7. **Quis est qui appropinquat?** |
| 8. **Cuius est imago haec?** (This one is from the Vulgate Latin New Testament.) |
| 9. **Equus cuius onus leve est velocius proficiscetur quam alter.** |
| 10. **Ignavus puer libro qui melior est non utitur.** |

### B. Harder

| |
|---|
| 1. The ambassadors whom I wanted to see have already set out as quickly as possible for [towards] the city. |
| 2. Those whose houses are very big are the richest citizens in Rome and much richer than we are. |
| 3. Hannibal of Carthage died more than one hundred years before Julius Caesar. Which of them was the better general? |
| 4. I have seen the judge whose virtuous son did this. I have also seen the soldiers you have been giving many presents to and by whom you have been given a few weapons which are useful presents. |
| 5. The Romans always gave very good laws to the countries that they had conquered. |

C. Translate the following short passage into English. Remember to do so in two stages.

**Quis umquam multiplicem Gaii Iulii Caesaris praestantiam superavit? Hic enim vir Romae se facundum sermone, lepidum**

litteris, sapientem in rebus publicis praebebat. In bello autem, armorum et equitandi peritissimus laborisque patientissimus, fere invincibilis exstitit. In agmine nonnumquam equo, saepius pedibus, milites suos anteibat, capite detecto, sive sole ardente, sive sub imbre. Longissima itinera incredibili celeritate faciebat, neque eum retardabant flumina.

Post bella civilia Caesar dictator in perpetuum creatus est. Antonius, Caesaris in omnibus expeditionibus comes, et tunc in consulatu collega, ei in sella aurea sedenti diadema, insigne regium, imposuit. Hac de causa contra eum coniuratio Cassio et Bruto ducibus ex invidia facta est. Idibus Martiis in senatum Caesarem assidentem coniurati circumsteterunt illicoque unus ex eis, quasi aliquid rogaturus, propius accessit eumque apprehendit. Mox Cassius dictatorem paulo infra iugulum vulnerat. Videns Marcum Brutum, quem loco filii habebat, in se irruentem dixit Caesar 'Tu quoque fili mi!' atque ita tribus et viginti plagis vulneratus sub ipsa Pompeii statua cecidit.

D. Parse and then translate into English these untranslated-Latin English idioms: **quid pro quo**, **in flagrante delicto**, **status quo ante**, **quo vadis**?

E. Translate into Latin:

    (1) Of a blazing crime.
    (2) I heard many slips of the tongue.

---

## CHAPTER SEVENTEEN

Subjunctives, imperatives, infinitives and
gerunds; commands, more advanced questions,
and exclamations

## ACCIDENCE – WHAT MUST BE
### *LEARNT BY HEART*

### Subjunctive mood

We have now arrived at the final demanding item of accidence
that I shall be asking you to learn by heart; and in terms of volume
of material, it is more than any previous chapter has imposed on
you. Specifically, I ask you to turn to pages 181–84 of the
Reference Grammar and – hold your breath as I give you the task
– learn by heart all four of the subjunctive tenses in both the
Active Voice and the Passive Voice of the four verbs of the four
conjugations. Do not move on from here until that is done.

Yes, there is a considerable body of material to be learnt in this
task; but no, the task is not nearly as daunting as it may at first
appear to be.

In the first place, although the endings are considerably different from the endings of the indicative mood, there is a pattern in
them which you will by now have become accustomed to.

In the second place, in both the Active and the Passive Voices,
there is sufficient similarity between one conjugation and another
to make it much easier to learn the rest once you have learnt the
first of them, the subjunctive of **amo**.

In the third place, you cannot fail to have become more profi-
cient in the learning of Latin declensions and conjugations by
heart than you were when you started Chapter Nine.

In the fourth place, I believe you will enjoy the deep satisfaction of taking on the task with the knowledge that, once it is

completed, there will be no more of this kind of task. Granted, there are some irregular verbs yet to come, not to mention a fair number of **Principal Parts** of the regular verbs that must be memorised, but these tasks are slight indeed compared with what you will have achieved

So away you go to page 181, and please make sure that you resist any temptation to return here before the job is done. I shall have another memorising task for you immediately on your return, but one that is only minimally demanding by comparison with this one.

## Imperative mood

Have you now completely committed to memory the entire subjunctive mood, both active and passive, of all the regular conjugations, dear diligent and honest reader? Cross your heart?! To continue then. . . .

First go to pages 179 and 180, and look at and learn the imperatives of **sum** and **amo**, including their meanings. Then go to page 184 and learn the remaining imperatives of the four conjugations. This should not take long.

## Exclamations or interjections

Go to page 196 and learn by heart the small number of common interjections given there.

### SYNTAX – WHAT MUST BE *UNDERSTOOD*

## Subjunctive mood

The subjunctive mood differs from the indicative mood in this. The indicative mood is for events or states that *actually happen* (including 'will happen' and 'have happened') and *are* (including 'will be' and 'have been'). The subjunctive mood is used when, by contrast, what is needed to be expressed is doubt, improbability, uncertainty, a recommendation, a condition, a purpose, or in some cases an order. That is much ground to cover, and no attempt will be made here to cover more than a small fraction of it.

The subjunctive can express *an exhortation*. 'Let everyone hear my words.' **Omnes mea verba audiant.**

It can express a *wish for the future*. 'May the Queen live (for ever).' **Vivat regina.**

It is needed *in a subsidiary clause beginning with 'since'*, in Latin **cum**. 'Since you are learning Latin, you will be happier.' **Cum linguam Latinam discas, felicior eris.**

It is needed *in a subsidiary clause beginning with 'when'*, which – sometimes confusingly when translating from Latin into English – is also **cum**. Thus, to use the example given in Chapter Fourteen, 'When we arrived in Italy . . .' is **Cum in Italiam venerimus . . .** (perfect subjunctive).

It can be *deliberative*, as in **Quid faciam**, 'What am I to do?'

It is used in what are called Final Clauses, which are clauses which express *purpose*. These clauses are introduced either by the conjunction **ut**, meaning 'in order that', when the purpose is positive, or by the conjunction **ne**, meaning 'lest' when the purpose is negative. 'We work in order that we may learn Latin well' or 'We work to learn Latin well' are both translated by **Laboramus ut linguam Latinam bene discamus**. 'We work in order that we may not be punished' or 'We work so as not to be punished' or 'We work lest we be punished' are all translated by **Laboramus ne puniamur**.

It can be used to express *an order in the negative*, again introduced by the conjunction **ne**, which here means 'not' rather than 'lest' and must be followed by the perfect subjunctive. 'Do not fear Latin.' **Ne linguam Latinam timueris.**

It is important always to satisfy yourself that you know why a verb in a subordinate clause is in the subjunctive.

**Note.** In English we often abbreviate 'in order to' to the simple word 'to' as in 'Paulus is studying to learn.' Wherever the meaning implies purpose this 'in order to' must be mentally supplied. Latin expresses 'Paulus is studying to learn' as if it were 'Paulus is studying *in order that* he may learn.'

## Imperative mood

The most basic use of the imperative mood is simple. 'Love Latin' is **Ama linguam Latinam**. Addressing the Latin language, 'Be loved, Latin' is **Amare, lingua Latina** (in the vocative case, of course).

A negative command is less straightforward than in English. The straightforward 'not' in the English negative command, as in 'Don't do that', does not work in Latin. It is replaced by two alternatives. One is the use of **nolo** in the imperative, followed of course by the prolative infinitive as in 'Do not be afraid of Latin', **Linguam Latinam noli timere**. (The verb in the imperative tends to come first, and even **Noli linguam Latinam timere** would be quite usual.) The other alternative is the one just mentioned above: **nē** followed by the perfect subjunctive.

## Questions, more elaborate, and also exclamations

In Latin, questions must always begin with an interrogative word of some sort. Inversion of the subject and the verb does *not* have the effect of turning a statement into a question as it does in English and in many other languages. And:

(a) With the simple questions of which we met a few in Chapter Twelve, all that is needed is to start a sentence with an interrogative word – as in **Quis es et quid facis?**, 'Who are you and what are you doing?' – or to add **-ne** to the first word of the sentence – as in **Miseretne te eius?**, 'Do you pity him?' or 'Are you sorry for him?' Note that *this* interrogative suffix **-ne** has a short **e** unlike the word **ne** that we have just learnt.

(b) When the question anticipates the answer 'no' – as in, for instance, 'Do you dare deny the usefulness of Latin?' – the sentence is begun with **num**. **Num linguae Latinae utilitatem negare audes?**

(c) When the question implies or invites the answer 'yes' – as in, for instance 'Isn't it delightful to know Latin!' – the sentence is begun with **nonne**, the reason (which should help you to remember which is which) being that such questions will always contain the word **non**, put first in the sentence and with **-ne** attached to it. **Nonne Latine scire delectat!**

(d) When the question is about two alternatives, **utrum** introduces the first of those alternatives, and **an** introduces the second. For instance: **Utrum lingua Latina delectabilior**

**est an Graeca?** which of course means: 'Which is more delightful, Latin or Greek?'

(e) As in English, many of the interrogative opening words are also used in exclamations, as in, **Quam celeriter is eaque linguam Latinam discunt!**, 'How quickly he and she are learning Latin!'

## EXERCISES ON WHAT HAS BEEN LEARNT SO FAR

### A. Easy

| |
|---|
| 1. Do not be sad, Julius. |
| 2. The barber has come to shave the beards of the soldiers. |
| 3. The Africans fear lest the city of Carthage be destroyed by the Romans. |
| 4. Alas, careless barber, do not injure my ear! |
| 5. Was not Carthage destroyed by the Romans? (The answer expected is 'yes': Carthage *was* destroyed by the Romans.) |
| 6. **Caesar senatui locuturus audiatur.** |
| 7. **Ne puer cum puella pugnet.** |
| 8. **Ite et interrogate diligenter de puero ut et ego veniens adorem eum.** (Another passage from the Latin New Testament.) |
| 9. **Ea puella laudanda erat quae cum semel librum legisset eum denuo lectura erat.** |
| 10. **Cum Caesar imperator sit, omnes ei pareant.** |

### B. Harder

| |
|---|
| 1. We who have learnt Latin and now speak well in Latin shall teach all the others, if they want to learn it, so-that they may be able to read books written in Latin. |
| 2. Why are you very unhappy, Claudia? Do you not like Latin now? |
| 3. Both last year and yesterday I came to see Claudius and to enjoy his wisdom. |

| |
|---|
| 4. Julius, come here and speak now. Come here, Julius, and speak now. |
| 5. Fight very bravely, my good friend, and do not flee, so that Britain may rule a large part of the world again. |
| 6. I have never seen the very lazy boy by whom this was said which ought not to have been said. |
| 7. Woe to Carthage! Carthage must be soon destroyed! Let us be brave and let them not be cowardly! |
| 8. Since our crime is so light and always was so, may we not be so greatly punished. |
| 9. For two years I have begged you not to stay in Rome and now at last I order you to come. |
| 10. Will the enemy attack our forces next year, or will they rest for the whole of a year? |

C. Give two different translations of: **Num noster exercitus cras hostes oppugnabit?**

D. Give three different translations of: **Nonne noster exercitus cras hostes oppugnabit?**

E. Translate into English: **summus mons, media urbs, reliquus hic liber**.

F. Parse and then translate into English these untranslated-Latin expressions: **benedictus benedicat** (a grace before a meal), **requiescat in pace, exeunt, velis nolis** (the origin of the expression 'willy-nilly'), **pari passu, primus inter pares, nota bene, vide, carpe diem, caveat, caveat emptor, imprimatur, exeat, stet quod vide, habeas corpus, vae victis, ave atque vale!**

G. Write down an English verb derived from **cras** and an English adjective derived from **pugno**.

## CHAPTER EIGHTEEN

No more accidence, but: subsidiary clauses of all kinds; indirect statements and sequence of tenses

## SYNTAX – WHAT MUST BE *UNDERSTOOD*

### Clauses

A main clause, as we know, is a clause that can stand by itself. Important further information can be added to what is in a main clause by additional clauses, groups of words which can provide more detail than can a single part of speech. These are subsidiary clauses, which can be defined, therefore, as groups of words containing verbs, which perform the function of nouns, adjectives and adverbs.

Here now are the different kinds of subsidiary clauses in increasing order of difficulty.

### Adjectival clauses, also known as relative clauses

These, obviously enough, do the work of describing nouns and pronouns. They are introduced by the relative pronoun **qui**, the declension and use of which you have already learnt. Two other things that you have learnt, and are especially important to remember, are:

(1) The relative pronoun must be placed immediately after the noun or pronoun that it relates to.

(2) Much more often than in English, relative clauses can be replaced by participles.

### Noun clauses

Very often, in English as well as in Latin, either the subject in a sentence or the object in a sentence can be a clause. A simple sentence is: 'The soldier fears something terrible.' A more elaborate sentence is: 'The soldier fears that he will be killed in the battle.' In the first sentence, the object is 'something terrible'. In the second sentence, the object is 'that he will be killed in the battle'. That type of clause is therefore known as a noun clause. When it is a statement of that kind, it is called an Indirect Statement. A direct statement would be: 'He will be killed in the battle.'

For indirect statements, a construction called 'Accusative and Infinitive' is used, the name arising because, unexpectedly, the *subject* of the indirect statement goes into the accusative and the verb in the indirect statement goes into the infinitive.

Examples: 'My friends are approaching.' **Amici mei appropinquant.** 'I know that my friends are approaching.' **Scio amicos meos appropinquare.**

The tense of the infinitive is the tense of the original words, the direct statement. Therefore, 'I knew that my friends were always trustworthy' translates into **Sciebam amicos meos fideles semper esse** and, for that matter, 'I knew that my friends wanted to be always trustworthy' translates into **Sciebam amicos meos fideles semper esse velle**, since **velle**, as I hope you remember, is the *present* infinitive of **volō**.

When a third person personal pronoun in a clause refers to the subject, **se** must be used in the indirect statement. Therefore, if we take the sentence 'My friends said that *they* wanted to learn Latin', this must first of all be translated in your mind as 'My friends said themselves to want to learn Latin' and, that done, you can put it into Latin as **Amici mei dixerunt se linguam Latinam discere velle**.

**Dico** is only used for *positive* indirect statements. In the case of *negative* indirect statements, **nego** is used and the indirect statement is written in positive form. Therefore 'My friends said that they did *not* want to learn Latin' would first be transformed in one's mind into 'My friends denied that they wanted to learn Latin' from which it would readily translate into **Amici mei negaverunt se linguam Latinam discere velle**. If an indirect statement has both subject and object, as in that last sentence, it is – unusually in Latin – important that the two are in the right order, the subject first and object second, since of course both are in the accusative case and one would otherwise often not know which was which.

If the infinitive in an indirect statement includes a participle, as do active future infinitives and passive perfect infinitives, the participle must, as can be expected, agree with the subject, which will be in the accusative. 'We know that Rome has been attacked' is therefore **Scimus Romam oppugnatam esse** and 'We know that Rome is about to attack' is **Scimus Romam oppugnaturam esse**. If you have remembered that future participle passives are formed by using the indeclinable supine together with **īrī** you will see that 'We know that Rome is about to be attacked' is **Scimus Romam oppugnatum iri**.

Finally, care needs to be taken with verbs of promising, hoping and threatening. In English these are followed by the infinitive, as in 'I hoped to read Latin easily.' Latin is more precise in this respect, so the sentence must be re-translated as 'I hoped that I would read Latin easily', and from there into **Sperabam me linguam Latinam facile lecturum esse**.

## Adverbial clauses

There is much to learn about adverbial clauses, but I shall restrict what is taught in this book to Final Clauses, which provide a good enough introduction to make many other kinds of clauses more straightforward than they might otherwise be found.

## Final clauses

### Sequence of tenses

The term *sequence of tenses* means that there must be a sort of *agreement* between (a) the tense of the verb in the *main* clause and (b) the tense of the verb in any *subsidiary* clause. Therefore, for instance:

(a) 'I say that I am not finding learning grammar desperately difficult' uses the *present* tense in both clauses.
(b) If, however, the words 'I say' in that sentence are put into the *past* tense, the words 'I am' must *also* go into the past tense,

and the sentence must become: 'I *said* that I *was* not finding learning grammar desperately difficult.'

A difficulty with this sequence-of-tenses principle is that the *past* tense in the subordinate clause often refers to the *present* time, as in 'The new-fangled teachers *did not realise* that grammar *was* such an important subject.' In reality, what 'the new-fangled teachers' did not realise, of course, is that grammar *is* such an important subject. The word 'was' in that sentence is used in order to make the tense of the verb in the subordinate clause agree with the tense of the verb in the main clause.

## EXERCISES ON WHAT HAS BEEN LEARNT SO FAR

### A. Easy

| |
|---|
| 1. Claudius says that the burden of learning Latin is heavy. |
| 2. Mark Antony denies that Caesar was justly killed. |
| 3. Do you think that the girls will outdo the boys? (The enquirer anticipates a negative answer.) |
| 4. Julius, do you believe that there are many gods or only one? |
| 5. Who denies that the army of the Romans will destroy Carthage? |
| 6. **Non tam praeclarum est scire Latine quam turpe nescire.** (Slightly adapted from Cicero.) |
| 7. **Audivistisne Caesarem Romam rediisse?** |
| 8. **Speramus te mox in Italiam venturum esse.** |
| 9. **Pompeii milites creduntur dormire.** |
| 10. **Carthaginem deletam esse audivimus.** |

### B. Harder

| |
|---|
| 1. We saw him fighting bravely, but he was soon defeated and we then saw the enemy about to kill him. |
| 2. You will become a good teacher of Latin, but perhaps you have become a good teacher already. |

3. After the walls had been destroyed, the citizens became captives whose fathers and mothers were always unhappier than their brothers and sisters were.

4. Having sold their chariots, the farmer who had been a slave and had been freed, walked through the middle of the city with his son who was a soldier, and left the town with the whole army. (Translate the first clause – 'Having sold their chariots' – in two different ways; that is, with two different syntactical constructions.)

5. **Nulli se dicit mulier mea nubere malle quam mihi, non si se Iuppiter ipse petat. Dicit: sed mulier cupido quod dicit amanti, in vento et rapida scribere oportet aqua.**
(This is a complete, authentic and un-retouched epigram by the poet Catullus (*c.* 84–54 BC) and you may be proud of your progress if you succeed in translating it. For reasons of poetic metre and style the author has separated the adjective **cupido** from the participle **amanti** which it agrees with, here meaning 'one who loves'. The adjective **rapida** is also separated from its noun.)

C. Write down (a) a noun and an adjective derived from **lego** when it means 'I read'; (b) a noun and a verb derived from the same word **lego** when it means 'I choose'; and (c) a word which, with a small difference in pronunciation, is both a noun and verb, derived from the First Conjugation **lēgō**.

## CHAPTER NINETEEN

# Word Order

I HAVE NOT seen word order discussed in any depth in any Latin textbook written during the last century and more. It is, however, an important subject as soon as we move on from the elementary stages of Latin; and this is another chapter that I suggest you will want to return to often when translating either way until you are able to apply almost without thought what it teaches.

For those well enough acquainted with standard Latin word order for any unusual word order to jump off the page as the Latin-writing author intends, the effects are genuinely dramatic. They indicate emphasis and other rhetorical effects which are sometimes equivalent to our exclamation marks, italicisations and occasional extravagances of language such as 'super-efficient'. That should cause no surprise. All written language, after all, is a collection of conventions, which affect the reader as the writer intends as long as the conventions are known by both parties. What it does mean, however, is that our study of Latin is very incomplete if we have an incomplete knowledge of what the writer intends whenever the word order is varied from the norm.

## 1. THE GENERAL RULES

1. The two most important positions in a sentence are the beginning of it and the end of it.

2. Latin, much more than English, very much more 'goes in for' long and involved sentences which include sometimes several clauses.

3. Experienced Latin writers usually connect each such sentence with one or more standard connecting words.

   The most usual standard connecting words are: the relative pronoun, **qui**; the demonstratives, **hic**, **is**, **ille** and **iste**; the conjunctions **et**, **ac** and **atque**, all meaning 'and'; **namque**, **nam** and **enim**, meaning 'for'; **itaque** and **igitur**, meaning 'therefore'; **at**, **vērō** and **autem**, meaning 'but'; **tamen**, meaning 'however'; **nec** and **neque**, meaning 'nor'; the adverbs **intereā** and **interim**, meaning 'meanwhile'; and **tum**, **deinde** and **inde**, meaning 'then'.

Note, however, that the conjunctions **enim** meaning 'for'; **igitur** meaning 'therefore'; **autem** meaning 'moreover' or 'but'; and **vērō** meaning 'indeed', 'in fact' or 'but'; should never be the first word in a sentence, but normally the second word.

4. When a word or phrase needs special emphasis in a sentence, for the purpose of indicating that it is the most important word or phrase there, it should either (a) come at the very beginning of the sentence or (b) come immediately after one of the words, listed above, that are used for showing the connection of the sentence with what has just come before it. In other words, the most important word in the sentence should be put at or near the beginning of the sentence, so that the reader has it in mind while reading the rest of the sentence.

This 'most important word or phrase' does not necessarily mean a *grammatical* subject, a word in the nominative case. It can apply also to what is the subject in another sense: what the statement is really about. An example would be in English 'Rome takes its name from Romulus', which Latin could render as **A Romulo Roma nomen ducit** in order to highlight Romulus as the subject the sentence is chiefly about.

5. The sentence should end with a word that is either essential to the *construction* of the sentence or important to its *sense*. Very much by contrast with English sentences, a well-constructed Latin sentence must 'force' the reader to go to the end of it in order to establish a clear understanding of it. This means that verbs often come at the end of sentences, as we have seen and shall be seeing.

6. In the rest of the sentence, between the beginning and the end of it, words must be arranged so that those most closely connected to each other are nearest together. This of course tends to be what should be done in English as well – for instance,

adverbs usually come immediately before or after verbs, adjectives or other adverbs that they qualify. It is not always the case in English, however. For instance, where we should say: 'Two soldiers were sent to Caesar with a gift', in Latin this would be **Duo milites cum dono ad Caesarem missi sunt**.

## 2. THE RULES FOR WHEN NO EMPHASIS IS NEEDED

1. The subject comes first in the sentence. The finite verb – the verb which is actually acting as a verb rather than as a noun or an adjective – comes last. Examples: (1) **Caesar Gallos vicit.** 'Caesar defeated the Gauls.' (2) In a longer sentence: **Caesar, etsi in his locis hiemes maturae sunt, in Britanniam proficisci contendit.** 'Although the winters in these regions are early, Caesar hastened to set out for Britain.'

2. Two exceptions to the rule just given are:

    (a) Forms of the verb **sum** may stand *anywhere* in the sentence. Thus 'God is good' can be either **Deus est bonus** or **Deus bonus est**.

    (b) Much more often than not, the imperative comes first. Thus 'Fight bravely, soldiers' is **Pugnate, milites, fortiter**.

3. A noun in the vocative case normally does not come first. This provides another reason for **Pugnate, milites, fortiter** being the best word order.

4. A relative pronoun comes first in its own clause, or second if preceded by a preposition. It should also be placed immediately after the antecedent to which it refers and which it is replacing. Example: **Imperatorem qui praeerat exercitui a quo hostes victi sunt vidi** (**praesum** takes the dative), 'I have seen the general *who* commanded the army *by which* the enemy was defeated.'

5. Ordinary adjectives – technically termed adjectives of quality – and nouns and pronouns in the genitive, and also possessive pronouns, come immediately *after* the noun to which they belong or which they modify.

Examples: **vir bonus**, 'a good man'; **magister meus**, 'my teacher'; **Caesar sapiens captivos hostium uxoresque eorum liberavit,** 'Wise Caesar freed the prisoners of the enemy and their wives.'

6. Adjectives of *number*, *quantity* and *size*, however, and also *demonstrative* and *interrogative pronouns*, come immediately *before* the nouns and pronouns to which they belong. Examples: **multi homines**, 'many men'; **parvi liberi**, 'the small children'; **hic vir**, 'this man'; **quis vir**, 'which man'; **quam in patriam**, 'into which country'.

7. Adverbs, including **non**, come immediately *before* the verbs and adjectives which they modify. Example: **Milites fortiter pugnaverunt,** 'The soldiers fought bravely.' There is therefore a difference between **eum audire non possum** and **eum non audire possum**.

8. Not only adverbs but nouns and adjectives in the ablative *also* stand *before* the verbs and adjectives they modify. Example: **laude dignus**, 'worthy of praise'.

9. Except in the ablative, as mentioned above, nouns in all cases *other than* the nominative and vocative come immediately before the nouns to which they belong.

10. Prepositions come immediately in front of whatever it is that they are governing, unless there is a noun in the genitive which is describing another noun, in which case it can go between the preposition and the noun governed by the preposition. Examples: **propter regem**, 'because of the king'; **propter regis sapientiam**, 'because of the wisdom of the king'.

11. Almost all of these rules can be broken for the sake of emphasis, or for the sake of the sentence reading or sounding better, as for instance in what now follows.

## 3. THE RULES FOR WHEN EMPHASIS IS NEEDED

1. Emphasis can be achieved by changing the word order. Perhaps the best way of showing how this works is by a series of examples. **Amanda linguam Latinam amat** could be fairly translated

as 'Amanda loves Latin'; **Amat Amanda linguam Latinam** as 'Amanda really *loves* Latin'; **Linguam Latinam Amanda amat** as 'It is *Latin* that Amanda loves'; and **Linguam Latinam amat Amanda** as 'Latin is loved even by – good heavens! – *Amanda*!'

Whether the displaced words are put at the beginning or the end does not create the same effect. As I have tried to show, moving a word out of its usual place up to the beginning has the effect of 'sharpening' that word. By contrast, putting it at the end produces a sort of crashing climax.

When questions are indicated by adding **-ne** to the end of the first word in the clause, the word to be most emphasised is put first. Thus **Eane Romam amat?** means 'Does *she* like Rome?', while **Romamne ea amat?** means 'Does she like *Rome?*' and I leave you to translate **Amatne ea Romam?**

Although some of the above translations are extreme cases, selected to illustrate the effects of changing the word order, none of them is really exaggerated. Because Latin is in many ways a very 'spare' language, it can achieve, in ways such as those illustrated above, effects on the reader which could only be achieved in English with the use of much more vivid wording.

2. Another way of creating emphasis is by separating two words that would normally come together, as in **Ingens eos amor linguae Latinae invasit** meaning 'A really *huge* love of Latin seized them.'

3. A comparable effect can also be produced by putting next to each other words that would normally be separated, as in **Nostri Latinam linguam liberi nunc amant**, 'Our children now like the *Latin* language.'

While there are other rules of word order as well, these are easily sufficient for the Latin covered in this book. The word-order rules are, incidentally, as good an example as could be wanted of why learning to translate Latin into English is an indispensable step in the learning of how to read Latin in the original. Without any practice at using these rules for *writing* Latin, most people would not even *notice* any variation in word order from the norm, let alone register in their minds *the effect* of it.

## EXERCISES ON WHAT HAS BEEN
## LEARNT SO FAR

A. The following passage is the story of Regulus. It is an example of the fidelity to the pledged word over any other consideration – the certain prospect of unspeakable, long-drawn-out torture unjustly administered on the one hand, and having to abandon a wife and family who are dear to him, on the other hand – that was once the hallmark of a gentleman not so long ago in our own time and would put any public figure to shame today.* Happy the society that is capable of producing such uncompromising nobility, and of holding it up for countless future generations as a model for children to be brought up on and for adults to revere.

Here, now, is the exercise. I advise you to set aside plenty of time for it, which will be needed if you are to get the most out of it. Done as I recommend it, the exercise will be very much more valuable to you than would be a much more superficial effort at translating a large number of such passages.

1. First read it, trying to understand it as you go along, and noting in your notebook the beginning of any sentences, clauses or phrases which you do not understand.

2. Next, and this will be much the most time-consuming, parse it clause by clause and word by word. This is not needed for every translation you do. I give the exercise as one that is useful for developing your knowledge of English and Latin grammar, your powers of analysis, and even your ability to persevere.

3. Now translate it word for word.

* As it is virtually forgotten today, it is perhaps worth putting on record that the noblest pagan morality united with traditional Christian morality in teaching that the pledged word, even if not supported by an oath, was binding in all circumstances however extreme, with only two exceptions. One is that the pledge was simply impossible to keep, perhaps because the subject-matter of the pledge no longer existed. The other was if the pledge was unquestionably immoral, as would be a promise to help someone else to steal. There were no other exceptions, not even in defence of one's country.

4. Now produce a translation that you can be proud of as a piece of literature. I think that there are no passages that will cause any special difficulty in translating them literally. There are, however, a number of constructions which are good Latin but which do not translate well directly into English, for instance participles with infinitives. It is perhaps as well also to remind you to make sure you remember the rule relating to **nego** given in Chapter Eighteen.

M. Atilius Regulus, vir omnium constantissimus, cum exercitum in Africam duxisset, hostium insidiis cum quingentis militibus captus est. Romae autem eodem tempore nobiles quidam Poenorum forte retinebantur. Hos Poeni captivis Romanis mutare volebant; itaque Regulum Romam ad senatum miserunt, ut hoc efficeret: nam virum tanta auctoritate rem senatui facile persuasurum esse credebant. Is tum missus est ea condicione ut aut capti Poeni redderentur aut rediret ipse Carthaginem. Haec se facturum esse iuravit.

Sciebat quidem se facile impetrare posse, ac salutem libertatemque sibi adipisci. Sed cum in senatum introductus esset et iussa Poenorum exposuisset, tam turpem libertatis condicionem accipere noluit. Negavit enim utile esse captivos reddere; eos enim adulescentes esse et bonos duces futuros; se iam confectum esse senectute: eos, cum ad patriam rediissent, rursus bello civitatem Romanam vexaturos esse; se suumque exercitum civibus adeo iam nocuisse, ut supplicium mererentur.

Tanta ei auctoritas fuit, ut captivi Poeni Romae retinerentur: ipse, quia promiserat se rediturum esse, statim proficisci parat. Sciebat quidem se ad hostium supplicia redire; sciebat mortem sibi Carthagine paratam esse; sed, quia iuraverat se aut impetraturum esse aut rediturum, neque amicorum precibus neque uxoris liberorumque lacrimis retentus est.

B. Write down a common lady's name derived from **amo** and another common name derived from **miror**, and parse and give the meaning of each name in the original Latin.

## CHAPTER TWENTY

# Rather Less Seriously

NEARING THE CLOSE of this book as we are, I am now going to defy precedent, as far as this book is concerned, and put the exercises first. Also defying precedent, I shall include the answers to each of them. You will deserve the homage of the academic world if you arrive unaided at the answers to *any* of them, let alone to *all* of them.

Most of the following are not original with me, and indeed some of them are classic traditional schoolboy jokes of the past.

1. **Meā māter māla sūs ēst.** This sentence is in more strictly classical Latin than any other sentence in this book, in that, just as when the classical authors were writing their Latin masterpieces, it has no punctuation where it would normally be included today; not *quite* as strict though, because the classical authors put no gaps between words either.

   In searching for the answer, I trust you eliminated at once the superficially obvious translation, 'My mother is a bad pig.' Not only is it inconceivable in a book which up to this point has never in even the tiniest degree lacked seemliness and good taste, it is also incompatible with three of the five vowels marked as long. What are evidently needed, therefore, are alternative translations of words where the apparent translations must be incorrect. From there it is a short step to coming up with: 'Go, mother, the pig is eating the apples.' **Meā** is the imperative of the verb **meo, meare**, to go.

2. Now that you have a clue provided by the previous sentence which might not have occurred to you otherwise, struggle away at these two: **Mālo mālo malo malo** and, more elaborate but along the same lines, **Mālo mālo cum mālo malo malo.**

Answers: 'I'd rather be [literally, 'I prefer', with 'to be' under-
stood] in an apple tree than a bad man in adversity' and 'I'd
rather be in an apple tree with a bad apple than a bad man in
adversity'.

3 More elaborate still: **Non mālo mālo in mālo alta sed mālo
bono in mālo alto frui mālo.** *If* you have come up with 'I prefer
to enjoy, not a bad apple in a high apple tree, but a good apple
on a ship mast', we can both be congratulated on what you
have succeeded in learning from this book.

4. Ladies, some valuable advice from your mother: **Semper ubi
sub ubi**. 'Always wear underwear.'

5. I expect to your relief, you are expected to understand this fine
piece of post-classical verse without even parsing or translating it. My guess is that the second sentence is the only one you
will need to puzzle over for more than a split second in order
to 'see' it. Just this once I suggest that you abandon the
Restored Classical Pronunciation and pronounce the words as
our grandfathers would have done for the word 'Caesar' and
whenever you see the letter 'j'. **Caesar adsum jam forti. –
Antonius sed passus sum. – Caesar aderat forti. – Brutus
adsum jam. – Caesar sic in omnibus. – Brutus sic intram.**

6. Teacher of Roman history: 'When was Rome built?' Pupil: 'At
night.' Teacher: 'Why did you say that?' Pupil: 'Because my
dad always says that Rome wasn't built in a day!'

7. Finally, there are doubtless boys among my readers who will
relish pointing out to girls that Latin has no room for the idea
of women acting in communion or any related concept, and
that English is even today guilty of the same discriminatory
bias. While the **lingua Latina** has given us the English words
'fraternise' and 'fraternal', to this day she has given us no
equivalents such as 'sororise' or goodness-knows-what.

# The Point at Which We Have Now Arrived

THAT IS LATIN then, or at least very much more than merely a start on it. If you have treated this book as I have constantly urged you to, you will by now be a very different person from the person you were when you first opened it – and different, moreover, in a way, as well as to a degree, that you will have reason to rejoice at. Your character will be altered as well as your mind. In addition you will be able to know and understand much more than was possible to you before, unless somehow you already possessed all the best gifts of intellect and character in super-abundant measure. You cannot fail to be able to focus and concentrate more attention more closely, to analyse and problem-solve more effectively, to persevere more – er – perseveringly, and to think more clearly.

That is what Latin is very much about, after all, as always used to be recognised. That is why, despite its having no evident practical use, Latin and the traditional method of teaching it survived as the primary and central element of the best education for so long, despite repeated efforts either to wipe it out or to dumb it down sufficiently to eliminate the beneficial elements of studying it.

I very much hope that you will continue with unabated enthusiasm the journey that you have started. If, while you are doing so, you happen to find appealing the idea of joining to your labours an activity which is in many ways even more mentally demanding than what you have been doing throughout this book, you might like to turn any attention you have to spare to starting classical Greek!

# Answers to Translation Exercises

## CHAPTER NINE

A. 1. **Reginam amo**. 2. **Angliae regina non es**. 3. **Filius amicum superat**. 4. **Mox pugnabimus**. 5. **Domini eritis**. 6. **Reginae amici Iulium laudant**. 7. England is the country of the queen. 8. We shall often praise the lord. 9. (The) prisoners never sing. 10. You will ask for a letter.

B. 1. **Puellae reginam amant sed regina puellas non amat**. 2. **Puellae amicum amo et puellarum amicos amabimus**. 3. **Reginae puellas numquam laudabunt puellaeque aut reginas nunc amant aut (reginas) numquam amabunt**. 4. **Regina amicos amat et amici puellae sunt**. 5. **Puella numquam regina erit sed reginam semper amabit. Filii amicos superant sed mox saepe cantabunt**. 6. **Amici amicos numquam superant neque filii umquam puellas superant. sed regina saepe filios laudat**. 7. **Iulius Caesar amicus Pompeii numquam erit neque Pompeius filium Iulium vocat**. 8. Claudius frees the prisoners and the prisoners praise Claudius. 9. We shall prepare letters for the queen but we shall not give money to the girls. 10. Either we love the (female) friend of the court or we do not love the (female) friend of the court.

C. 1. **Aegrotat**, Third person singular present indicative active of **aegroto**. He is ill. 2. **Concordat**, Third person singular present indicative active of **concordo**. He agrees. 3. **Extant**, Third person plural present indicative active of **exsto** or **exto**. They are still in existence. 4. **Ignoramus**, First person plural present indicative active of **ignoro**. We are ignorant; we do not know. 5. **Aqua vitae**, Nominative singular of **aqua**, and genitive singular of **vita**. Water of life.

2. **Iulius Caesar (suum) filium amicumque fili amat. Amicus (sui) filii filiam Pompeii non amat sed reginam amat.**

## CHAPTER TEN

A. 1. I love the queen. 2. You are not the queen of England. 3. The son outdoes his friend. 4. We shall soon fight. 5. You will be lords. 6. The friends of the queen praise Julius. 7. **Reginae patria Anglia est**. 8. **Dominum saepe laudabimus**. 9. **Captivi numquam cantant**. 10. **Epistulam rogabitis**.

B. 1. The girls love the queen, but the queen does not love the girls. 2. I love the friend of the girl, and we shall love the friends of the girls. 3. Never will queens praise girls, and girls either love queens now or will never love queens. 4. The queen loves her friends and her friends are girls. 5. The girl will never be queen but she will always love the queen. The sons are outdoing their friends but will soon often be singing. 6. Friends never outdo friends and sons never outdo girls, but the queen often praises her sons. 7. Julius Caesar will never be a friend of Pompey, and Pompey is not calling his son Julius. 8. **Claudius captivos liberat et captivi Claudium laudant**. 9. **Epistulas reginae parabimus sed pecuniam puellis non dabimus**. 10. **Aut amicam curiae amamus aut amicam curiae non amamus**.

C. **Adsum**, first person singular present tense indicative of **adsum**. I am present. **Advocatus diabolic**, nominative singular of **advocatus**, and genitive singular of **diabolus**. Advocate of the devil (someone officially appointed by the Catholic Church to produce every possible objection to the canonisation of someone as a saint, to make sure in advance that every possible objection to the canonisation has been considered).

## CHAPTER ELEVEN

A. 1. **Pompeii castra oppugnare scimus**. 2. **Mali liberi amicos videbunt**. 3. **Heri servus equum duxerat**. 4. **Cras equus servum duxerit**. 5. **Oppida bonae patriae nostrae pulchra sunt**.

B. 1. **Regina numquam multa verba Latina dicet. Patriam semper rexit et nonnumquam servavit**. 2. **Magister ianuam aperuit et multos bonos servos videt**. 3. **Mox multam sapientiam habebo et multa verba Latina audivero**. 4. **Liberi mali trans longum murum errant sub pulchra luna. Ibi multos equos nigros vident sed nulla arma habent**. 5. **Amici nostri prosperi nunc in magnis castris sunt cum liberis tuis, Iuli. Servorum consilia timent sed magistrorum sapientiam semper amaverunt**.

C. **Ab initio**, preposition **a** or **ab** taking the ablative, and ablative singular of **initium**. From the beginning; at the outset. **Terra firma**, nominative singular of **terra**, and nominative feminine singular of **firma**. Firm land; dry land. **Persona non grata**, nominative singular of **persona**, adverb **non**, nominative feminine singular of **gratus**. Person not in favour; person who is unacceptable. **Et cetera**, conjunction **et**, and nominative neuter plural of **ceterus**. And the rest.

D. **Liber**, library. **Līber**, liberty. **Murus**, mural. **Equus**, equine. **Magister**, magisterial and magistrate. **Servus**, serve, servant and servile.

## CHAPTER TWELVE

A. 1. **Hunc virum [or hominem] vides.** 2. **Hanc patriam regina amabit.** 3. **Laudatne servum ille puer?** 4. **Amicos Pompeii vicimus et castra eorum vastavimus.** 5. **Illa castra magna pulchraque erant.** 6. **Hae puellae nulla castra amant.** 7. **Nullus Romanus duas habet patrias.** 8. You will have fought against three towns. 9. Has Pompey lost his (own) sword? 10. Does that master praise Latin?

B. 1. **Pulchrae reginae mox malos pueros monebunt.** 2. **Mille quinquaginta viri diu contra tria milia virorum pugnaverunt.** 3. **Unum castrum una [or singula] castra in lingua Latina non est.** 4. **Nunc adsum. Isne mox aderit et illi quoque aderuntne?** 5. **Advocatus diaboli numquam homo [or vir] malus est.** 6. **Duo castra bina castra in lingua Latina non sunt.** 7. **Oppidum oppugnavit hique se suumque oppidum defenderunt. Ipsae mulieres [or feminae] idem oppidum defendebant.** 8. **Tonsor speculum suum tenet et magister suam barbam in eius speculo videt.** 9. If you (will) see me I shall already have seen you. 10. Yesterday the slaves saw Caesar and today (they saw) Pompey; they praised the latter but they loved the former.

C. **Terra firma, terram firmam** and **terrarum firmarum. Persona non grata, personam non gratam** and **personarum non gratarum. Et cetera, et ceteri** and **et ceterorum.**

D. Contrary, contradict.

## CHAPTER THIRTEEN

A. 1. **Regina amatur.** 2. **Boni libri saepe leguntur.** 3. **Hic liber facilis lectu est.** 4. **Imperatoris [*or* ducis] nomen diu ignorabatur [*or* nesciebatur].** 5. **Barbarorum castra tandem delebuntur.** 6. **Vix ulli cives in ingentibus montibus inveniuntur.** 7. **Si audax imperator olim laudabatur denuo [*or* iterum] laudabitur.** 8. Once England was well governed. 9. I have come to see. 10. Beautiful girls, today you are praised.

B. 1. **Tristis est quia aegrotat.** 2. **Multa sunt hodie facienda [*or* quae hodie fieri debent].** 3. **Suggestio falsi a malis numquam difficilis fuit neque umquam erit. Audivistine tu ipse cuius opiniones scire volo falsorum suggestiones ab improbis?** 4. **Puellae pulchrae et parvae terrebantur a ferocibus civibus et militum armis.** 5. **Mens sana in corpore sano: haec sententia utiliter dici potest et saepe ab omnibus audienda est.**

C. **Alma mater**, nourishing mother. (Usually, metaphorically, a person's school or university.) **Annus mirabilis**, wonderful year, used to describe a special year, one in which more than one memorable thing has happened. **Rara avis**, a rare bird. (A kind of person or thing rarely encountered.) **Suggestio falsi**, suggestion of (something) false. (As a legal term, a positive misrepresentation, which does not go as far as a lie, but is a conscious concealment of truth.) **Suppressio veri**, suppression of something true. (A misrepresentation by concealment of one or more facts that ought to be made known in the interest of justice.) **Tempus fugit**, time flees. Time flies. **Corpus delicti**, the body of the crime. (Once the corpse of someone murdered; now, metaphorically, the factual evidence, at least apparent, of a crime.) **Repetitio mater memoriae (est)**. Repetition is the mother of memory or of the ability to remember. (A maxim never to be forgotten, good reader, while you are working your way through *Gwynne's Latin*.) **Rigor mortis**, stiffness of death. (Stiffening of the body after death.) **Sui generis**, of its own kind. Unique. **Eiusdem generis**, of the same kind. (In law, a rule of construction and interpretation which applies to documents and statutes.) **Dramatis personae**, people of a drama. (The characters in a play; the cast of a play.) **Fons et origo**, the spring or fountain and the origin. (The source and the origin of something.)

D. **Fontem et originem** and **fontium et originum; almam matrem**
and **almarum matrum; annum mirabilem** and **annorum mirabil-
ium; raram avem** and **rararum avium; suggestionem** and **suggestio-
num; suppressionem** and **suppressionum; rigorem** and **rigorum.**

E. Abduct. Abduction. Abductor. Adduce. Adduceable. Aducent.
Adduct. Adduction. Adductor. Aqueduct. Conductor. Conducive.
Conduciveness. Conductible. Unconducive. Deduce. Deducible.
Deducibility. Deduction. Deductive. Undeducible. Duct. Educe.
Educt. Eduction. Educible. Induce. Inducement. Induct. Induction.
Inductive. Inductor. Introduce. Introduction. Introductory. Producer.
Producible. Producibility. Product. Production. Productive.
Productivity. Unproductive. Reduce. Reducible. Reducibility.
Reduction. Irreducible. Irreducibility. Subduce. Subduct. Subduction.
Traduce. Traducer. Traducible. Viaduct.

F. (a) Audience and audition. Video! – and visible. (b) Transfer and
translation.

## CHAPTER FOURTEEN

A. 1. **Caesar magna virtute pugnabat et dignitat loquebatur.** 2.
**Classem sine mora vicit.** 3. **Quarto die tonsor veniet duosque
dies manebit.** 4. **Duobus diebus omnium militum longas barbas
totonderit.** 5. **Hic tonsor velocius tondet quam frater.** 6. **Iuli,
amor sapientiae tuus par est desiderio tuo honoris.** 7. **Captivi a
regina liberabuntur.** 8. While the soldiers listen, Caesar talks. 9.
You are using this book badly if you do not commit everything to
memory. 10. The wise man walking in the garden exhorts his
disciples.

B. 1. **Caesar hostes principio anni oppugnaverat, et (eos) una mense
superaverat [*or* vicerat].** 2. **Cicero ultimo anno duas horas nonnumquam loquebatur, atque eodem anno consul creatus est.** 3.
**Mater mea a Britannia abiit et Romam iit ut Caesarem
Ciceronemque videret eosque loqui [*or* loquentes] audiret; post
multos annos Roma abiit.** 4. **Salve, Iuli! Estne pater tuus domi?
Mene videre vult? Non in Italia habito sed Londinio. Romam cras
proficiscar.** 5. **Pueri si ignavi erant a magistro sapiente [*or* sapienti]
semper puniebantur.** 6. **Mihi nomen Marcus est et sunt mihi tres
equi sed solum duo canes. Proximo autem anno alio cane [*or* cani]
potiar.** 7. **Caesar non pugnans in proelio contra Romae hostes sag-**

**ittis sed a Bruto necatus (or occisus or interfectus) est. 8. Omnibus militibus dormientibus [or Dum omnes milites dormiebant] hostes lentissime adiverunt (or appropinquaverunt) et quam celerrime castra (eorum) oppugnaverunt. 9. (In) urbem cras inibo, ex eadem urbe post duobus diebus exibo, et trans montem tunc iter faciam. 10. Meus vetus pater domi nunc est Romae. Mater tua quando domum pervenit?**

C. **Non sequitur**, adverb; third person singular indicative of deponent verb **sequor**. It does not follow. (An inference or conclusion that does not follow from its premises in the work quoted; a claim that is illogical.) **Res ipsa loquitur**, nominative singular of the Fifth Declension **res**; nominative feminine singular of the intensive pronoun **ipse**; third person singular indicative of deponent verb **loquor**. The thing itself speaks. (The thing speaks for itself; in legal terminology, something so obvious that it does not need to be proved.) **Dei gratia**, genitive singular; ablative singular. By God's grace. **Bona fides**, nominative feminine singular of **bonus**; nominative singular of **fides**. Good faith (genuineness). **Bona fide**, ablative feminine singular of **bonus** and ablative singular of **fides**. In good faith. (Genuine or genuinely; without deception.) **Viva voce**, ablative feminine singular of **vivus** and ablative singular of **vox**. With the living voice. (Oral, as in an oral examination.) **Casus belli**, nominative singular of **casus** and genitive singular of **bellum**. Occasion of war. (Action justifying war; an excuse for war.) **Tabula rasa**, nominative singular of **tabula**, and nominative feminine singular of the past participle of Third Conjugation **rado**. A erased tablet. (An empty slate; metaphorically, an empty page; figuratively, the human mind at birth, which at that point has no inborn impressions of any kind.) **Deo volente**, ablative absolute construction. Ablative singular of **Deus**; ablative masculine singular of present participle active of **volo**. God willing. **Ipso facto**, ablative neuter singular of intensive pronoun **ipse**; ablative singular of **factum**. In the fact itself (by that very fact). **Locum tenens**, accusative singular of **locus**, nominative masculine singular of present participle active of **teneo**. Holding the place. (Acting deputy, especially for a member of the clergy or for a doctor; acting as substitute.) **Mutatis mutandis cives feliciores fiebant**, ablative absolute construction with ablative neuter plural of past participle passive of **muto** and ablative neuter plural of gerundive of **muto**. Nominative plural of **civis**, nominative masculine pural of comparative of **felix** and third person plural of imperfect indicative of **fio**. The things that ought to be changed having been changed (or after the necessary changes had been made), the citizens became happier. **Mens sana in corpore sano**, nominative singular of **mens**; nominative feminine singular of **sanus**, preposition **in** taking the ablative; ablative singular of **corpus** and ablative neuter singular of **sanus**. Sound or healthy mind in sound or healthy body.

D. **Bona fides, bonam fidem, bonarum fiderum. Casus, casum, casuum. Tabula rasa, tabulam rasam, tabularum rasarum.**

E. **Sunt multi casus belli.**

F. Culpable. Timid. Odium. Odious.

## CHAPTER FIFTEEN

A. 1. **Potesne me iam videre, Iuli?** 2. **Iuli, potesne nunc me audire?** 3. **Mecum venire mavisne an cum eis ire?** 4. **Oppida nostra maiora sunt quam bina Caesaris castra.** 5. **Magna onera tuli quia olim servus factus sum.** 6. **Servis in Senatu loqui non licet.** 7. **Caesari Romam quam velocissime ire placuit.** 8. **Caesare vivo Roma Britanniam regere non incepit.** 9. Latin ought to be learnt by those who are wiser. 10. O daughter more beautiful than your beautiful mother.

B. 1. **Ab initio hunc librum legere facile fuit.** 2. **Ipse me in speculo videre non volui, sed saepe hoc vitare non potui.** 3. **Milites Romani dicuntur fortissime ferocissimeque pugnavisse et alteram urbem pugnaturi esse quae prope Romam est.** 4. **Saepe senex eorum meminisse non potest quae facienda erant.** 5. **Abire volo et (abire) conor sed (abire) numquam potui quod abire mihi non licet.** 6. **Timeo ne senes numquam linguam Latinam bene discant.** 7. **Veterrimi legati multa inutilia de Romanis et de urbe Roma locuti sunt.** 8. **Servi felices latum et altum murum multos menses in media Britannia aedificabant. Hic murus lapidibus magnis aedificatur.** 9. **Multum de lingua Latina scire volo quam multos annos docuisti antequam eam discere amare incipere possum.** 10. **Alii linguam Latinam amant alii eam non amant sed omnes linguam Latinam discere debent [or oportet]. Eam omnes docere licet. Eorum me miseret qui eam discere nolunt quosque eam discere taedet aut piget.**

C. Dative masculine plural of demonstrative pronoun **is**; dative masculine plural of adjective **Germanus**; correlative conjunction **neque**; genitive singular of **consilium**; genitive neuter singular of gerundive of **habeo**; correlative conjunction **neque**; accusative plural of the neuter word **arma** (only existing in the plural); genitive singular neuter of gerund of **capio**; third person singular neuter of perfect tense active indicative of **capio**. There was given to those Germans the time neither to hold consultation nor to take up arms.

D. (a) **Agenda**, gerundive. Things to be done or ought to be done. **Corrigendum**, gerundive. That which ought to be corrected. **Modus operandi**, gerund. Manner of working. **Modus vivendi**, gerund. Manner or way of living. **Nil desperandum**, gerundive. Nothing meet for the despairing of or worthy of despair. (b) Nominative neuter singular of demonstrative pronoun **hic**; nominative singular of **telum**; dative singular of gerund of **pugno**; nominative neuter singular of **utilis**; and third person singular of present tense of **sum**. This weapon is useful for fighting.

E. When Caesar had now conquered almost the whole of Gaul, he decided to set out for Britain because the Britons had often sent help to the Gauls. Accordingly he first set off with all his forces into the territory of the Morini because the crossing to Britain from there was very short. To that place he ordered his ships from wherever they might be in neighbouring states, and the fleet which he had built for the war of the Veneti, to come together.

F. **Nolle prosequi**, present infinitive of **nolo**; present infinitive of deponent **prosequor**. Not to wish to pursue. Not to wish to proceed. (An Attorney General stops a prosecution by entering a 'Nolle prosequi', for instance when he judges that there is not enough evidence to make it worth proceeding.) **Prima facie**, ablative feminine singular of primus; ablative singular of **facies**. At first sight; *hence*, apparently. **Reductio ad absurdum**, nominative singular of **reductio**; preposition **ad** taking the accusative; accusative neuter singular of **absurdus**. Reduction to the absurd; (The reduction to absurdity; proof of the falsity of, for instance, a principle, by proving that the principle leads to a logical result that is absurd and therefore impossible). **Deus ex machina**, nominative singular of **deus**; preposition **e** or **ex** taking the ablative case; ablative singular of **machina**. God out of a machine. (First used to represent a Greek theatrical convention, where a god would swing onto the stage, high up in a machine, solving humanly insoluble problems and thus resolving the action of a play. Now used to describe a wholly outside person who puts matters right. Also, a providential interposition.) **In vino veritas**, preposition **in**, taking the ablative; ablative singular of **vinum**; nominative singular of **veritas**. In wine, truth. (The truth comes out when a person has had too much to drink.)

G. **Do**, dative. **Incipio**, incipient. **Possum**, potential.

## CHAPTER SIXTEEN

A. 1. **Regina quae in Britannia regit audax est.** 2. **Onus quod servi ferebant grave erat.** 3. **Exercitus cuius Caesar erat dux ab omnibus timebatur.** 4. **Numquam bonorum quae didicimus obliviscemur.** 5. **Is cui omnes parent potens est.** 6. What was your reason for seeing Rome? 7. Who is it that who is approaching? 8. Whose image is this? 9. The horse whose burden is light will advance more swiftly than the other. 10. The lazy boy does not use the book which is better.

B. 1. **Legati quos videre volebam ad urbem quam celerrime iam profecti sunt.** 2. **Ii quorum domus maximae cives ditissimi Romae sunt multoque divitiores nobis [quam nos].** 3. **Hannibal Carthaginiensis pluribus [*or* plus] quam centum annis ante Iulium Caesarem mortuus est. Uter melior dux erat?** 4. **Iudicem vidi cuius filius honestus hoc fecit. Milites quoque vidi quibus multa dona dedisti et a quo pauca tela tibi data sunt quae dona utilia sunt.** 5. **Romani civitatibus quas vicerant leges optimas semper dabant.**

C. Who has ever surpassed the manifold excellence of Gaius Julius Caesar? For this man showed himself at Rome to be eloquent in speech, elegant in writing and wise in statesmanship. In war, however, he proved almost invincible, being most expert in fighting and in riding and exceedingly patient of labour. When on the march he went before his soldiers, sometimes riding, more often on foot, bareheaded alike under burning sun or rain. He accomplished the longest journeys with incredible speed and even rivers did not detain him.

After the civil wars Caesar was made perpetual dictator. Anthony, who accompanied Caesar in all his expeditions and was then his fellow-consul, set the symbol of kingship, a golden diadem, on his head while he sat in a golden seat. For this reason a conspiracy inspired by envy was formed against him, under the leadership of Cassius and Brutus. On the Ides of March the conspirators surrounded Caesar as he sat in the Senate and at once one of them drew closer as though to ask him something and seized him. Thereupon Cassius wounded the Dictator a little below the throat. Seeing Marcus Brutus, who was as a son to him, rush upon him, Caesar said, 'You too, my son!' and thus wounded in twenty-three places he fell beneath the very statue of Pompey.

D. **Quid pro quo**, nominative neuter singular of relative pronoun **quis**; proposition **pro** taking the ablative; ablative neuter singular of relative pronoun **quis**. What for what. (One thing for another; something in return, an equivalent.) **In flagrante delicto**, in the blazing crime. (While the crime is ablaze; in the act of committing a crime; caught red-handed.) **Status quo ante**, the state in which before. (The same state as before, as in the common usage 'maintaining the status quo'. It is often shortened to **status quo**.) **Quo vadis?** Interrogative adverb **quo**, second person singular present indicative of Third Conjugation **vado**. Where are you going *or* hastening to?

E. (1) **Delicti flagrantis.** (2) **Multos linguae lapsus audivi.**

## CHAPTER SEVENTEEN

A. 1. **Noli tristis esse, Iuli.** 2. **Tonsor ut militum barbas tondeat venit.** 3. **Africani ne urbs Carthago a Romanis deleatur timent.** 4. **Eheu, tonsor incaute, ne aurem meam laeseris!** 5. **Nonne Carthago a Romanis deleta est?** 6. Let Caesar, who is about to speak to the Senate, be heard. 7. Let not a boy fight with a girl. 8. Go and enquire diligently about the boy in order that I also may come and adore him. 9. That girl was worthy to be praised who when she had read the book once was about to read it again. 10. Since Caesar is general, let all obey him.

B. 1. **[Nos] qui linguam Latinam didicimus et latine nunc bene loquimur omnes ceteros si eam discere volunt docebimus, ut libros latine scriptos legere possint.** 2. **Cur infelicissima es, Claudia? Nonne lingua Latina tibi nunc placet [*or* Nonne linguam Latinam nunc amas]?** 3. **Et anno ultimo et heri veni ut Claudium viderem utque eius sapientia fruerer.** 4. **Huc veni et nunc loquere, Iuli. Huc veni, Iuli, et nunc loquere.** 5. **Fortissime pugna, mi bone amice, et noli fugere, ut Britannia magnam mundi partem iterum (*or* denuo) regat.** 6. **Puerum ignavum numquam vidi, a quo hoc dictum est quod non dicendum erat [*or* non dici] debebat.** 7. **Vae Carthagini!**

**Carthago mox delenda est! Fortes simus neque illi ignavi sint!** 8.
**Cum crimen nostrum tam leve sit atque semper esset, ne tantopere
puniamur.** 9. **Duos annos te oravi ne Romae moreris teque nunc
tandem venire iubeo.** 10. **Hostesne copias nostras anno proximo
oppugnabunt, an totum annum requiescent?**

C. Our army will not be attacking the enemy tomorrow, will it?
Surely our army will not attack the enemy tomorrow?

D. Our army will attack the enemy tomorrow, will it not? Surely our
army will attack the enemy tomorrow? Is our army not attacking the
enemy tomorrow?

E. **Summus mons**, the top of the mountain *or* the highest mountain.
**Media urbs**, the middle of the city. **Reliquus hic liber**, the rest of
this book.

F. **Benedictus benedicat** (a grace before a meal), nominative masculine singular of past participle passive of **benedico**; and third person
singular of the present subjunctive active of **benedico**. May the
Blessed One bless. **Requiescat in pace**, third person singular of the
present subjunctive active of **requiesco**; preposition **in** taking the
ablative; ablative singular of **pax**. May he/she rest in peace. **Exeunt**,
third person plural present indicative of **exeo**. They are going out or
away. It is the plural of **exit**. **Velis nolis**, may you wish, may you not
wish. (Whether you like it or not. It is the origin of the expression
willy-nilly.) **Pari passu**, ablative masculine singular of **par**, and ablative singular of **passus**. With equal pace. (At the same pace; on the
same terms; at an equal rate of progress; simultaneously.) **Primus
inter pares**, nominative masculine singular of **primus**; preposition
**inter** taking the accusative; accusative masculine plural of **par**. First
among equals. (The senior member of a group of colleagues, or their
spokesman.) **Nota bene**, second person singular imperative active of
**noto**; adverb from **bonus**. Note well. (Observe what follows, usually
used to draw attention to what has immediately gone before.) **Vide**,
second person singular imperative active of **video**. See (in the imperative – often used in books with reference to what is elsewhere). **Carpe
diem**, second person singular present imperative active of **carpo**;
accusative singular of **dies**. Pluck the day; seize the day. (Enjoy the
moment; make the most of life.) **Caveat**, third person singular active
subjunctive of **caveo**. **Caveat emptor**, third person singular active
subjunctive of **caveo**. Let the buyer beware. **Imprimatur**, third person

plural active subjunctive of Third Conjugation **imprimo**. Let it be printed. **Exeat**, third person singular active subjunctive of **exeo**. He may go out or let him go out. (In schools and university colleges, this was until recently commonly used to indicate permission for temporary absence.) **Quod vide**, accusative neuter singular of the relative pronoun **quis** or **qui**. Second person singular imperative active of **video**. Which see (for instance, instructing the reader to look for the word just mentioned in the glossary). **Stet**, third person singular active subjunctive of **sto**. Let it stand. (Do not delete, for instance cancelling an alteration in proofreading.) **Habeas corpus**, second person singular active subjunctive of **habeo**; accusative singular of **corpus**. You are to have (produce) a body. **Vae victis!** Interjection **vae**; dative masculine plural of **vinco**. Woe to the victors! **Ave atque vale!** Interjection **ave**; coordinating conjunction **atque**; interjection **vale**. Hail and farewell!

G. To procrastinate and repugnant.

## CHAPTER EIGHTEEN

A. 1. **Claudius onus linguae latinae discendae grave esse dicit.** 2. **Marcus Antonius negat Caesarem juste occisum [*or* interfectum *or* necatum] esse.** 3. **Num putas puellas pueros superaturas esse?** 4. **Iuli, credisne multos esse deos an unum tantum?** 5. **Quis negat Romanorum exercitum Carthaginem deleturum esse?** 6. It is not so honourable to know Latin as shameful not to know it. 7. Have you heard that Caesar has returned to Rome? 8. We hope that you will soon come to Italy. 9. The soldiers of Pompey are believed to be sleeping. 10. We have heard that Carthage has been destroyed.

B. 1. **Eum fortiter pugnantem vidimus, sed mox victus est; deinde hostem vidimus eum interfecturum [*or* necaturum *or* occisurum].** 2 **Linguae latinae magister bonus fies, sed forsitan magister bonus iam factus es.** 3. **Muris deletis, cives captivi facti sunt quorum patres matresque infeliciores semper erant quam fratres sororesque [*or* fratribus sororibusque].** 4. **Curribus venditis / Cum currus vendidissent, agricola, qui servus fuerat et liberatus erat, per mediam urbem ambulavit cum filio qui miles erat et ex oppido abierunt.** 5. My woman says that she prefers to be married to no one rather than me, not even if Jupiter himself should seek her; but what a woman says to an ardent lover should be written in the wind and in rapid water.

C. (a) Legend and legible. (b) Election and legislate. (c) Delegate.

## CHAPTER NINETEEN

A. M. Atilius Regulus, the most constant of all men, when he had led
his army into Africa, was captured, together with fifty soldiers, by an
ambush of the enemy. Moreover at the same time certain nobles of
the Carthaginians were by chance being kept in Rome. The
Carthaginians wanted to exchange these men with their Roman prisoners; and so they sent Regulus to Rome to the Senate in order that
he might bring this about; for they believed him to be a man of so
great authority (as) to be able easily to persuade the matter to the
Senate (persuade the Senate in the matter). He therefore was sent
under the condition that either the captured Carthaginians would be
returned or he himself would return to Carthage. These things he
swore that he would do.

He knew himself, indeed, to be able to accomplish them easily,
and to acquire freedom for himself. But when he had been introduced to the Senate and had explained the orders of the Carthaginians,
he was unwilling to accept such a disgraceful condition of freedom
(for himself). For he denied it to be useful to return the prisoners; for
they were growing men and about to be (would be) good future
leaders; he himself to be worn out with old age; them, when they had
returned to their country, again to be about to be (would be) annoying in the war against the Roman state; and they, what is more, to
have already harmed himself and his army, so that they deserved
torture/punishment.

So great was his influence that the Carthaginian prisoners were
kept in Rome: he, because he had promised to be about to (that he
would) give himself back, at once prepares to set out. He knew
himself indeed to be returning to torture of (by) the enemy; he knew
death for himself at Carthage to have been prepared; but, because he
had sworn either to be about to (to) obtain the request or to return,
he was held back by neither the prayers of his friends nor the tears of
his wife and children.

B. Amanda. Nominative feminine singular of the gerundive, meaning
'worthy to be loved'. Miranda. Nominative feminine singular of the
gerundive, meaning 'worthy to be admired'.

# Reference Grammar

**Note.** This Reference Grammar makes extensive use of the classic works of Dr Benjamin Hall Kennedy, which cannot be too highly recommended.

## NOUNS

*Abbreviations*: *sing.* or *s.* stands for the singular number, *plur.* or *pl.* for plural, *nom.* for the nominative case, *voc.* for vocative, *acc.* for accusative, *gen.* for genitive, *dat.* for dative, *abl.* for ablative, *m.* for the masculine gender, *f.* for feminine, *n.* for neuter, and *c.* for common (which means either masculine or feminine according to the sex of the person referred to).

### FIRST DECLENSION

**mēnsa, mēnsae**, f., table

|       | *Singular* | *Plural* |
|-------|-----------|----------|
| Nom.  | mēnsa     | mēnsae   |
| Voc.  | mēnsa     | mēnsae   |
| Acc.  | mēnsam    | mēnsās   |
| Gen.  | mēnsae    | mēnsārum |
| Dat.  | mēnsae    | mēnsīs   |
| Abl.  | mēnsā     | mēnsīs   |

Latin nouns ending in **-as** which were originally Greek nouns ending in **-as** go like **mēnsa** after the nominative and vocative singular, other than that the accusative singular often ends with the Greek ending **-an** rather than **-am**. An example is **Aenēās**, which is usually declined **Aenēās, Aenēā** (note the long **a**), **Aenēan, Aenēae, Aenēae, Aenēā**.

## SECOND DECLENSION

**annus, anni,** m., year

|      | Singular | Plural  |
| ---- | -------- | ------- |
| Nom. | annus    | annī    |
| Voc. | anne     | annī    |
| Acc. | annum    | annōs   |
| Gen. | annī     | annōrum |
| Dat. | annō     | annīs   |
| Abl. | annō     | annīs   |

**magister, magistri,** m., master

|      | Singular  | Plural      |
| ---- | --------- | ----------- |
| Nom. | magister  | magistrī    |
| Voc. | magister  | magistrī    |
| Acc. | magistrum | magistrōs   |
| Gen. | magistrī  | magistrōrum |
| Dat. | magistrō  | magistrīs   |
| Abl. | magistrō  | magistrīs   |

**puer, puerī,** m., boy

|      | Singular | Plural   |
| ---- | -------- | -------- |
| Nom. | puer     | puerī    |
| Voc. | puer     | puerī    |
| Acc. | puerum   | puerōs   |
| Gen. | puerī    | puerōrum |
| Dat. | puerō    | puerīs   |
| Abl. | puerō    | puerīs   |

**bellum, bellī,** n. war

|      | Singular | Plural  |
| ---- | -------- | ------- |
| Nom. | bellum   | bella   |
| Voc. | bellum   | bella   |
| Acc. | bellum   | bella   |
| Gen. | bellī    | bellōrum |
| Dat. | bellō    | bellīs  |
| Abl. | bellō    | bellīs  |

**Deus**, meaning 'god', has vocative singular **deus**, nominative and vocative plural **deī** or **dī**, genitive plural **deōrum** or **deum**, dative and ablative plural **deīs** or **dīs**. The plural of **locus**, m., 'place', is **loca**, n. (like the plural of **bellum, bellī**). **Dea**, 'goddess', and **filia**, 'daughter', have dative and ablative plural **deīs** or **deābus** and **filiīs** or **filiābus** – the forms in -**ābus** are used to avoid confusion with **deus** and **filius**.

## THIRD DECLENSION

Third Declension nouns are in two separate classes, with some endings differing very slightly.

**Class 1.** Nouns which go substantially like **iūdex**.

Here is the declension of **iūdex**. It is important to remember that what counts with any Third Declension noun is its *stem*, indicated by the difference between the nominative and the genitive singular. Thus, in **iūdex**, the stem is **iūdic-** and the endings are what follow that stem.

**iūdex, iūdicis,** c., judge    **nōmen, nōminis,** n., name

|       | Singular | Plural | Singular | Plural |
|-------|----------|--------|----------|--------|
| Nom.  | iūdex    | iūdicēs | nōmen   | nōmina |
| Voc.  | iūdex    | iūdicēs | nōmen   | nōmina |
| Acc.  | iūdicem  | iūdicēs | nōmen   | nōmina |
| Gen.  | iūdicis  | iūdicum | nōminis | nōminum |
| Dat.  | Iūdicī   | iūdicibus | nōminī | nōminibus |
| Abl.  | iūdice   | iūdicibus | nōmine | nōminibus |

**pater, patris,** m., father

|       | Singular | Plural |
|-------|----------|--------|
| Nom.  | pater    | patrēs |
| Voc.  | pater    | patrēs |
| Acc.  | patrem   | patrēs |
| Gen.  | patris   | patrum |
| Dat.  | patrī    | patribus |
| Abl.  | patre    | patribus |

The above models and a little common sense will tell you how to decline any of the following nouns: **rādix, rādicis,** f., root; **rēx, rēgis,** m., king; **vōx, vōcis,** f., voice; **mīles, mīlitis,** c., soldier; **virtūs, virtūtis,** f., virtue; **seges, segetis,** f., corn; **pēs, pedis,** m., foot; **lapis, lapidis,** m., stone; **caput, capitis,** n., head; **sacerdos, sacerdōtis,** c., priest or priestess; **prīnceps, prīncipis,** c., chief; **flōs, flōris,** m., flower; **honōs, honōris,** m., honour; **opus, operis,** n., work; **tempus, temporis,** n., time; **corpus, corporis,** n., body; **genus, generis,** n., race (of people); **crūs, crūris,** n., leg; **iūs, iūris,** n., law; **consul, consulis,** m., consul; **sōl, sōlis,** m., sun; **amor, amōris,** m., love; **ōrātor, ōrātōris,** m., speaker; **carcer, carceris,** m., prison; **frāter, frātris,** m., brother; **māter, mātris,** f., mother; **aequor, aequoris,** n., sea; **ebur, eboris,** n., ivory; **leō, leōnis,** m., lion; **latrō, latrōnis,** m., robber; **ratiō, ratiōnis,** f., reason; **virgō, virginis,** f., virgin; **ordō, ordinis,** f., order; **homō, hominis,** m., man; **carmen, carminis,** n., song.

**Class 2.** These are nouns which go substantially like **iūdex** *but* have **-ium** in the genitive plural and, in the case of neuter nouns, also have **-ia** in the nominative plural.

**mōns, montis,** m., mountain    **cīvis, cīvis,** c. citizen

|  | Singular | Plural | Singular | Plural |
|------|---------|--------|----------|--------|
| Nom. | **mōns** | **montēs** | **cīvis** | **cīvēs** |
| Voc. | **mōns** | **montēs** | **cīvis** | **cīvēs** |
| Acc. | **montem** | **montēs** | **cīvem** | **cīvēs** |
| Gen. | **montis** | **montium** | **cīvis** | **cīvium** |
| Dat. | **montī** | **montibus** | **cīvī** | **cīvibus** |
| Abl. | **monte** | **montibus** | **cīve/-ī** | **cīvibus** |

**animal, animālis,** n., animal

|  | Singular | Plural |
|------|---------|--------|
| Nom. | **animal** | **animālia** |
| Voc. | **animal** | **animālia** |
| Acc. | **animal** | **animālia** |
| Gen. | **animālis** | **animālium** |
| Dat. | **animālī** | **animālibus** |
| Abl. | **animālī** | **animālibus** |

From the above you can work out without difficulty how the following go: **dēns, dentis,** m., tooth; **urbs, urbis,** f., city; **ars, artis,** f., art; **frōns, frontis,** f., forehead; (and confusingly) **frōns, frondis,** f., leaf; **amnis, amnis,** m., river; **ignis, ignis,** m., fire; **avis, avis,** f., bird; **imber, imbris,** m., shower; **linter, lintris,** f., boat; **nūbēs, nūbis,** f., cloud; **cubīle, cubīlis,** n., couch; **conclāve, conclāvis,** n., room; **sedīle, sedīlis,** n., seat; **tribūnal, tribūnālis,** n., tribunal; **calcar, calcāris,** n., spur; **exemplar, exemplāris,** n., pattern.

Here are some rules which may help the memory on whether the genitive plural is **-um** or **-ium**.

1. Third Declension nouns of which the genitive singular has more syllables than the nominative singular (for instance, **iūdex, iūdicis,** and **mīles, mīlitis**) have the genitive plural in **-um**.

2. Where the genitive singular has the same number of syllables as has the nominative singular (for instance, **cīvis, cīvis** and **nūbes, nūbis**) the genitive plural ends in **-ium**.

3. Nouns of which the nominative has one syllable but has a stem ending in two consonants (for instance **mōns, montis**) have genitive plural in **-ium**.

4. **Pāter, māter, frāter, iuvenis, senex, canis, sēdēs** have genitive plural in **–um**.

5. Neuter nouns in **-e, -al, -ar** have genitive plural in **-ium** (except **mare**); they also have ablative singular in -ī.

6. Nouns ending in in **-tās**, such as **cīvitās, clāritās, celebritās** and **celeritās,** have genitive plural in **-um** or **-ium.**

## FOURTH DECLENSION      FIFTH DECLENSION

|  | **gradus, gradūs,** m., step | | **genū, genūs,** n., knee | | **rēs, reī,** f., thing | |
|---|---|---|---|---|---|---|
|  | *Singular* | *Plural* | *Singular* | *Plural* | *Singular* | *Plural* |
| Nom. | gradus | gradūs | genū | genua | rēs | rēs |
| Voc. | gradus | gradūs | genū | genua | rēs | rēs |
| Acc. | gradum | gradūs | genū | genua | rem | rēs |
| Gen. | gradūs | graduum | genūs | genuum | reī | rērum |
| Dat. | graduī | gradibus | genū | genibus | reī | rēbus |
| Abl. | gradū | gradibus | genū | genibus | rē | rēbus |

Like **gradus** go **frūctus, frūctūs,** m., fruit; **senātus, senātūs,** m., senate; **manus, manūs,** f., hand. Like **genū** goes **cornū, cornūs,** n., horn. Like **rēs** go **aciēs, aciēī,** f., line of battle; **diēs, diēī,** m., day; **faciēs, faciēī,** f., face; **fidēs, fideī,** f., faith; **seriēs, seriēī,** f., series; **spēs, speī,** f., hope.

Just two nouns are joint nouns of different declensions, declined in both their parts: **iūsiūrandum, iūrisiūrandī,** meaning an oath, is a Third and Second Declension noun, and **rēspūblica, reīpūblicae,** f., meaning public interest, republic or state, is a Fifth and First Declension noun.

## IRREGULAR NOUNS

|  | **domus, domūs,** f., home | | **vīs, ——,** f., force | |
|---|---|---|---|---|
|  | *Singular* | *Plural* | *Singular* | *Plural* |
| Nom. | domus | domūs | vīs | vīrēs |
| Voc. | domus | domūs | vīs | vīrēs |
| Acc. | domum | domūs, domōs | vim | vīrēs |
| Gen. | domūs, domī | domuum, domōrum | —— | vīrium |
| Dat. | domuī, domō | domibus | —— | vīribus |
| Abl. | domō | domibus | vī | vīribus |

**domus** also has a locative quite often used, **domī,** *at home*.

Surely most interesting of all:

**Imppiter, Iovis,** m., Jupiter

*Singular*
Nom.    **Iuppiter**
Voc.    **Iuppiter**
Acc.    **Iovem**
Gen.    **Iovis**
Dat.    **Iovī**
Abl.    **Iove** (Hence the old English interjection 'By Jove!' For the
             fascinating reason why this word alone in Latin is so
             bizarrely declined, I refer you to the website.)

*Locative case.* Where it survives, the locative case is similar in form to the dative except in the Second Declension singular, where it is similar to the genitive. Thus the locative of **Carthagō** is **Carthaginī** and of **domus** is **domī**.

## ADJECTIVES AND ADVERBS
## ADJECTIVES

The Principal Parts given before each declension suffice to identify how it declines. These parts vary depending on whether the adjective has identical masculine and feminine.

### FIRST AND SECOND DECLENSION ADJECTIVES

**bonus, -a, um,** good.

|       | *Singular* |        |        | *Plural* |         |         |
|-------|------------|--------|--------|----------|---------|---------|
|       | M.         | F.     | N.     | M.       | F.      | N.      |
| Nom.  | **bonus**  | **bona** | **bonum** | **bonī** | **bonae** | **bona** |
| Voc.  | **bone**   | **bona** | **bonum** | **bonī** | **bonae** | **bona** |
| Acc.  | **bonum**  | **bonam** | **bonum** | **bonōs** | **bonās** | **bona** |
| Gen.  | **bonī**   | **bonae** | **bonī** | **bonōrum** | **bonārum** | **bonōrum** |
| Dat.  | **bonō**   | **bonae** | **bonō** | **bonīs** | **bonīs** | **bonīs** |
| Abl.  | **bonō**   | **bonā** | **bonō** | **bonīs** | **bonīs** | **bonīs** |

**niger, nigra, nigrum,** black.

|       | *Singular* |         |          | *Plural* |          |          |
|-------|------------|---------|----------|----------|----------|----------|
|       | M.         | F.      | N.       | M.       | F.       | N.       |
| Nom.  | **niger**  | **nigra** | **nigrum** | **nigrī** | **nigrae** | **nigra** |
| Voc.  | **niger**  | **nigra** | **nigrum** | **nigrī** | **nigrae** | **nigra** |
| Acc.  | **nigrum** | **nigram** | **nigrum** | **nigrōs** | **nigrās** | **nigra** |
| Gen.  | **nigrī**  | **nigrae** | **nigrī** | **nigrōrum** | **nigrārum** | **nigrōrum** |
| Dat.  | **nigrō**  | **nigrae** | **nigrō** | **nigrīs** | **nigrīs** | **nigrīs** |
| Abl.  | **nigrō**  | **nigrā** | **nigrō** | **nigrīs** | **nigrīs** | **nigrīs** |

**tener, tenera, tenerum,** tender

|  | *Singular* | | | *Plural* | | |
|---|---|---|---|---|---|---|
|  | M. | F. | N. | M. | F. | N. |
| Nom. | tener | tenera | tenerum | tenerī | tenerae | tenera |
| Voc. | tener | tenera | tenerum | tenerī | tenerae | tenera |
| Acc. | tenerum | teneram | tenerum | tenerōs | tenerās | tenera |
| Gen. | tenerī | tenerae | tenerī | tenerōrum | tenerārum | tenerōrum |
| Dat. | tenerō | tenerae | tenerō | tenerīs | tenerīs | tenerīs |
| Abl. | tenerō | tenerā | tenerō | tenerīs | tenerīs | tenerīs |

Examples of adjectives going like **bonus** are **cārus,** dear; **dubius,** doubtful; **dūrus,** hard; **magnus,** big; **parvus,** small; and **meus,** my (except that the vocative masculine singular is **mī**). Like **tener** are **līber,** free; and **miser,** wretched. Like **niger** are **pulcher,** beautiful; and **noster** and **vester,** our and your (plural) respectively.

## THIRD DECLENSION

**trīstis, trīstis, trīste,** sad

|  | *Singular* | | *Plural* | |
|---|---|---|---|---|
|  | M. and F. | N. | M. and F. | N. |
| Nom. and Voc. | trīstis | trīste | trīstēs | trīstia |
| Acc. | trīstem | trīste | trīstēs | trīstia |
| Gen. | trīstis | | trīstium | |
| Dat. | trīstī | | trīstibus | |
| Abl. | trīstī | | trīstibus | |

Going like **trīstis** are **aequālis,** equal; **brevis,** short; **facilis,** easy; **difficilis,** difficult; and **omnis,** all.

**fēlix, fēlix, fēlicis,** happy, fortunate

|  | *Singular* | | *Plural* | |
|---|---|---|---|---|
|  | M. and F. | N. | M. and F. | N. |
| Nom. and Voc. | fēlīx | fēlix | fēlicēs | fēlicia |
| Acc. | fēlicem | fēlix | fēlicēs | fēlicia |
| Gen. | fēlicis | | fēlicium | |
| Dat. | fēlicī | | fēlicibus | |
| Abl. | fēlicī | | fēlicibus | |

**vetus, vetus, veteris**, old

|  | Singular | | Plural | |
|---|---|---|---|---|
|  | M. and F. | N. | M. and F. | N. |
| Nom. and Voc. | **vetus** | **vetus** | **veterēs** | **vetera** |
| Acc. | **veterem** | **vetus** | **veterēs** | **vetera** |
| Gen. | **veteris** | | **veterum** | |
| Dat. | **veterī** | | **veteribus** | |
| Abl. | **vetere** | | **veteribus** | |

Like **vetus, veteris** in principle are **dīves, dīvitis**, rich; **inops, inopis**, poor; **memor, memoris**, mindful; **pauper, pauperis**, poor.

**ingēns, ingēns, ingentis,** huge

|  | Singular | | Plural | |
|---|---|---|---|---|
|  | M. and F. | N. | M. and F. | N. |
| Nom. and Voc. | **ingēns** | **ingēns** | **ingentēs** | **ingentia** |
| Acc. | **ingentem** | **ingēns** | **ingentēs** | **ingentia** |
| Gen. | **ingentis** | | **ingentium** | |
| Dat. | **ingentī** | | **ingentibus** | |
| Abl. | **ingentī** | | **ingentibus** | |

Very important: all present participles of verbs are declined like **ingēns**; for instance, **amans**, loving.

**ācer, ācris, ācre,** keen

This, with the nominative and vocative feminine singular differing from those of the others, is most easily learnt in a slightly different form from the others in the singular.

|  | Singular | | | Plural | |
|---|---|---|---|---|---|
|  | M. | F. | N. | M. and F. | N. |
| Nom. and Voc. | **ācer** | **ācris** | **ācre** | **ācrēs** | **ācria** |
| Acc. | **ācrem** | **ācrem** | **ācre** | **ācrēs** | **ācria** |
| Gen. | **ācris** | **ācris** | **ācris** | **ācrium** | |
| Dat. | **ācrī** | **ācrī** | **ācrī** | **ācribus** | |
| Abl. | **ācrī** | **ācrī** | **ācrī** | **ācribus** | |

Like **ācer** is **celeber**, famous.

## COMPARISON OF ADJECTIVES AND ADVERBS

To form the comparative and superlative of a Latin *adjective* remove the ending from its genitive singular and add **-ior** for the comparative and **-issimus** for the superlative.

| Positive | Comparative | Superlative |
|---|---|---|
| **lātus**, wide | **lātior**, wider, rather wide | **lātissimus**, widest, very wide |
| **fēlīx**, fortunate | **fēlīcior**, more fortunate, rather fortunate | **fēlīcissimus**, most fortunate, very fortunate |

If the positive ends in **-er**, the superlative ends in **-errimus**:

| | | |
|---|---|---|
| **tener**, tender | **tenerior** | **tenerrimus** |
| **ācer**, keen | **ācrior** | **ācerrimus** |

The superlatives of **facilis**, easy; **difficilis**, difficult; **similis**, like; **dissimilis**, unlike; **humilis**, humble; and **gracilis**, slender, end in **-illimus**:

| | | |
|---|---|---|
| **facilis**, easy | **facilior** | **facillimus** |

The following have irregular comparatives and superlatives:

| | | |
|---|---|---|
| **bonus**, good | **melior**, better | **optimus**, best |
| **magnus**, great | **maior**, greater | **maximus**, greatest |
| **malus**, bad | **peior**, worse | **pessimus**, worst |
| **multus**, much | **plūs**, more | **plūrimus**, most |
| **parvus**, small | **minor**, less | **minimus**, least |
| **vetus**, old | **vetustior**, older | { **veterrimus**, oldest<br>{ **vetustissimus** |
| **senex**, old | **senior** or **nātū maior** (literally greater by birth) | **nātū maximus** |
| **iuvenis**, young | **iūnior** or **nātū minor** (less by birth) | **nātū minimus**, youngest |

Comparative adjectives are declined as follows:

|  | *Singular* | | *Plural* | |
|---|---|---|---|---|
|  | M. and F. | N. | M. and F. | N. |
| Nom. and Voc. | **trīstior** | **trīstius** | **trīstiōrēs** | **trīstiōra** |
|  | **trīstior** | **trīstius** | **trīstiōrēs** | **trīstiōra** |
| Acc. | **trīstiōrem** | **trīstius** | **trīstiōrēs** | **trīstiōra** |
| Gen. | **trīstiōris** | | **trīstiōrum** | |
| Dat. | **trīstiōrī** | | **trīstiōribus** | |
| Abl. | **trīstiōre** | | **trīstiōribus** | |

**Plūs**, more, is different from the other comparatives in two respects. 1. In the singular, it is not used as an adjective, but only as a neuter noun, while, in the plural, it is used as an adjective. 2. It also declines irregularly, as follows:

|  | *Singular* | *Plural* | |
|---|---|---|---|
|  |  | M. and F. | N. |
| Nom., Voc., Acc. | **plūs** | **plūrēs** | **plūra** |
| Gen. | **plūris** | **plūrium** | |
| Dat. | —— | **plūribus** | |
| Abl. | **plūre** | **plūribus** | |

Superlative adjectives are all declined like **bonus**.

## ADVERBS

*Positive adverbs* are formed by removing the ending from the genitive singular of the adjective and adding -**ē** for adjectives of the First and Second Declensions and -**iter** for the Third Declension. Thus **dūrus**, hard, becomes **dūrē**, hard ('hardly', in its modern English meaning of 'scarcely' would be incorrect here), and **fēlīx**, happy, becomes **fēliciter**, happily. There are numerous exceptions to this rule, which will be found in the vocabularies. *Comparative adverbs* are formed by changing the ending of the corresponding comparative adjective from -**ior** to -**ius**, the superlative by changing the ending of the corresponding superlative adjective from -**us** to -**ē**. Thus the comparative adverb is the same as the neuter of the comparative adjective.

| *Positive* | *Comparative* | *Superlative* |
|---|---|---|
| **lātē,** widely | **lātius,** more widely, rather widely | **lātissimē,** most widely, very widely |
| **fēlīciter,** happily | **fēlīcius** | **fēlicissimē** |
| **ācriter,** sharply | **ācrius** | **ācerrimē** |
| **facile,** easily | **facilius** | **facillimē** |
| **bene,** well | **melius** | **optimē** |

Exceptions:

**magnopere**, greatly    **magis**, more (in degree)    **maximē**, most
**multum**, much    **plūs**, more (in quantity)    **plūrimum**, most

A few adverbs have no corresponding adjective. For instance:

**saepe**, often    **saepius**    **saepissimē**
**diū**, for a long time    **diūtius**    **diūtissimē**

## SOME FURTHER IMPORTANT ADVERBS, MOST OF THEM WITH NO COMPARATIVES OR SUPERLATIVES

**DEGREE, ETC.: satis**, enough. **frustra**, in vain. **vix**, sarcely.

**PLACE: hīc**, here. **ibi**, there. **eō**, thither. **procul**, far away.

**TIME: aliquandō**, sometimes. **hodiē**, today. **nōndum**, not yet. **nunquam**, never. **nūper**, lately (superlative **nuperrimē**). **ōlim**, once upon a time. **rūrsus**, again. **semper**, always. **simul**, at the same time. **tandem**, at last. **umquam**, ever.

## PRONOUNS

### PERSONAL PRONOUNS

| *First Person* (I; we) | | | *Second Person* (thou; you) | |
|---|---|---|---|---|
| | *Singular* | *Plural* | *Singular* | *Plural* |
| Nom. | **ego** | **nōs** | **tū** | **vōs** |
| Acc. | **mē** | **nōs** | **tē** | **vōs** |
| Gen. | **meī** | **nostrī** *or* **nostrum** | **tuī** | **vestrī** *or* **vestrum** |
| Dat. | **mihi** | **nōbīs** | **tibi** | **vōbīs** |
| Abl. | **mē** | **nōbīs** | **tē** | **vōbīs** |

The Personal Pronouns have no vocative case. **Nostrum** and **vestrum** are used to indicate a whole divided into parts, as in 'most *of us*' and 'all *of you*'. **Nostrī** and **vestrī** are used for all other constructions.

*Third Person* (he, she, it; they)

|       | M.   | F.   | N.   | M.        | F.        | N.        |
|-------|------|------|------|-----------|-----------|-----------|
| Nom.  | is   | ea   | id   | eī, iī, ī  | eae       | ea        |
| Acc.  | eum  | eam  | id   | eōs       | eās       | ea        |
| Gen.  | eius | eius | eius | eōrum     | eārum     | eōrum     |
| Dat.  | eī   | eī   | eī   | eīs, iīs  | eīs, iīs, | eīs, iīs, |
| Abl.  | eō   | eā   | eō   | eīs, iīs  | eīs, iīs  | eīs, iīs, |

## REFLEXIVE PRONOUNS

| | *First Person* | | *Second Person* | | *Third Person* | |
|-------|------|------|------|------|------|------|
| | *Sing.* | *Pl.* | *Sing.* | *Pl.* | | |
| Acc.  | mē   | nōs  | tē   | vōs  | sē or sēsē | Note. The **sēsē** |
| Gen.  | meī  | nostrī *or* nostrum | tuī | vestrī *or* vestrum | suī | singular and plural are the same in form. |
| Dat.  | mihi | nōbīs | tibi | vōbīs | sibi | |
| Abl.  | mē   | nōbīs | tē   | vōbīs | sē or sēsē | |

**Nostrum** and **vestrum** are distinguished in usage from **nostrī** and **vestrī** as stated above.

## EMPHATIC PRONOUNS

Emphasising whichever person is involved (myself, ourselves, yourself, yourselves, himself, herself, itself, themselves).

|       | *Singular* | | | *Plural* | | |
|-------|--------|--------|--------|---------|---------|---------|
|       | M.     | F.     | N.     | M.      | F.      | N.      |
| Nom.  | ipse   | ipsa   | ipsum  | ipsī    | ipsae   | ipsa    |
| Acc.  | ipsum  | ipsam  | ipsum  | ipsōs   | ipsās   | ipsa    |
| Gen.  | ipsīus | ipsīus | ipsīus | ipsōrum | ipsārum | ipsōrum |
| Dat.  | ipsī   | ipsī   | ipsī   | ipsīs   | ipsīs   | ipsīs   |
| Abl.  | ipsō   | ipsā   | ipsō   | ipsīs   | ipsīs   | ipsīs   |

## DEMONSTRATIVE PRONOUNS

**is**, that, declined exactly as the Third Person **is, ea, id**, declined above.

**hic**, this, these; also he, she and they

|       | *Singular* |       |       | *Plural* |       |       |
|-------|------|------|------|------|------|------|
|       | M.   | F.   | N.   | M.   | F.   | N.   |
| Nom.  | hic  | haec | hoc  | hī   | hae  | haec |
| Acc.  | hunc | hanc | hoc  | hōs  | hās  | haec |
| Gen.  | huius | huius | huius | hōrum | hārum | hōrum |
| Dat.  | huic | huic | huic | hīs  | hīs  | hīs  |
| Abl.  | hōc  | hāc  | hōc  | hīs  | hīs  | hīs  |

**ille** that, those (most usually more indicating 'that *or* those over there' than do **is, ea, id**, which indicate the more ordinary use of 'that' and 'those'); also he, she, they

|       | *Singular* |       |       | *Plural* |       |       |
|-------|------|------|------|------|------|------|
|       | M.   | F.   | N.   | M.   | F.   | N.   |
| Nom.  | ille | illa | illud | illī | illae | illa |
| Acc.  | illum | illam | illud | illōs | illās | illa |
| Gen.  | illīus | illīus | illīus | illōrum | illārum | illōrum |
| Dat.  | illī | illī | illī | illīs | illīs | illīs |
| Abl.  | illō | illā | illō | illīs | illīs | illīs |

**iste** declines like **ille**. It is **is tc** abbreviated, meaning 'that of yours', 'that near you', and sometimes used in speeches to indicate someone a speaker is opposing and an opposite person to **hic**, a person on the speaker's side)

## PRONOMINAL ADJECTIVES

**alter**, one *or* other of two

|       | *Singular* |       |       |
|-------|--------|---------|---------|
|       | M.     | F.      | N.      |
| Nom.  | alter  | altera  | alterum |
| Acc.  | alterum | alteram | alterum |
| Gen.  | alterīus | alterīus | alterīus |
| Dat.  | alterī | alterī  | alterī  |
| Abl.  | alterō | alterā  | alterō  |

|       | *Plural* |       |       |
|-------|--------|---------|---------|
|       | M.     | F.      | N.      |
| Nom.  | alterī | alterae | altera  |
| Acc.  | alterōs | alterās | altera  |
| Gen.  | alterōrum | alterārum | alterōrum |
| Dat.  | alterīs | alterīs | alterīs |
| Abl.  | alterīs | alterīs | alterīs |

**Neuter,** neither of two, and **uterque,** each of two, decline like **alter** but omit the **e** before the **r**.

**alius** (one *or* other of more than two)

*Singular*

|      | M.      | F.      | N.      |
|------|---------|---------|---------|
| Nom. | alius   | alia    | aliud   |
| Acc. | alium   | aliam   | aliud   |
| Gen. | alīus   | alīus   | alīus   |
| Dat. | aliī    | aliī    | aliī    |
| Abl. | aliō    | aliā    | aliō    |

*Plural*

|      | M.       | F.       | N.       |
|------|----------|----------|----------|
| Nom. | aliī     | aliae    | alia     |
| Acc. | aliōs    | aliās    | alia     |
| Gen. | aliōrum  | aliārum  | aliōrum  |
| Dat. | aliīs    | aliīs    | aliīs    |
| Abl. | aliīs    | aliīs    | aliīs    |

In the plural **alius** means 'some', 'others'.

**idem,** the same

|      | *Singular* | | | *Plural* | | |
|------|---------|---------|---------|----------|----------|----------|
|      | M.      | F.      | N.      | M.       | F.       | N.       |
| Nom. | idem    | eadem   | idem    | eīdem    | eaedem   | eadem    |
| Acc. | eundem  | eandem  | idem    | eōsdem   | eāsdem   | eadem    |
| Gen. | eiusdem | eiusdem | eiusdem | eōrundem | eārundem | eōrundem |
| Dat. | eīdem   | eīdem   | eīdem   | eīsdem   | eīsdem   | eīsdem   |
| Abl. | eōdem   | eādem   | eōdem   | eīsdem   | eīsdem   | eīsdem   |

## RELATIVE PRONOUN

**quī,** who, which

|      | *Singular* | | | *Plural* | | |
|------|-------|-------|-------|-------------|-------------|-------------|
|      | M.    | F.    | N.    | M.          | F.          | N.          |
| Nom. | quī   | quae  | quod  | quī         | quae        | quae        |
| Acc. | quem  | quam  | quod  | quōs        | quās        | quae        |
| Gen. | cuius | cuius | cuius | quōrum      | quārum      | quōrum      |
| Dat. | cui   | cui   | cui   | quīs *or* quibus | quīs *or* quibus | quīs *or* quibus |
| Abl. | quō   | quā   | quō   | quīs *or* quibus | quīs *or* quibus | quīs *or* quibus |

## INTERROGATIVE PRONOUNS

**Quis,** who?, is **quis, quis, quid** in the nominative singular, and otherwise declines like **quī**.

**Uter,** which of two?, declines like **alter** but omits the **e**.

## INTERROGATIVE ADJECTIVE

**Quī,** which, what?, declines like **quī,** relative.

## PREPOSITIONS

### The prepositions and their cases – the commonest ones

Taking the accusative case: **ad,** to, towards. **ante,** before. **apud,** at the house of. **circum,** round. **contrā,** against. **inter,** among. **per,** through. **post,** after. **propter,** on account of. **trāns,** across.

Taking the ablative case: **a, ab,** by (agent), from. **cum** with, in the company of. **dē,** concerning. **ē, ex,** out of. **sine,** without.

With accusative or ablative according to its meaning or use: **in** + acc.. into. **in** + abl., in. **sub** + acc., under, when motion is involved. **sub** + abl., under, when stationary position is involved.

### The prepositions and their cases – all the important ones

These prepositions take the **accusative case: ad,** to, at towards. **adversus,** against opposite to. **ante,** before. **apud,** at, near, among. **circā, circiter,** about. **circum,** around. **cis, citrā,** on this side of. **clam,** unknown to. **contrā,** against. **extrā,** outside of. **in,** into (motion). **infrā,** below. **inter,** between. **intrā,** amidst, within. **iuxtā,** next to, beside. **ob,** on account of. **per,** through. **pōne,** behind. **post,** after, behind. **praeter,** beside, past. **prope,** near. **propter,** near, on account of. **secundum,** next, along, according to. **sub,** under (motion). **subter,** under (motion). **super,** over, upon (motion). **suprā,** above. **trāns,** across. **ultrā,** beyond. **versus,** towards.

These prepositions take the **ablative case: a, ab,** by, from. **coram,** in the presence of. **cum,** with. **dē,** from, concerning. **ex,** out of, from. **in,** into (at rest). **palam,** in sight of. **prae,** before, in front of. **pro,** on behalf of, for. **sine,** without. **sub,** under (at rest). **subter,** under (at rest). **super,** over, upon (at rest).

## NUMERALS

| Arabic Numeral (not used in Latin) | Roman Symbol | Cardinals (one, two, etc.) | Ordinals (first, second, etc.) |
|---|---|---|---|
| 1 | I | ūnus | prīmus |
| 2 | II | duo | secundus (alter) |
| 3 | III | trēs | tertius |
| 4 | IV | quattuor (quatuor) | quārtus |
| 5 | V | quinque | quīntus |
| 6 | VI | sex | sextus |
| 7 | VII | septem | septimus |
| 8 | VIII | octō | octāvus |
| 9 | IX | nŏvem | nōnus |
| 10 | X | decem | decimus |
| 11 | XI | ūndecim | ūndecimus |
| 12 | XII | duodecim | duodecimus |
| 13 | XIII | tredecim | tertius decimus |
| 14 | XIV | quattuordecim | quārtus decimus |
| 15 | XV | quīndecim | quīntus decimus |
| 16 | XVI | sēdecim | sextus decimus |
| 17 | XVII | septendecim | septimus decimus |
| 18 | XVIII | duodēvīgintī | duodēvīcēnsimus |
| 19 | XIX | ūndēvīgintī | ūndēvīcēnsimus |
| 20 | XX | vīgintī | vīcēnsimus |
| 21 | XXI | vīgintī ūnus *or* ūnus et vīgintī | vīcēnsimus prīmus *or* ūnus et vīcēnsimus |
| 30 | XXX | trīgintā | trīcēnsimus |
| 40 | XL | quadrāgintā | quadrāgēnsimus |
| 50 | L | quinquāgintā | quīnquāgēnsimus |
| 60 | LX | sexāgintā | sexāgēnsimus |
| 70 | LXX | septuāgintā | septuāgēnsimus |
| 80 | LXXX | octōgintā | octōgēnsimus |
| 90 | XC | nōnāgintā | nōnāgēnsimus |
| 100 | C | centum | centēnsimus |

CC, **ducentī, ducentae, ducenta** (as also the rest up to **nōngentī**); CCC, **trecentī**; CCCC, **quadringentī**; D, **quingentī**; DC, **sexcentī** (**sescentī**); DCC, **septingentī**; DCCC, **octingentī**; DCCCC, **nōngentī**; M, **mille**; MM, **duo milia**; MMM, **tria milia**; $\overline{\text{X}}$, **decem milia**.

|       | *Singular* |       |       | *Plural* |         |         |
| ----- | ------ | ------ | ------ | ------ | ------ | ------ |
|       | M.     | F.     | N.     | M.     | F.     | N.     |
| Nom.  | ūnus   | ūna    | ūnum   | ūnī    | ūnae   | ūna    |
| Acc.  | ūnum   | ūnam   | ūnum   | ūnōs   | ūnās   | ūna    |
| Gen.  | ūnīus  | ūnīus  | ūnīus  | ūnōrum | ūnārum | ūnōrum |
| Dat.  | ūnī    | ūnī    | ūnī    | ūnīs   | ūnīs   | ūnīs   |
| Abl.  | ūnō    | ūnā    | ūnō    | ūnīs   | ūnīs   | ūnīs   |

|       | *Singular* |       |       | *Plural* |      |
| ----- | ---------- | ----- | ------ | ------------ | ---- |
|       | M.         | F.    | N.     | M. and F.    | N.   |
| Nom.  | duo        | duae  | duo    | trēs         | tria |
| Acc.  | duōs, duo  | duās  | duo    | trēs         | tria |
| Gen.  | duōrum     | duārum | duōrum | trium       |      |
| Dat.  | duōbus     | duābus | duōbus | tribus      |      |
| Abl.  | duōbus     | duābus | duōbus | tribus      |      |

Cardinals from **ducentī** to **nongentī** and ordinals are declined like **bonus**.

**Mīlle** does not decline, but its plural **mīlia** declines as follows:

| Nom., Acc. | mīlia    |
| ---------- | -------- |
| Gen.       | mīlium   |
| Dat., Abl. | mīlibus  |

A noun qualified by '*two* thousand', etc., in English, though not a noun qualified by '*one* thousand', in English, goes into the genitive in Latin. Thus **a mille militibus**, by a thousand soldiers, but **a duobus milibus militum**, by two thousand soldiers.

*Distributives* (one each, etc.): **singulī, bīnī, ternī, quaternī, quīnī, sēnī, septēnī, octōnī, novēnī, dēnī,** etc. (like **bonus**).

*Adverbs* (once, twice, etc.): **semel, bis, ter, quater, quīnquiēns, sexiēns,** etc. (ending in -**ēns** or -**ēs**).

## CONJUGATION OF VERBS

(No translation is given for the subjunctive mood because translating it depends so much on what it is being used for in any particular instance.)

**sum**, I am

|  | INDICATIVE |  | SUBJUNCTIVE | |
|---|---|---|---|---|
| *Present* | **sum** | I am, I am being | *Present* | **sim** |
| | **es** | you are, thou art | | **sīs** |
| | **est** | he, she, it is, etc. | | **sit** |
| | **sumus** | we are | | **sīmus** |
| | **estis** | you are | | **sītis** |
| | **sunt** | they are | | **sint** |
| *Future* | **erō** | I shall be | *Imperfect* | **essem** |
| | **eris** | you will be, thou wilt be | | **essēs** |
| | **erit** | he, she, it will be, etc. | | **esset** |
| | **erimus** | we shall be | | **essēmus** |
| | **eritis** | you will be | | **essētis** |
| | **erunt** | they will be | | **essent** |
| *Imperfect* | **eram** | I was, I was being | *Perfect* | **fuerim** |
| | **erās** | you were, thou wast | | **fuerīs** |
| | **erat** | he, she, it was, etc. | | **fuerit** |
| | **erāmus** | we were | | **fuerīmus** |
| | **erātis** | you were | | **fuerītis** |
| | **erant** | they were | | **fuerint** |
| *Perfect* | **fuī** | I have been, I was | *Pluperfect* | **fuissem** |
| | **fuistī** | you have been, thou wast | | **fuissēs** |
| | **fuit** | he, she, it, was, etc. | | **fuisset** |
| | **fuimus** | we have been, we were | | **fuissēmus** |
| | **fuistis** | you have been, you were | | **fuissētis** |
| | **fuērunt** | they have been, they were | | **fuissent** |

| *Future* | **fuerō** | I shall have been |
|---|---|---|
| *Perfect* | **fueris** | you will have been, thou wilt have been |
| | **fuerit** | he, she, it, will have been, etc. |
| | **fuerimus** | we shall have been |
| | **fueritis** | you will have been |
| | **fuerint** | they will have been |

**IMPERATIVE**
**es** be *(singular)*
**este** be *(plural)*

**INFINITIVES**
*Present* **esse** to be
*Perfect* **fuisse** to have been
*Future* **futūrus esse**
*simp.* or **fore**

| *Pluperfect* | **fueram** | I had been | |
|---|---|---|---|
| | **fuerās** | you had been, thou wast | **PARTICIPLES** |
| | **fuerat** | he, she, it had been, etc. | *Present* —— |
| | **fuerāmus** | we had been | *Perfect* —— |
| | **fuerātis** | you had been | *Future* **futūrus** about |
| | **fuerant** | they had been | to be |

## First Conjugation: amō, I love

## ACTIVE VOICE

### INDICATIVE MOOD

| PRESENT | FUTURE | IMPERFECT |
|---|---|---|
| I love, I am loving, | I shall love, | I was loving, |
| I do love | I shall be loving | I used to love |
| **amō** | **amābō** | **amābam** |
| **amās** | **amābis** | **amābās** |
| **amat** | **amābit** | **amābat** |
| **amāmus** | **amābimus** | **amābāmus** |
| **amātis** | **amābitis** | **amābātis** |
| **amant** | **amābunt** | **amābant** |

| PERFECT | FUTURE PERFECT | PLUPERFECT |
|---|---|---|
| I loved, I have loved | I shall have loved | I had loved |
| **amāvī** | **amāverō** | **amāveram** |
| **amāvistī** | **amāveris** | **amāverās** |
| **amāvit** | **amāverit** | **amāverat** |
| **amāvimus** | **amāverimus** | **amāverāmus** |
| **amāvistis** | **amāveritis** | **amāverātis** |
| **amāvērunt** | **amāverint** | **amāverant** |

### INFINITIVE MOOD

PRESENT **amāre**, to love
PERFECT **amāvisse**, to have loved
FUTURE **amātūrus esse**, to be
about to love

GERUND **amandum, amandī**,
n., the loving

### IMPERATIVE MOOD

*Sing.* **amā**, love  *Pl.* **amāte**, love

**PARTICIPLES**
PRESENT **amāns**, loving
FUTURE **amātūrus, -a, -um,**
about to love

## SUBJUNCTIVE MOOD

| PRESENT | IMPERFECT | PERFECT | PLUPERFECT |
|---|---|---|---|
| amem | amārem | amāverim | amāvissem |
| amēs | amārēs | amāverīs | amāvissēs |
| amet | amāret | amāverit | amāvisset |
| amēmus | amārēmus | amāverīmus | amāvissēmus |
| amētis | amārētis | amāverītis | amāvissētis |
| ament | amārent | amāverint | amāvissent |

## PASSIVE VOICE

### INDICATIVE MOOD

| PRESENT | FUTURE | IMPERFECT |
|---|---|---|
| I am loved, I am being loved | I shall be loved | I was being loved |
| amor | amābōr | amābar |
| amāris | amāberis | amābāris |
| amātur | amābitur | amābātur |
| amāmur | amābimur | amābāmur |
| amāminī | amābiminī | amābāminī |
| amantur | amābuntur | amābantur |

| PERFECT | FUTURE PERFECT | PLUPERFECT |
|---|---|---|
| I have been loved, I was loved | I shall have been loved | I had been loved |
| amātus sum | amātus erō | amātus eram |
| amātus es | amātus eris | amātus erās |
| amātus est | amātus erit | amātus erat |
| amātī sumus | amātī erimus | amātī erāmus |
| amātī estis | amātī eritis | amātī erātis |
| amātī sunt | amātī erint | amātī erant |

| INFINITIVE MOOD | IMPERATIVE MOOD |
|---|---|
| PRESENT **amārī,** to be loved | *Sing.* **amāre,** be loved *Pl.* **amāminī** |
| PERFECT **amātus esse**, to have been loved | PERFECT |
| FUTURE **amātum īrī**, to be about to be loved | PARTICIPLE **amātus**, loved, having been loved |
| GERUNDIVE **amandus**, fit to be loved | |

## SUBJUNCTIVE MOOD

| PRESENT | IMPERFECT | PERFECT | PLUPERFECT |
|---------|-----------|---------|------------|
| amer | amārer | amātus sim | amātus essem |
| amēris | amārēris | amātus sīs | amātus essēs |
| amētur | amārētur | amātus sit | amātus esset |
| amēmur | amārēmur | amātī sīmus | amātī essēmus |
| amēminī | amārēminī | amātī sītis | amātī essētis |
| amentur | amārentur | amātī sint | amātī essent |

## REGULAR VERBS

Against the background, so to speak, of the First Conjugation **amō**, the other three conjugations are not difficult to understand, since there is much overlap. Below they are set out together in a table, making it easy to compare them. To make it easier still, the stems are separated from the endings, which are sometimes identical and always very similar.

## INDICATIVE

### ACTIVE

**PRESENT**

| | | | | | |
|---|---|---|---|---|---|
| amō | amā-s | ama-t | amā-mus | amā-tis | ama-nt |
| mone- ō | monē-s | mone-t | monē-mus | monē-tis | mone-nt |
| reg- ō | reg-is | reg-it | reg-imus | reg-itis | reg-unt |
| audi- ō | audī-s | audi-t | audī-mus | audī-tis | audi-unt |

**FUTURE SIMPLE**

| | | | | | |
|---|---|---|---|---|---|
| amā- bō | -bis | -bit | -bimus | -bitis | -bunt |
| monē- bō | -bis | -bit | -bimus | -bitis | -bunt |
| reg- am | -ēs | -et | -ēmus | -ētis | -ent |
| audi- am | -ēs | -et | -ēmus | -ētis | -ent |

**IMPERFECT**

| | | | | | |
|---|---|---|---|---|---|
| amā- bam | -bās | -bat | -bāmus | -bātis | -bant |
| monē- bam | -bās | -bat | -bāmus | -bātis | -bant |
| reg- ēbam | -ēbās | -ēbat | -ēbāmus | -ēbātis | -ēbant |
| audi- ēbam | -ēbās | -ēbat | -ēbāmus | -ēbātis | -ēbant |

## PERFECT

| amāv- | ī | -istī | -it | -imus | -istis | -ērunt |
|-------|---|-------|-----|-------|--------|--------|
| monu- | ī | -istī | -it | -imus | -istis | -ērunt |
| rēx- | ī | -istī | -it | -imus | -istis | -ērunt |
| audīv- | ī | -istī | -it | -imus | -istis | -ērunt |

## FUT. PERFECT

| amāv- | ero | -eris | -erit | -erimus | -eritis | -erint |
|-------|-----|-------|-------|---------|---------|--------|
| monu- | ero | -eris | -erit | -erimus | -eritis | -erint |
| rēx- | ero | -eris | -erit | -erimus | -eritis | -erint |
| audīv- | ero | -eris | -erit | -erimus | -eritis | -erint |

## PLUPERFECT

| amāv- | eram | -erās | -erat | -erāmus | -erātis | -erant |
|-------|------|-------|-------|---------|---------|--------|
| monu- | eram | -erās | -erat | -erāmus | -erātis | -erant |
| rēx- | eram | -erās | -erat | -erāmus | -erātis | -erant |
| audīv- | eram | -erās | -erat | -erāmus | -crātis | -erant |

## PASSIVE

### PRESENT

| am- | or | -āris | -ātur | -āmur | -āminī | -antur |
|-----|----|-------|-------|-------|--------|--------|
| mon- | eor | -ēris | -ētur | -ēmur | -ēminī | -entur |
| reg- | or | -eris | -itur | -imur | -iminī | -untur |
| aud- | ior | -īris | -ītur | -īmur | -īminī | -iuntur |

### FUTURE SIMPLE

| amā- | bor | -beris | -bitur | -bimur | -biminī | -buntur |
|------|-----|--------|--------|--------|---------|---------|
| mone- | bor | -beris | -bitur | -bimur | -biminī | -buntur |
| reg- | ar | -ēris | -ētur | -ēmur | -ēminī | -entur |
| audi- | ar | -ēris | -ētur | -ēmur | -ēminī | -entur |

### IMPERFECT

| amā- | bar | -bāris | -bātur | -bāmur | -bāminī | -bantur |
|------|-----|--------|--------|--------|---------|---------|
| mone- | bar | -bāris | -bātur | -bāmur | -bāminī | -bantur |
| reg- | ēbar | -ēbāris | -ēbātur | -ēbāmur | -ēbāminī | -ēbantur |
| audī- | ēbar | -ēbāris | -ēbātur | -ēbāmur | -ēbāminī | -ēbantur |

### PERFECT

| amāt- | us sum | -us es | -us est | -ī sumus | -ī estis | -ī sunt |
|-------|--------|--------|---------|----------|----------|---------|
| monit- | us sum | -us es | -us est | -ī sumus | -ī estis | -ī sunt |
| rēct- | us sum | -us es | -us est | -ī sumus | -ī estis | -ī sunt |
| audīt- | us sum | -us es | -us est | -ī sumus | -ī estis | -ī sunt |

## FUT. PERFECT

| amāt- | us erō | -us eris | -us erit | -ī erimus | -ī eritis | -ī erunt |
| monit- | us erō | -us eris | -us erit | -ī erimus | -ī eritis | -ī erunt |
| rēct- | us erō | -us eris | -us erit | -ī erimus | -ī eritis | -ī erunt |
| audīt- | us erō | -us eris | -us erit | -ī erimus | -ī eritis | -ī erunt |

## PLUPERFECT

| amāt- | us eram | -us erās | -us erat | -ī erāmus | -ī erātis | -ī erant |
| monit- | us eram | -us erās | -us erat | -ī erāmus | -ī erātis | -ī erant |
| rēct- | us eram | -us erās | -us erat | -ī erāmus | -ī erātis | -ī erant |
| audīt- | us eram | -us erās | -us erat | -ī erāmus | -ī erātis | -ī erant |

# SUBJUNCTIVE

## ACTIVE

### PRESENT

| am- | em | am-ēs | am-et | am-ēmus | am-ētis | am-ent |
| mone- | am | monē-ās | mone-at | monē-āmus | monē-ātis | mone-ant |
| reg- | am | reg-ās | reg-at | reg-āmus | reg-ātis | reg-ant |
| audi- | am | audī-ās | audi-at | audī-āmus | audī-ātis | audi-ant |

### IMPERFECT

| amā- | rem | -rēs | -ret | -rēmus | -rētis | -rent |
| monē- | rem | -rēs | -ret | -rēmus | -rētis | -rent |
| rege- | rem | -rēs | -ret | -rēmus | -rētis | -rent |
| audī- | rem | -rēs | -ret | -rēmus | -rētis | -rent |

### PERFECT

| amāv- | erim | -erīs | -erit | -erīmus | -erītis | -erint |
| monu- | erim | -erīs | -erit | -erīmus | -erītis | -erint |
| rēx- | erim | -erīs | -erit | -erīmus | -erītis | -erint |
| audīv- | erim | -erīs | -erit | -erīmus | -erītis | -erint |

### PLUPERFECT

| amāv- | issem | -issēs | -isset | -issēmus | -issētis | -issent |
| monu- | issem | -issēs | -isset | -issēmus | -issētis | -issent |
| rēx- | issem | -issēs | -isset | -issēmus | -issētis | -issent |
| audīv- | issem | -issēs | -isset | -issēmus | -issētis | -issent |

## PASSIVE

### PRESENT

| am- | er | -ēris | -ētur | -ēmur | -ēminī | -entur |
|-----|-----|-------|-------|-------|--------|--------|
| mone- | ar | -āris | -ātur | -āmur | -āminī | -antur |
| reg- | ar | -āris | -ātur | -āmur | -āminī | -antur |
| audi- | ar | -āris | -ātur | -āmur | -āminī | -antur |

### IMPERFECT

| amā- | rer | -rēris | -rētur | -rēmur | -rēminī | -rentur |
|------|-----|--------|--------|--------|---------|---------|
| monē- | rer | -rēris | -rētur | -rēmur | -rēminī | -rentur |
| rege- | rer | -rēris | -rētur | -rēmur | -rēminī | -rentur |
| audī- | rer | -rēris | -rētur | -rēmur | -rēminī | -rentur |

### PERFECT

| amāt- | us sim | -us sīs | -us sit | -ī sīmus | -ī sītis | -ī sint |
|-------|--------|---------|---------|----------|----------|---------|
| monit- | us sim | -us sīs | -us sit | -ī sīmus | -ī sītis | -ī sint |
| rēct- | us sim | -us sīs | -us sit | -ī sīmus | -ī sītis | -ī sint |
| audīt- | us sim | -us sīs | -us sit | -ī sīmus | -ī sītis | -ī sint |

### PLUPERFECT

| amāt- | us essem | -us essēs | -us esset | -ī essēmus | -ī essētis | -ī essent |
|-------|----------|-----------|-----------|------------|------------|-----------|
| monit- | us essem | -us essēs | -us esset | -ī essēmus | -ī essētis | -ī essent |
| rēct- | us essem | -us essēs | -us esset | -ī essēmus | -ī essētis | -ī essent |
| audīt- | us essem | -us essēs | -us esset | -ī essēmus | -ī essētis | -ī essent |

## IMPERATIVE

| ACTIVE | | PASSIVE | |
|--------|--------|---------|---------|
| *Sing. 2nd* | *Plur. 2nd* | *Sing. 2nd* | *Plur. 2nd* |
| amā | amā-te | amā-re | amā-minī |
| monē | monē-te | monē-re | monē-minī |
| reg-e | reg-ite | reg-ere | reg-iminī |
| audī | audī-te | audī-re | audī-minī |

## PRINCIPAL PARTS OF VERBS

You have learnt the 'model' verbs for the four conjugations. The first two Principal Parts of a verb will indicate to which conjugation they belong.

1. **First Conjugation verbs** have first person singular present indicative active ending: -ō and the infinitive in -āre. The long ā of the infinitive is the clue to the stem of the verb and its conjugation.

2. **Second Conjugation verbs** have first person singular present indicative active ending -eō and the infinitive -ēre. The long ē is the indicator for Second Conjugation verbs.

3. **Third Conjugation verbs** have first person singular present indicative active ending -ō or -iō and the infinitive -ere. The short e in the infinitive is the indicator for Third Conjugation verbs.

4. **Fourth Conjugation verbs** have first person singular present indicative active ending -iō and the infinitive -īre. The long ī in the infinitive is the indicator for Fourth Conjugation verbs.

As you learn new verbs and memorise the Principal Parts you will find some variants from our models in the formation of the stem of the Perfect Indicative Active and the Supine:

So, First Conjugation

|  | **amō** | -āre | **amāvī** | **amātum** | love |
|-----|---------|------|-----------|------------|------|
| but | **dō** | -āre | **dedī** | **datum** | give |

Second Conjugation

|  | **moneō** | -ēre | **monuī** | **monitum** | advise |
|-----|-----------|------|-----------|-------------|--------|
| but | **sedeō** | -ēre | **sēdī** | **sessum** | sit |
|  | **videō** | -ēre | **vīdī** | **vīsum** | see |

Third Conjugation

|  | **regō** | -ere | **rēxī** | **rēctum** | rule |
|-----|----------|------|------------|-------------|-------|
| but | **currō** | -ere | **cucurrī** | **cursum** | run |
|  | **scrībō** | -ere | **scrīpsī** | **scrīptum** | write |

Fourth Conjugation

|  | **aperiō** | -īre | **aperuī** | **apertum** | open |
|-----|-----------|------|-----------|-------------|------|
| but | **veniō** | -īre | **vēnī** | **ventum** | come |

Once you have identified the conjugation and know the perfect stem and the supine, the conjugation of the endings follows the models you have learnt.

## DEPONENT VERBS

There is a group of verbs in Latin which have passive forms but active meanings. They are called deponent verbs because they have 'laid aside' (**dēpōnō, -ere**) their passive *meanings* but have retained their passive *forms*. They are translated only in the Active Voice. The Third Declension **ūtor**, I use, is the most frequently given in books, or sections of books, on grammar.

**ūtor, ūti, ūsus,** use

| TENSE | INDICA-TIVE | | SUBJUNC-TIVE | IMPERA-TIVE |
|---|---|---|---|---|
| Present | **ūtor** | I use, I am using | **ūtar** | **ūtere**, use (*s.*) |
| | **ūteris** | you (*s.*) use, you (*s.*) are using | **ūtāris** | **ūtimini**, use (*pl.*) |
| | **ūtitur** | he uses, he is using | **ūtātur** | |
| | **ūtimur** | we use, we are using | **ūtāmur** | |
| | **ūtiminī** | you (*pl.*) use, you (*pl.*) are using | **ūtāminī** | |
| | **ūtuntur** | they use, they are using | **ūtantur** | |
| Fut. Simple | **ūtar** | I shall use | | |
| | **ūtēris** | you (*s.*) will use | | |
| | **ūtētur** | he will use | | |
| | **ūtēmur** | we shall use | | |
| | **ūtēminī** | you (*pl.*) will use | | |
| | **ūtentur** | they will use | | |
| Imperfect | **ūtēbar** | I was using | **ūterer** | |
| | **ūtēbāris** | you (*s.*) were using | **ūterēris** | |
| | **ūtēbātur** | he was using | **ūterētur** | |
| | **ūtēbāmur** | we were using | **ūterēmur** | |
| | **ūtēbāminī** | you (*pl.*) were using | **ūterēminī** | |
| | **ūtēbantur** | they were using | **ūterentur** | |
| Perfect | **ūsus sum** | I have used, I used | **ūsus sim** | |
| | **ūsus es** | you (*s.*) have used, you (*s.*) used | **ūsus sīs** | |
| | **ūsus est** | he has used, he used | **ūsus sit** | |
| | **ūsī sumus** | we have used, we used | **ūsī sīmus** | |
| | **ūsī estis** | you (*pl.*) have used or you (*pl.*) used | **ūsī sītis** | |
| | **ūsī sunt** | the have used, they used | **ūsī sint** | |

Fut. Perfect **ūsus erō**    I shall have used
       **ūsus eris**    you (*s.*) will have used
       **ūsus erit**    he will have used
       **ūsī erimus**    we shall have used
       **ūsī eritis**    you (*pl.*) will have used
       **ūsī erunt**    they will have used

Pluperfect  **ūsus eram**    I have used        **ūsus essem**
       **ūsus erās**    you (*s.*) had used    **ūsus essēs**
       **ūsus erat**    he had used       **ūsus esset**
       **ūsī erāmus**    we had used       **ūsī essēmus**
       **ūsī erātis**    you (*pl.*) had used    **ūsī essētis**
       **ūsī erant**    they had used     **ūsī essent**

## THE VERB INFINITE

*Infinitives* Present **ūtī**, use. Perfect **ūsus esse**, to have used. Future **ūsūrus esse**, to be about to use.

*Supines* **ūsum**, to use. **ūsū**, in *or* for using.

*Gerund* **ūtendum**, using.

*Participles* Present **ūtēns**, using. Future **ūsūrus**, about to use. Perfect **ūsus**, having used.

*Gerundive* **ūtendus**, fit to be used.

The conjugation of all deponent verbs is completely regular

First Conjugation:    **cōnor, cōnārī, cōnātus sum**, I try, attempt
Second Conjugation:    **polliceor, pollicērī, pollicitus sum**, I promise
Third Conjugation:    **ūtor, ūtī, ūsus sum**, I use
Fourth Conjugation:    **orior, orīrī, ortus sum**, I rise, arise

As has been seen with **ūtor**, deponent verbs have retained a few regular active forms:

(a) The present active participle: **ūtens, -entis** = using
(b) The future active participle: **ūsūrus, -a, -um** = about to use
(c) The future active infinitive: **ūsūrus esse** = to be about to use

**Note.** Because deponent forms are translated actively, they can have no 'fourth Principal Part' (i.e., they have no perfect *passive* participle). Instead, the participle form contained in the third Principal Part (**cōnātus, pollicitus, locūtus, ortus**, etc.) is a perfect *active* participle.

This participle fills a much-needed gap in the language and accordingly is frequently used. Thus:

**conātus** = having tried　　　**pollicitus** = having promised
**locūtus** = having spoken　　**ortus** = having arisen

There are deponent verbs of all conjugations, the Third Conjugation being the most common. Once **utor** is understood, how the others go is easy to work out as long as the Principal Parts are known.

## SEMI-DEPONENT VERBS

Four verbs in Latin have active forms in the first two Principal Parts, but are deponent verbs in the third Principal Part (i.e. the perfect tense). They too are translated only in the Active Voice. These verbs are:

**audeō, -ēre, ausus sum**, to dare　**gaudeō, -ēre, gāvisus sum**, to rejoice
**fidō, -ere, fisus sum**, to trust　　**soleō, -ēre, solitus sum**, to be
　　　　　　　　　　　　　　　　　accustomed to

## IRREGULAR VERBS

**possum,** I can *or* I am able, goes very like **sum**

### INDICATIVE

| *Present* | *Future* | *Imperfect* |
|---|---|---|
| possum | poterō | poteram |
| potes | poteris | poterās |
| potest | poterit | poterat |
| possumus | poterimus | poterāmus |
| potestis | poteritis | poterātis |
| possunt | poterunt | poterant |

*Present* and *Imperfect Subjunctive*: **possim, possem,** like **sum**.

*Perfect, Future Perfect* and *Pluperfect Indicative, Perfect* and *Pluperfect Subjunctive* formed regularly from perfect **potuī**.

*Present Infinitive:* **posse**. There is no *Imperative* or *Supine*.

**ferō,** I bear

Its **Principal Parts** are the most remarkable of any Latin verb: **ferō, ferre, tulī, lātum**.

The first three tenses active and passive are as follows:

*Present tense indic. active*: **fero, fers, fert, ferimus, fertis, ferunt.**

*Future simple and imperfect indic. active*: **feram,** etc., and **ferēbam,** etc.

*Present indicative passive*: **feror, ferris, fertur, ferimur, feriminī, feruntur.**

*Present subjunctive active*: **feram, ferās,** etc. *Present subjunctive passive*: **ferar, ferāris,** etc.

*Imperfect subjunctive active*: **ferrem, ferrēs,** etc. *Imperfect subjunctive passive*: **ferrer, ferrēris,** etc.

*Imperative active, sing. and plur.*: **fer** and **ferte**. *Imperative passive:* **ferre** and **ferimini**.

*Present infinitive active*: **ferre**; and *passive:* **ferrī**. *Present participle active*: **ferēns.**

*Gerund*: **ferendum**. *Gerundive*: **ferendus.**

The other forms are regularly conjugated from the *perfect stem*, **tulī**, and the *supine stem* **lātum**.

The *third person singular of the present indicative passive* **fertur** is sometimes used to mean 'he *or* it is said'.

**eō,** I go

INDICATIVE

| Present | Future | Imperfect | Perfect |
|---------|--------|-----------|---------|
| eō | ībō | ībam | iī |
| īs | ībis | ībās | īstī |
| it | ībit | ībat | iit |
| īmus | ībimus | ībāmus | iimus |
| ītis | ībitis | ībātis | īstis |
| eunt | ībunt | ībant | iērunt |

*Present* and *Imperfect Subjunctive* **eam** (similar to Second Conjugation) and **īrem** (similar to Fourth Conjugation).

*Future Perfect* and *Pluperfect Indicative*, *Perfect* and *Pluperfect Subjunctive* formed regularly from perfect **īvī**; the **v** may be omitted, therefore **iī**.

| | |
|---|---|
| *Present Infinitive* | **īre** |
| *Imperative* | sing. **ī** plur. **īte** |
| *Supine* | **itum** |

**volō,** I wish, I am willing; **nōlō,** I do not wish, I am unwilling; **mālō,**
I prefer

### INDICATIVE

| *Present* | **volō** | **nōlō** | **mālō** |
|---|---|---|---|
| | **vīs** | **nōn vīs** | **māvīs** |
| | **vult** | **nōn vult** | **māvult** |
| | **volumus** | **nōlumus** | **mālumus** |
| | **vultis** | **nōn vultis** | **māvultis** |
| | **volunt** | **nōlunt** | **mālunt** |
| *Future* | **volam** | **nōlam** | **mālam** |
| *Imperfect* | **volēbam** | **nōlēbam** | **mālēbam** |

(Continue as in the Third Conjugation.)

### SUBJUNCTIVE

| *Present* | **velim** | **nōlim** | **mālim** |
|---|---|---|---|
| *Imperfect* | **vellem** | **nōllem** | **māllem** |

(Continue with the same endings as in the present and imperfect
subjunctive tenses of **sum.**)

The Perfect, Future Perfect and Pluperfect Indicatives and the
Perfect and Pluperfect Subjunctives are regular, based on the perfect
indicatives **voluī, noluī, maluī**.

| *Present Infinitive:* | **velle** | **nōlle** | **mālle** |
|---|---|---|---|
| *Imperative:* sing. | —— | **nōlī** | —— |
| plur. | —— | **nōlīte** | —— |
| *Supine:* | —— | —— | —— |

**edō,** I eat, **edere** (*or* **ēsse**), **ēdī, ēsum**

| Pres. Indic. Act.: | **edō, ēs, ēst, edimus, ēstis, edunt** |
|---|---|
| Imperf. Subj. Act.: | **ēssem, ēssēs, ēsset, ēssēmus, ēssētis, ēssent** |
| Imperat. Act.: | **ēs, ēstō; ēstō; ēste, ēstōte; eduntō** |
| Infin. Pres.: | **ēsse** |
| Pres. Indic. Pass.: | **ēstur** |
| Imperf. Subj. Pass.: | **ēssētur** |

Note that, although there is considerable resemblance between **edō**
and **sum,** very often they are distinguished by **edō** having a long
vowel of **ēs-** where **sum** has a short vowel **es-**.

**fīō,** I become, *or* I am made, **fierī.**

**Fīō** is used in place of the Passive Voice of **faciō,** I make. Note carefully where the **ī** of the stem becomes short in the Present Indicative and throughout the Imperfect Subjunctive.

|  | INDICATIVE | SUBJUNCTIVE | IMPERATIVE |
|---|---|---|---|
| *Present* | **fīō** | **fīam** | |
| | **fīs** | **fīās** | |
| | **fit** | **fiat** | (**fī**) |
| | (**fīmus**) | **fīāmus** | (**fīte**) |
| | (**fītis**) | **fīātis** | |
| | **fīunt** | **fīant** | |
| *Future Simple* | **fīam** | | |
| | **fīēs** | | |
| | **fīet** | | |
| | **fīēmus** | | |
| | **fīētis** | | |
| | **fīent** | | |
| *Imperfect* | **fīēbam** | **fierem** | |
| | **fīēbās** | **fierēs** | |
| | **fīēbat** | **fiieret** | |
| | **fīēbāmus** | **fierēmus** | |
| | **fīēbātis** | **fierētis** | |
| | **fīēbant** | **fierent** | |
| *Present Infinitive* | **fierī** | | |

**Fīō** has no other forms. For 'I have become' Latin uses simply **sum,** I am, and **factus sum** for I have been made.

**Note** When **fīō** means 'I become', the Future Infinitive and Future Participle are **fore** and **futūrus.** When **fīō** means 'I am made', the Future Infinitive and the Gerundive are **factum īrī** and **faciendus.**

## DEFECTIVE VERBS

**Defective verbs** are so-called because of deficiencies in the number of their forms.

**Coepī,** I have begun; **meminī,** I remember; and **ōdī,** I hate, are used almost exclusively in the Perfect, Future Perfect and Pluperfect tenses only. **Meminī** and **ōdī,** although apparently Perfect in their *tenses,* are in fact Present in *meaning.*

### INDICATIVE

| | | | |
|---|---|---|---|
| Perfect | **coepī** | **meminī** | **ōdī** |
| Fut. Perfect | **coeperō** | **meminerō** | **ōderō** |
| Pluperfect | **coeperam** | **memineram** | **ōderam** |

### SUBJUNCTIVE

| | | | |
|---|---|---|---|
| Perfect | **coeperim** | **meminerim** | **ōderim** |
| Pluperfect | **coepissem** | **meminissem** | **ōdissem** |

### INFINITIVE, IMPERATIVE, PARTICIPLES

| | | | |
|---|---|---|---|
| Perfect Infinitive | **coepisse** | **meminisse** | **ōdisse** |
| Future Infinitive | **coeptūrus esse** | —— | **ōsūrus esse** |
| Imperative | —— | **mementō** | |
| | | **mementōte** | |
| Perfect Participle | **coeptus** | —— | **ōsus** (see below) |
| Future Participle | **coeptūrus** | —— | **ōsūrus** |

Unlike **meminī** and **ōdī**, **coepī** has the Perfect Passive **coeptus sum**, used mainly when **coepī** is followed by a Passive Infinitive – for instance, **Mea vōx tandem audīrī coepta est**, 'At last my voice began to get heard.' When the present of **coepī** is really needed, **incipiō**, I begin, can be used in its place. Note particularly that the Perfect Participle **ōsus** is, completely contrary to what one would expect, both Active and Present in its meaning.

**aiō,** I say yes, affirm, assert

PRESENT INDICATIVE

| | | | | | |
|---|---|---|---|---|---|
| aiō | ais | ait | —— | —— | aiunt |

IMPERFECT INDICATIVE

| | | | | | |
|---|---|---|---|---|---|
| aiēbam | aiēbās | aiēbat | aiēbāmus | aiēbātis | aiēbant |

PRESENT SUBJUNCTIVE

| | | | | | |
|---|---|---|---|---|---|
| —— | —— | aiat | —— | —— | aiant |

PRESENT PARTICIPLE
aiēns

**inquam,** I say

PRESENT INDICATIVE

| | | | | | |
|---|---|---|---|---|---|
| inquam | inquis | inquit | inquimus | inquitis | inquiunt |

IMPERFECT INDICATIVE

| | | | | | |
|---|---|---|---|---|---|
| —— | —— | inquiēbat | —— | —— | inquiēbant |

FUTURE SIMPLE INDICATIVE
—— inquiēs inquiet
PERFECT INDICATIVE
inquīstī inquit
IMPERFECT INDICATIVE
inque

## IMPERSONAL VERBS

**Impersonal Verbs** are limited in their forms and use the Third Personal Singular of each tense, the Infinitive and the Gerund. They cannot have a personal subject in the nominative, so that, for instance, 'I am vexed' is translated into Latin by the equivalent of 'it vexes me'.

The most important **Impersonal Verbs** are (in the Indicative Mood):

| Present | | Infinitive | Perfect | Followed by |
|---|---|---|---|---|
| **miseret** | it moves to pity | **miserēre** | **miseruit** | Accusative of person and genitive of cause |
| **piget** | it vexes | **pigēre** | **piguit** | Acc. of person and genitive of cause |
| **paenitet** | it repents | **paenitēre** | **paenituit** | Acc. of person and genitive of cause |
| **pudet** | it shames | **pudēre** | **puduit** | Acc. of person and genitive of cause |
| **taedet** | it wearies | **taedēre** | **taeduit** | Acc. of person and genitive of cause |
| **decet** | it is becoming | **decēre** | **decuit** | Acc. of person and infin. Impersonal subject |
| **dēdecet** | it is unbecoming | **dēdecēre** | **dēdecuit** | Acc. of person and infin. Impersonal subject |
| **libet** | it pleases | **libēre** | **libuit** | Dative, sometimes with infin. as impers. subject |
| **licet** | it is awful | **licēre** | **licuit** | Dat., sometimes with infin. as impers. subject |
| **oportet** | it behoves | **oportēre** | **oportuit** | See note 2 overleaf. |
| **rēfert** | it concerns, it matters | **rēferre** | **rēttulit** | See note 3 overleaf. |

Note 1. Examples: **Miseret te captivorum**, 'You pity the prisoners.'
**Taedet me linguae Latinae docere**, 'Teaching Latin wearies me'.

Note 2. **Oportet** is used with an accusative and then an infinitive
clause, or with the subjunctive alone.  Example: **Me te linguam
Latinam docere oportet** *or* **Me te linguam Latinam doceas oportet**,
'It behoves me to teach you Latin' *or* 'I ought to teach you Latin.'

Note 3. With **rēfert** the person 'concerned' is, on the face of it mys-
teriously, expressed by the feminine ablative singular of a possessive
adjective irrespective of the sex of the person. The degree of the
concern is expressed by an adverb of degree or by a genitive of value.
Example: **Mea magnopere refert**, 'It concerns me greatly.'

The following Impersonal Verbs relate to weather and time.

| | | | |
|---|---|---|---|
| **fulgurat** | it lightens | **tonat** | it thunders |
| **ningit** | it snows | **lūcēscit** | it dawns |
| **pluit** | it rains | **vesperāscit** | it grows late |

A very special case is **intersum**. Ordinarily it means 'I lie between',
but the third person singular present tense **interest** means 'it concerns' or 'it is of importance', and is used impersonally.  As if that is
not complicated enough, the person or thing concerned goes either
in the genitive or in the ablative feminine of the relevant possessive
pronoun. Thus 'This very greatly concerns you and me' could be, for
instance, **meī et tuī vehementer interest**, or **meā tuāque interest**.
(Other useful adverbs often found qualifying **interest** are **multum,
quantum, tantum, maximē** and **magnopere**.)

## MORE IRREGULAR VERBS

There are in fact some hundreds of irregular verbs, and many of them
are among the verbs that are most commonly used. In standard books
on Latin grammar, lists of them occupy several pages.

Lack of space makes it impossible to include lists here. Those
verbs that are needed in this book will be found in their appropriate
places in the vocabulary section, complete with their Principal Parts,
and I recommend that you pause and learn each one as you come
across it, for the reason that any verb there will be a commonly used
one. Lists of others, again showing their Principal Parts and meanings, can easily be found elsewhere, for instance in the two Kennedy
Latin primers.

## CONJUNCTIONS

Conjunctions fall into two distinct categories: coordinating conjunctions, which separate words, phrases and clauses of equal value, and subordinating conjunctions, which introduce clauses which are either subordinate to two main clauses or subordinate to other subordinate clauses. There are many more subordinating conjunctions than coordinating conjunctions. Under the heading of coordinating conjunctions, there is a further category, correlative conjunctions, where conjunctions are used in pairs.

The **coordinating conjunctions** in turn fall into five main categories.

1. Connecting conjunctions: **et, -que, atque, ac**, and; **nec, neque,** nor; **etiam, quoque,** also.
2. Separating conjunctions: **aut, vel**, or, either; **sīve, seu**, whether, or.
3. Opposing conjunctions: **sed, at**, but; **atquī**, but yet; **tamen**, yet, however, nevertheless; **vērum, vērō**, but, morevover.
4. Conjunctions indicating cause: **nam, enim, etenim**, for.
5. Conjunctions introducing conclusions: **ergō, itaque, igitur,** therefore.

**Subordinating conjunctions** are:

Consecutive: **ut**, so that. **ut nōn**, so that not. **quīn**, that not, but that.

Final or 'purpose': **ut**, in order that. **nē**, lest. **nēve, neu**, and that not, and lest. **ut nē**, that not, lest.

Causal: **quod** *and* **quia**, because. **cum**, since. **quoniam** *and* **si quidem**, inasmuch as.

Temporal: **cum, quandō, ubi** *and* **ut**, when. **dum, dōnec** *and* **quoad**, while, so long as. **dum, dōnec** *and* **quoad**, until. **antequam** and **priusquam**, before that. **postquam**, after that. **simul ac**, as soon as. **quotiēns**, as often as.

Conditional: **sī**, if. **sīve** and **seu**, whether, or if. **sī modo**, if only. **nisi, nī**, unless. **sī nōn**, if not. **modo** *and* **tantum**, only. **modo** *and* **dummodo**, provided that.

Concessive: **etsī** *and* **etiamsī**, even if, although. **tametsī**, although. **quamquam** *and* **utut**, however, although. **cum**, whereas, although. **ut** *and* **licet**, granting that, although. **quamvīs**, although, however much.

Comparative: **ut, utī, sicut, velut, veluti** *and* **ceu**, as. **quōmodo** *and* **quemadmodum**, as, how. **quam**, than, as. **quasi (quam sī)** *and* **ut sī (velut sī)**, as if. **ceu** *and* **tamquam**, as though.

Correlative conjunctions, which come in pairs, include:

| | |
|---|---|
| **et ... et** | |
| **-que ... -que** | both ... and |
| **-que ... et** | |
| **aut ... aut** | either ... or |
| **vel ... vel** | |
| **neque ... neque** | |
| **nec ... nec** | neither ... nor |
| **nēve ... nēve** | |
| **sīve ... sīve** | whether ... or |
| **seu ... seu** | |
| **sic ... ut** | so ... as |
| **ut ... ita** | as ... so |
| **ita ... ut** | so ... that |

## INTERJECTIONS

An Interjection is an exclamatory word, used either to draw attention or to express feeling. The most usual are: **Edepol!** My word, goodness me! **En** and **ecce!** Behold, look! **Heu** and **ēheu!** Alas! **Quam!** What! **Salve** (*sing.*) and **salvēte** (*plur.*)! Greetings! **Vae!** Woe! **Vae tibi!** Woe is you! **Vale!** Farewell, goodbye!

# Vocabulary

## ENGLISH–LATIN

able, I am, **possum, posse, potuī**
absurd, **absurdus, -a, -um**
about, **dē** + abl.
above (adv.), **suprā**
above (preposition), **super** + acc.
or abl.
absence, **absentia, -iae,** f.
accept, I, **accipiō, -cipere, -cēpī,
-ceptum**
accomplish, I, **exsequor, -sequī,
-secutus sum; efficiō, -ere,
-fēcī, -fectum; impetrō, -āre,
-āvī, -ātum**
according to, **secundum**
account of, on, **ob** + acc.
accustomed, I am, **sōleō, solēre,
solitus sum**
acquire, I, **adipiscor, -piscī,
adeptus sum**
across, **trans** + acc.
act, **factum, -ī,** n.
add, I, **addō, addere, addidī,
additum**
admire, I, **miror, -ārī, -ātus sum;
admīror, -ārī, -ātus sum**
advance, I, **prōgredior, -gredī,
-gressus sum**
advice, **cōnsilium, -iī,** n.
advise, I, **moneō, -ēre, -uī, -itum**
advocate, **advocātus, -ī,** m.
after (conjunction), **postquam**
after (preposition), **post** + acc.
afterwards, **postea**
afraid (of), I am, **timeō, -ēre, -uī;
vereor, -ērī, -itus sum**
Africa, **Africa, -ae,** f.
again, **rūrsus, iterum, dēnuō**
against, **contrā** + acc.; **versus;
adversus**
ago, **abhinc**
agree, I, **concordō, -āre, āvī, ātum;**

cōnsentiō, -sentīre, -sēnsī,
-sēnsum
alas!, **vae!, eheu!, heu!**
alive, **vīvus, -a, -um**
all, **omnis, -e**
allow, I, **patior, patī, passus sum**
allowed, it is, **licet, licēre, licuit** or
**licitum est**
ally, **socius, sociī,** m.
almost, **ferē, paene**
alone, **sōlus, -a, -um**
along, **secundum**
already, **iam**
also, **etiam, quoque**
alter, I, **mūtō, -āre, -āvī, -ātum**
although, **etiamsī, etsī, tametsī,
quamquam, utut, cum, licet, ut,
quamvīs**
always, **semper**
ambassador, **legātus, -ī,** m.
ambush, **īnsidiae, -ārum,** f. pl.
among, **inter** + acc; **apud** + acc.
and, **et, ac, atque, -que** (at the end
of a word)
and that not, **nēve, neu**
anger, **īra, -ae,** f.
announce, I, **nūntiō, -āre, -āvī,
-ātum**
annoy, I, **vexō, -āre, -āvī, -ātum**
another, **alius, -a, -ud**
another time, at, **aliās**
appear to be, I, **exsistō -ere, -stitī**
(irreg.)
apple, **mālum, - ī,** n.
apple-tree, **mālus, - ī,** m.
appoint, I, **lēgō, -āre, -āvī, -ātum**
approach, **adeō, adīre, -īvī, -itum;
accēdō, accēdere, accessī,
accessum; appropinquō, -āre,
-āvī, -ātum**
argument, **argūmentum, - ī,** n.

arise, I, **orior, orīrī, ortus sum**

arms, **arma, -ōrum,** n. pl.

army, **exercitus, -ūs,** m.

army on the march, **agmen, agminis,** n.

around, **circa, circum,** +acc.

arrive, I, **perveniō, -venīre, -vēnī, -ventum**

arrow, **sagitta, -ae,** f.

as, **ut, utī, velut, veluti, sicut, quemadmodum, quam**

as ... so, **ut ... ita**

as if, as it were, **quasi, ut sī, velut sī**

as often as, **quotiēns**

as soon as, **simul ac**

as though, **tamquam**

ashamed, be (impersonal), **pudet, puduit**

ask, I, **rogō, -āre, -āvī, -ātum**

assault, I, **invādō, invādere, invāsī, invāsum**

at, **ad** + acc.

at length, at last, **tandem**

at the house of, **apud** + acc.

attack, *or* attack in words, **petītiō, -iōnis,** f.

attack, I, **oppugnō, -āre, -āvī, -ātum; prōsequor, -sequī, -secutus sum,**

attend, be present at, **assideō, -idēre, -ēdī, -essum,**

attention, pay, **operam do, dare, dedī, datum**

augur, **augur, -uris,** c.

avoid, I, **vītō, -āre, -āvī, -ātum**

away, I go, **abeō, abīre, -īvī, -itum**

back, **tergum, -ī,** n.

back, go, **revertor, -ī, reversus sum**

bad, **malus, -a, -um**

baggage (especially of an army), **impedimentum, -ī,** n.

balance, **libra, -ae,** f.

barbarian, **barbarus, -ī,** m.

barber, **tōnsor, -ōris,** m.

battle, **proelium, -ī,** n.; **pugna, -ae,** f.

be, to, **sum, esse, fuī**

beak (in birds), **rōstrum, -ī,** n.

bear, I, **ferō, ferre, tulī, lātum**

beard, **barba, -ae,** f.

beautiful, **pulcher, pulchra, pulchrum**

beauty, **pulchritūdō, -inis,** f.

because, **quod, quia**

because of, on account of, **ob** + acc.; **propter** + acc.

become, I, **fīō, fierī, factus sum**

before (preposition), **ante** + acc.; **prae**

before that, **antequam, priusquam**

behold, look, **en! ecce!**

beg, I, **orō, -āre, -āvī, -ātum**

begin, I, **incipiō, incipere, incēpī, inceptum**

beginning, **prīncipium, -iī,** n.; **initium, initiī,** n.; **orīgō, orīginis,** f.; **repetītiō, -iōnis,** f.

behind, **pōne**

believe, I, **crēdō, -dere, -didī, -ditum** (+ dat.)

below (adv.), **infrā**

below (preposition), **sub** + acc. or abl.; **subter** + acc. or abl.

bequeath, I, **lēgō, -āre, -āvī, -ātum**

beside, **iuxtā; praeter**

better (adv.), **melius**

between, **inter** + acc.

beware, **caveō, cavēre, cāvī, cautum**

beyond, **ultrā**

big, **magnus, -a, -um**

binding, **nexus, ūs,** m.

bird, **avis, -is,** f.

black, **niger, nigra, nigrum**

blame, **culpa, -ae,** f.

blame, I, **culpō, -āre, -āvī, -ātom**

blaze, I, **flagrō, -āre, -āvī, -ātum**

bless (post-classical Latin), **benedīcō, -dīcere, -dīxī, -dictum**

blood, **sanguis, sanguinis,** m.

bloody, **sanguineus, -a, -um**

blow, I, **flagrō, -āre, -āvī, -ātum**

board, **tabula, -ae,** f.

boat, **linter, lintris,** f.

body, **corpus, -oris,** n.

book, **liber, librī,** m; **cōdex, cōdicis,** m.

born, I am, **nāscor, nāscī, nātus sum**

both ... and, **et ... et; -que ...
-que; que ... et**

bother about, **cūrō, -āre, -āvī,
-ātum**

boundary, **modus, -ī,** m.

boy, **puer, puerī,** m.

brave, **fortis, -e**

bravely, **fortiter**

break, I, **frangō, frangere, frēgī,
fractum**

brightness, fame, celebrity, **clāritās,
-ātis,** f.

bring, I, **ferō, ferre, tulī, lātum**

bring to, add, I, **addō, -ere, addidī,
additum**

bring back, I, **referō, referre,
rettulī, relātum**

bringing back, a, **reductiō, iōnis,** f.

Briton, **Britannus, -a, -um**

Britain, **Britannia, -iae,** f.

British, **Britannicus, -a, -um**

broad, **lātus, -a, -um**

brother, **frāter, frātris,** m.

build, I, **aedificō, -āre, -āvī, -ātum**

burden, **onus, oneris,** n.

burn, I, **flagrō, -āre, -āvī, -ātum**

busy, I am, **operor, operārī,
operātus sum**

but, **sed, at, vērum, vērō**

but yet, **atquī**

buy, I, **emō, emere, ēmī, emptum**

buyer, **emptor, -ōris,** m.

by, **ā/ab** + abl. if by an agent; abl.
only (without **ā/ab**) if by an
instrument

by reason of, **propter** + acc.

by the way, **obiter**

Caesar, **Caesar, Caesaris,** m.

call, I, **vocō, -āre, -āvī, -ātum**

camp, **castra, -ōrum,** n. pl.

captive, **captīvus, -ī,** m.

care, concern, **cūra, -ae,** f.

care for, I, **cūrō, -āre, -āvī, -ātum**

careless, **incautus, -a, -um**

carry on, I, **gērō, gerere, gessī,
gestum**

carry out, I, **exsequor, -sequī,
-secūtus sum**

Carthage, **Carthāgō, -inis,** f.

Carthaginian, **Carthāginiēnsis**

cat, **fēlēs, -is,** f.

cavity, **lacūna, -ae,** f.

cease, I, **dēsistō, -ere, -stitī,
-stitum**

celebrity (abstract), 'celeb-status'
(in the modern vernacular),
**clāritās, -ātis,** f.

censor, **cēnsor, -ōris,** m.

certain, a, **quīdam, quaedam,
quoddam**

chair (professor's, official),
**cathedra, -ae,** f.

chair, **sedīle, sedīlis,** n.

chamber, **camera, -ae,** f.

chance, **fors, forte** (only in nom.
and abl. sing.), f.

change, I, **mūtō, -āre, -āvī, -ātum**

character represented by an actor,
**persōna, -ae,** f.

chariot, **currus, -ūs,** m.

chariot-course, **stadium, stadiī,** n.

chief, **prīnceps, -cipis,** m.

children, **līberī, -ōrum,** m. pl.

citizen, **cīvis, -is,** c.

city, **urbs, urbis,** f.

civil, **cīvīlis, -e**

class, **classis, -is,** f.; classes into
which Roman citizens were
divided; when related to living
beings in general indicating
especially the highest class,
human beings, **genus, -eris,** n.

cloud, **nūbēs, nūbis,** f.

colleague, **collēga, -ae,** m.

come, I, **veniō, venīre, vēnī,
ventum**

come to, I, **adveniō, -venīre, -vēnī,
-ventum**

come together, I, **conveniō, -īre,
vēnī, ventum**

command (for instance of an
army), **imperium, -iī,** n.

command of, I am in, **praesum,
-esse, -fuī**

commit to memory, I, **memoriae
mandō, -āre, -āvī, -ātum**

companion, **comes, -itis,** c.

concerning, **dē** + abl

condition, **status, -ūs,** m.

condition, agreement, **condiciō,
-iōnis**, f.
confess, **cōnfiteor, -fitērī, fessus**
connecting, **nexus, -ūs**, m.
conquer, I, **vincō, vincere, vīcī,
victum**
consequence, **eventus, -ūs**, m.
conspiracy, **coniūrātiō, -iōnis**, f.
conspire, I, **coniūrō, -āre, -āvī,
-ātum**
constant, **cōnstans, -antis**
consul, **cōnsul, -is**, m.
contradict, **contrādīcō, -dīcere,
-dīxī, -dictum**
corn, **seges, segetis**, f.
correct, **corrigō, -rigere, -rēxī,
-rēctum**
council, **concilium, -iī**, n.
country (fatherland), **patria, -ae**, f.
country (as opposed to town), **rūs,
rūris**, n.
courage, **virtūs, virtūtis**, f.
court, **cūria, -ae**, f.
course (of life), **curriculum, ī**, n.
cover, I, **tegō, tegere, tēxī, tectum**
create, I, **creō, -āre, -āvī, -ātum**
crime, **dēlictum, -ī**, n.; **crīmen,
-inis**, n.
crisis, **articulus, -ī**, m.
cross, I, **trānseō, -īre, -īvī, -itum**
crossing, **trāiectus, -ūs**, m.
crowd, **celebritas, -ātis**, f.
cry, **clamor, -ōris**, m.

daily, **quotīdiē**
dare, I, **audeō, audēre, ausus sum**
dart, **tēlum, -ī**, n.
daughter, **filia, -ae**, f.
day, **diēs, diēī**, m.
dear, **cārus, -a, -um**
death, **mors, mortis**, f.
decide, I, **cōnstituō, -uere, -uī,
-ūtum**
declare, **praedīcō, -āre, -āvī, -ātum**
deed, **factum, -ī**, n.
deep, **altus, -a, -um**; **profundus,
-a, -um**
defeat, I, **vincō, vincere, vīcī, victum**
defend, I, **dēfendō, -fendere,
-fendī, -fensum**

deference, **officium, -iī**, n.
deficiency, **lacūna, -ae**, f.
delay, **mora, -ae**, f.
delay, I, **mōror, morārī, morātus
sum; retardō, -āre, -āvī, -ātum**
delight, I, **dēlectō, -āre**
delightful, **dulcis, -e**
deny, I, **negō, -āre, -āvī, -ātum**
depart, I, **abeō, -īre, -īvī or -iī,
-itum**
departure, **discessus, -ūs**, m.
descent, **genus, generis**, n.
deserve, **mereor, meruī, meritus
sum**
desire, **cupīdō, cupīdinis**, f.
desire, I, **cupiō, -ere, -īvī or -iī,
-ītum**
despair, I, **dēspērō, -āre, -āvī,
-ātum** (both transitive and
intransitive)
destitute, in need, **inops, inopis**
destroy, I, **dēleō, -ēre, -ēvī, -ētum**
detain, I, **retineō, -ēre, -uī, -entum**.
determine, I, **cōnstituō, -uere, -uī,
-ūtum**
determined (**pro rāta parte,**
determined according to a fixed
proportion, in proportion),
**rātus, -a, -um** (past participle
of **reor**)
device, **māchina, -ae**, f.
devil, **diabolus, -ī**, m.
die, I, **morior, morī, mortuus sum**
(future participle, **moriturus**);
(with **diem** or **mortem**, at least
understood), **obeō, -īre, -iī,
-itum**
difficult, **difficilis, -e**
difficulty, **difficultās, -ātis**, f.
dignity, **dignitās, -ātis**, f.
dine, I, **cēnō, -āre, -āvī, -ātum**
direction, in that, **versus**
disgraceful, **turpis, -e**
disgraceful, it is, **dēdecet, -ēre;
dēdecuit**
dishonest, **improbus, -a, -um**
disperse, I, **diffugiō, -ugere, -ūgī**
distinguish, I, **notō, -āre, -āvī,
-ātum**
distinguished, **īnsignis, -e**

divide, I, **dīvidō, -videre, -vīsī, -vīsum**

divine utterance, **fātum, -ī,** n.

do, I, **faciō, facere, fēcī, factum; agō, āgere, ēgī, actum**

document, **tabula, -ae,** f.

dog, **canis, -is,** m.

dominion, **imperium, -iī,** n.

donkey, **asinus, -ī,** m.

door, **ianua, -ae,** f.

drama, **drāma, drāmatis,** f.

dread, or object of dread, **horror, -ōris,** m.

drive, I, **agō, agere, ēgī, actum**

dutiful action, **officium, -iī,** n.

eager, **cupidus, -a, -um**

eager, I am, **studeō, -ēre, uī**

ear, **auris, -is,** f.

early, **mātūrus, -a, -um**

earn, I, **mereor, meruī, meritus sum**

earth (soil), **humus, -ī,** m.

easily, **facile**

easy, **facilis, -e**

eat, **edō, edere** or **esse, ēdī, ēsum**

either, **aut, vel**

either . . . or, **aut . . . aut; vel . . . vel**

elect (to office), I, **creō, -āre, -āvī, -ātum**

elegant, **lepidus, -a, um**

eloquent, **facundus, -a, um**

elsewhere, **aliās, alibī**

embezzlement, **suppressiō, –iōnis,** f.

empire, **imperium, -iī,** n.

employment, official, **officium, -iī,** n.

empty, **vacuus, -a, -um**

encourage, I, **hortor, -ārī, -ātus sum**

enemy, **hostis, -is,** c. In the plural, the enemy (collective)

engage in, I, **obeō, -īre, -iī, itum**

England, **Anglia, -ae,** f.

enjoy, I, **fruor, fruī, frūctus sum** or **fruitus sum** (direct object in the ablative); **gaudeō, gaudēre, gāvīsus sum** (direct object in the ablative)

enough, **satis**

enter, I, **ineō, inīre, iniī, initum;** (assault) **invādō, invādere, invāsī, invāsum; ingredior, ingredī, ingressus sum**

enter upon, I, **obeō, -īre, -iī, -itum**

entreaty, **precem** (no nom. sing.), **precis,** f.

entrust, I, **dēpōnō, dēpōnere, dēposuī, dēpositum**

envoy, **legātus, -ī,** m.

envy, **invidia, -ae,** f.

equal, **par, paris**

ergō, **therefore**

err, I, **errō, -āre, -āvī, -ātum**

error, **lapsus, -ūs,** m.

even if, **etiamsī, etsī**

event, **eventus, -ūs,** m.

ever, adv., **umquam**

example, **exemplum, -ī,** n.

exceedingly, **vehementer**

excellence, **praestantia, -ae,** f.

excite, I, **citō, -āre-, āvī, -ātum**

execute, I, **exsequor, -sequī, -secūtus sum**

exist, I, **exsistō -ere, -stitī** (irreg.)

experienced, expert, **perītus, -a, -um**

explain, I, **expōnō, -pōnere, -posuī, -positum**

expression (on face), look, **vultus, -ūs,** m.

extreme, **extrēmus, -a, -um**

fact, in, **vērō**

faint trace, **scintilla, -ae,** f.

faith, **fidēs, -ēī,** f.

fall, falling, **cāsus, -ī,** m.

fall (sliding), **lapsus, -ūs,** m.

fall, I, **cadō, cadere, cecidī, cāsum**

false, **falsus, -a, -um**

fame, **celebritās, -ātis,** f.; **clāritās, -ātis,** f.

family, **gēns, gentis,** f.

family (head of), **paterfamiliās, patrisfamiliās**

famous, **celeber, celebris, celebre**

far, **procul;** (adverb) **longe**

far and wide, **passim**

farewell!, **vale!**

farmer, **agricola, -ae,** m.

fate, **fātum, -ī,** n.

father, **pater, patris,** m.

fatherland, **patria, -ae,** f.

fault, **culpa, -ae,** f.

favour, **grātia, -iae,** f.

favour, I, **faveō, favēre, fāvī, fautum**

favourable, **secundus, -a, -um**

fear, **timor, -ōris,** m.

fear, I, **timeō, -ēre, -uī; vēreor, -ērī, -itus sum**

feel, I, **sentiō, -īre, sēnsī, sēnsum**

few, **paucus, -a, -um**

field, **ager, agrī,** m.

fierce, **ferōx, ferōcis**

fiercely, **ferōciter, ācriter**

fight, I, **pūgnō, -āre, -āvī, -ātum**

finally, **dēnique**

find, I, **inveniō, -venīre, -vēnī, -ventum**

find out, I, **cognoscō, -noscere, -nōvī, -nitum**

fine, **poena, -ae,** f.

finish, I, **cōnficiō, cōnficere, cōnfēcī, cōnfectum**

fire, **ignis, -is,** m.

fire, be on, **ardeō, -ēre, arsī, arsum**

firm, **cōnstans -antis**

first (adj.), **prīmus, -a, -um** (superlative of **priscus,** ancient)

first, at first (adv.), **prīmum**

first element, first principle, **prīncipium, -iī,** n.

fitting, fit for, a**ptus, -a, -um**

fitting, it is, **decet, -ēre, decuit**

fixed, **rātus, -a, -um** (past participle of **reor**)

flee, I, **fugiō, fugere, fūgī**

fleet, **classis, -is,** f.

flourish, I, **floreō, -ēre, -uī, -itum**

flower, **flōs, flōris,** m.

fly, I, **fugiō, fugere, fūgī**

follow, I, **sequor, sequī, secūtus sum**

follow, a company, I, **prōsequor, -sequī, -secūtus sum**

follow a corpse to the grave; follow to the end, I, **exsequor, -sequī, -secūtus sum**

following after, **posterior,**

posterius (comparative of **posterus** and **poster**)

foolish, **absurdus, -a, -um**

foot, **pēs, pedis,** m.

for (on behalf of), **prō** + abl.; (because of), **ob** +acc.

for (conjunction), **enim; etenim; nam**

forbid, I, **vetō, -āre, uī, -itum, prohibeō,- ēre, -ui, -itum**

force, **vis,** acc. sing. **vim,** no gen. sing., abl. sing. **vī;** plur. reg. except gen. plur. **virium,** f.

forces, **cōpiae, -ārum,** f. pl.

forefinger, **index, -dicis,** m.

forgetful, **immemor, -ōris**

former (comparative of **priscus,** ancient), **prior, prius,** gen. **priōris**

formerly, **quondam; ōlim**

fort, **castrum, castrī,** n.

fortunate, **fēlīx,** gen. **fēlīcis**

foster-child (adjective used as noun), **alumnus, -a, -um**

foundation, **prīncipium, -iī,** n.; **stirps, stirpis,** f.

fountain, **fōns, fōntis,** m.

free, **līberus, -a, -um**

free, to set, **līberō, -āre, -āvī, -ātum**

freedom, **lībertās, -ātis,** f.

frenzied excitement (post-classical), **dēlīrium, -iī,** n.

friend, **amīcus, ī,** m.

friend (female), **amīca, -ae,** f.

fright, **horror, -ōris,** m.

frighten, I, **terreō, -ēre, -uī, -itum**

from, **ā, ab** +abl.

from all sides, **undique**

front of, in, **prae**

fruit, **fructus, fructūs,** m.

full (of), **plēnus, -a, -um**

further on, **infrā**

gap, **lacūna, -ae,** f.

garden, **hortus, -ī,** m.

Gaul, **Gallia, -iae** f.

Gauls, the, **Gallī, -ōrum**

general, **imperātor, -is,** m.; **dux, ducis,** m.

genuine, **vērus, -a, -um**

gift, **dōnum, -ī,** n.

girl, **puella, -ae,** f.

give, I, **dō, dare, dedī, datum**

give back, **reddō, -ere, reddidī, redditum**

glass, **vitrum, -ī,** n.

glimmer, **scintilla, -ae,** f.

gnaws, that which, **rōstrum, -ī,** n.

go, I, **eō, īre, īvī** or **iī, itum; vādō, vādere, vāsī;** (only with prefixes) **-gredior, -ī, -gressus sum; meō, meāre**

go away, I, **abeō, -īre, -īvī** or **-iī, -itum**

go to, against, over, I, **obeō, -īre, -iī, itum; aggredior, -ī, -gressus sum**

god, **deus, -eī** (irregular), m.

goddess, **dea, -ae,** f.

good, **bonus, -a, -um**

goodbye! **valē!**

grain, **grānum, ī,** n.

granting that, **licet**

great, **magnus, -a, -um**

great, very, **summus, -a, -um**

greatly, **magnopere**

Greek, **Graecus, -a, -um**

ground, **humus, -ī,** m.

grow (intrans.), **crēscō, -ere, crēvī, crētum**

grow up, I, **adolēscō,-ere, adultus sum**

guiding principle, **index, -dicis,** m.

hail (greeting), **avē! salvē!**

hallucinations, **dēlirium, -iī,** n.

hand, **manus, -ūs,** f.

happen, I, **adveniō, -venīre, -vēnī, -ventum; ēveniō, ēvenīre, ēvēnī, ēventum**

happily, **fēlīciter**

happy, **fēlīx,** gen. **fēlīcis**

hard, **dūrus, -a, -um**

hardness, **rigor, rigōris,** m.

hasten, I, **vādō, vādere, vāsī**

hate, **ōdī, ōdisse**

hatred, **odium, -iī,** n.

have, I, **habeō, -ēre, -uī, -itum**

head, **caput, capitis,** n.

healing, art of or means of, **medicīna, -ae,** f.

healthy, **sānus, -a, -um**

hear, I, **audiō, -īre, -īvī, -ītum**

heavy, **gravis, -ie**

hello! **salvē!**

help, **auxilium, -ī,** n.

help, I, **iuvō, -āre, iūvī, iūtum**

help, one called in to, especially as adviser in a lawsuit, advocate, **advocātus, -ī,** m.

here, **hīc** (or **hūc** if the meaning is 'to this place')

here and there, **passim**

hero, **hērōs, -ōis,** m.

high, **altus, -a, -um**

highly, **valdē**

hinder, I, **impediō, -īre, -īvī, -ītum**

hindrance, **impedimentum, -ī,** n.

hither, **hūc**

hold, I, **teneō, tenēre, tenuī, tentum; hābeō, -ēre, -uī, -itum**

hold, I take hold of, **apprehendō, -endere, ensī, -ensum**

hollow, **lacūna, -ae,** f.

home, **domus, -ūs,** f.

honour, **honōs, -ōris,** m.

honour, done or given as, **honōrārius, -a, -um**

honourable, **praeclarus, -a, -um**

hope, **spēs, spēī,** f.

hope, I, **spērō, -āre, -āvī, -ātum**

hope, I am without, **dēspērō, -āre, -āvī, -ātum** (both transitive and intransitive)

horn, **cornū, cornūs,** n.

horse, **equus, -ī,** m.

hour, **hōra, -ae,** f.

house, **domus, -ūs,** f.

how, **quemadmodum**

how (in what manner)?, **quōmodo …?**

how (interrogative adverb used with another adverb), **quam**

how great, **quantus, -a, -um**

however, **tamen; quamquam, utut**

however much, **quamvīs**

huge, **ingēns, -tis**

hunger, **famēs, famis,** f.

hunt, chase, I, **vēnor, vēnārī, vēnātus**

hurry, I, **festīnō, -āre, -āvī, -ātum**

hurt, I, **noceō, -ēre, uī, -itum**
(+ dat.); **laedō, laedere, laesī,
laesum**
hypothesis, **hypothesis, -is,** f.

idle, **ignāvus, -a, -um**
if, **sī**
if not, **nisi, sī nōn**
if only, **sī modo**
ignorant, be ... of, **ignōrō, -āre,
-āvī, -ātum**
ill, I am, **aegrōtō, -āre, āvī, -ātum**
immediately, **statim, īlicō**
impediment, **impedimentum, -ī,** n.
impossible (medieval Latin, though
classical Latin had **possibilis,**
derived from **possum**),
**impossibilis, -ile**
in (within), **in** + abl.
in as much as, **siquidem**
in this way, **sīc; hōc modō**
in vain, **frustrā; nēquīquam**
incidentally, in passing, **obiter**
increase, I, **augeō, augēre, auxī,
auctum** (transitive)
incredible, **incredibilis**
indeed, **vērē, quidem**
indiscriminately, **passim**
infinite, **infinītus, -a, -um**
influence, **auctōritās, -ātis,** f.
informs or indicates, one that,
**index, -dicis,** m.
infrequent, **rārus, -a, -um**
injure, I, **laedō, laedere, laesī,
laesum**
inquire, I, **interrogō, -āre, -āvī,
-ātum**
insane, be, **dēlīrō, -āre**
inside, **intrā**
instantly, **īlicō**
intention, **cōnsilium, cōnsiliī,** n.
interchange, **vicis** (gen.; there is no
nom.), (abl.) **vice,** f.
interregnum, **interrēgnum, -ī,** n.
into, **in** + acc.
introduce, I, **intrōdūcō, -dūcere,
-duxī, -ductum**
invade, I, **invādō, invādere, invāsī,
invāsum**
invincible, **invincibilis**

iron, **ferrum, - ī,** n.
iron, of, **ferreus, -a, -um**
issue, **eventus, -ūs,** m.
Italy, **Italia, -ae,** f.
ivory, **ebur, eboris,** n.

javelin, **tēlum, -ī,** n.
join battle, I, **proelium committō,
-mittere, -mīsī, -missum**
join together, I, **iūngō, -ere, iūnxī,
iūnctum**
journey, **iter, itineris,** n.
judge, **iūdex, -icis,** c.
judge, I, **reor, rērī, rātus sum**
judgement-seat, **tribūnal, -ālis,** n.
Jupiter, **Iuppiter, Iovis,** m.
just, **iustus, -a, -um**
just as, **quasi**

keenly, **ācriter**
kernel of a nut, **nucleus, -iī,**
m. (diminutive of **nux, nucis,**
f., nut)
kill, I, **occīdō, occīdere, -cīdī,
-cīsum; interficiō, -ficere,
-fēcī,- fectum; necō, -āre, -āvī,
-ātum**
kiss, **ōsculum, -ī,** n.
kind, **almus, -a, um**
kind, **genus, generis,** n.
king, **rēx, rēgis,** m.
kingdom, **rēgnum, -ī,** n.
know, I, **sciō, scīre, scīvī, scītum**
know, not to, **nesciō, nescīre,
nescīvī, -ītum**
know (get to know), I, **nōscō,
nōscere, nōvī, nōtum**

labour, I, **labōrō, -āre, -āvī, -ātum;
operor, operārī, operātus sum**
lack, I, **egeō, -ēre, -uī**
land, **terrā, -ae,** f.
Latin (adj.) **Latīnus, -a, -um**
Latin (n.) **lingua Latīna**
Latin, skill in, **latinitās, ātis,** f.
language, **lingua, -ae,** f.
last, **ultimus, -a, -um**
last, at, **tandem**
lately, **nūper**
later, **posterior, posterius**

(comparative of **posterus** and **poster**)

laugh, I, **rīdeō, rīdēre, rīsī, rīsum**

Lavinia, **Lavinia -ae**, f. (a town in Latium, where Rome was eventually built)

Lavinian, **Lāvīnius, -a, -um**

law, **lex, lēgis**, m.; **iūs, iūris**, n.

lawful, it is, **licet, licēre, licuit** or **licitum est**

layout, **situs, -ūs**, m.

lazy, **ignāvus, -a, -um**

lead, I, **dūcō, dūcere, dūxī, ductum**

lead away, abduct, I, **abdūcō, abdūcere, abdūxī, abductum**

leader, **dux, ducis**, c.

learn, I, **discō, discere, didicī**

least, **minimus, -a, -um** (superlative of parvus)

leave, I (a thing), **relinquō, -linquere, -līquī, -lictum**; (a place), **abeō, īre, īvī** or **iī, ītum**

leg, **crūs, crūris**, n.

lesser, **minor, -ōris** (comparative of **parvus**)

lest, **nē; ut nē**

letter, **epistola** or **epistula, -ae**, f.

letter of the alphabet, pl. writing, literature, document, **littera, -ae**, f.

life, **vīta, -ae**, f.

light, **lūx, lūcis**, f.

light (in weight), **levis, -is**

light, become, **lūcēscō, -ere**

lighten (lightning), **fulgurō, -āre**

like, **similis, -e**

limit, **modus, -ī**, m.

line-of-battle, **aciēs, -ēī**, f.

lion, **leō, leōnis**, m.

little, **parvus, -a, -um; paulus, -a, -um**

littleness, **minūtia, -ae**, f.

live, I (I am alive), **vīvō, vīvere, vīxī, victum**

live, I (I dwell), **habitō, -āre, -āvī, -ātum; incolō, -colere, -coluī**

living, of a living person, **vīvus, -a, -um**

London, **Londinium, Londiniī**, n.

long, **longus, -a, -um**

long time, for a, **diū**

loose, **rārus, -a, -um**

loose or loosen, I, **solvō, -ere, solvī, solūtum**

lord, **dominus, -ī**, m.

loss, **lacūna, -ae**, f.

love, **amor, amōris**, m.

love, I, **amō, -āre, -āvī, -ātum**

lower down, **infrā**

machine, **machina, -ae**, f.

maiden, **virgō, virginis**, f.

make, I, **faciō, facere, fēcī, factum; creō, -āre, -āvī, -ātum**

man (as in mankind/human), **hōmō, hominis**, c.; (as opposed to woman), **vir, -ī**, m.

manifold, **multiplex, -icis**

manly, **virīlis, virīle**

manner, **modus, -ī**, m.

manuscript book, **cōdex, cōdicis**, m.

many, **multus, -a, -um**

march, **iter, itineris**, n.

March (the month of), **martius, -a, -um**

mark, mark out, I, **notō, -āre, -āvī, -ātum**

marry, I (of man), **dūcō, dūcere, dūxī, ductum (in matrimonium)**

marry, I (of the bride), **nūbō, nūbere, nūpsī, nūptum**

mast (of ship), **mālus, - ī**, m.

master, **magister, magistrī**, m.

matter, **rēs, rēī**, f.

meanwhile, **intereā, interim**

measure, **modus, -ī**, m.

meet, I, **congredior, -gredī, congressus sum**

meeting, **concilium,-iī**, n.

memory, **memoria, -ae**, f.

mental faculties, **mēns, mentis**, m.; in full possession of, **compos, -potis**

mention, I, **meminī, -isse**

merit, **dignitās, -ātis**

method, **modus, -ī**, m.

midday, **merīdiēs, -diēī**, m.

middle, **mēdius, -a, -um**

mile, **mille, milia** (plural of **mille**)
**passuum** (gen. plur. of **passūs**)*
mind, **animus, -ī,** m.; **mēns,**
**mentis,** m.
mindful, **memor, -ōris**
mirror, **speculum, - ī,** n.
mistaken, I am, **errō, -āre, -āvī,**
**-ātum**
modest, **pudicus, -a, -um**
moment, **articulus, -ī,** m.
money, **pecūnia, -ae,** f.
month, **mēnsis, -is,** m.
moon, **lūna, -ae,** f.
more, **plūs, plūris** (comparative of
**multus**)
more (adverb), **magis**
moreover, **autem, vērum, vērō**
mother, **māter, mātris,** f.
motto, **sententia, -ae,** f.
mountain, **mōns, mōntis,** m.
move, I, **moveō, movēre, mōvī,**
**mōtum** (trans.)
movement downwards (gradual),
**lapsus, -ūs,** m.
much, **multus, -a, -um**
must, I, **dēbeō, -ēre, -uī, -itum;**
(impersonal) **oportet**

name, **nōmen, nōminis,** n.;
surname, family name,
**cognōmen, -nōminis,** n.
nation, **populus, -ī,** m.
near, **prope** + acc., **propter** + acc.
need, I, **egeō, -ēre, -uī**
need, in, **inops, inopis**
neighbouring, **finitimus, -a, -um**
neither, never, **numquam**
neither . . . nor, **neque . . . neque,**
**nec . . . nec, nēve . . . nēve**
never, **numquam**
next, **proximus, -a, -um; posterior,**
**posterius** (comparative
of **posterus** and **poster**);
**secundum**
next to, **iuxtā**
no, **nullus, -a, -um**

no one, **nēmō, nēminis,** c.
noble, **nōbilis, -e**
noon, **merīdiēs, -diēī,** m.
nor, **nec, neque**
not, **nōn**
not know, I do, **ignōrō, -āre, -āvī,**
**-ātum**
not want, I do (I am unwilling),
**nōlō, nolle, nōluī**
not yet, **nōndum**
notable, **īnsignis**
nothing, **nihil,** n.; **nil,** n.
nourishing, **almus, -a, um**
now, **nunc, iam**
nursling (adj. used as noun),
**alumnus, -a, -um**

oath, **iūsiūrandum, -ī,** n.
oath, take, **iūrō, -āre, -āvī, -ātum**
obey, I, **pareō, -ēre, -uī, -itum** + dat.
observe, **notō, -āre, -āvī, -ātum**
obstruction, **impedīmentum, -ī,** n.
obtain request, I, **impetrō, -āre,**
**-āvī, -ātum**
occasion, **cāsus, -ī,** m.
occupied, I am, **operor, operārī,**
**operātus sum**
occurrence, **eventus, -ūs,** m.
of what sort, **quālis, -e**
offer, **dēferrō, dēferre, dētulī,**
**dēlātum**
often, **saepe**
old, **vetus, veteris;** (person) **senex,**
gen. **senis.**
old age, **senectūs, -ūtis,** f.
old man, **senex, senis,** m.
on, **in** + abl.
on account of, **ob** + acc.; **propter**
+ acc.
on guard against, be, **caveō, cavēre,**
**cāvī, cautum**
once (ordinal number), **semel**
once (formerly), **quondam**
once, at, **statim**
once upon a time, **ōlim**
one (number), **ūnus, -a, -um**
one, another, **alius, -a, -ud**
one, the other, **alter, -a, -um**
only, **sōlus, -a, -um,** gen. **solius,**
**modo, tantum**

* The Roman mile was 142 yards
shorter than is the English mile.

open, I, **aperiō, aperīre, aperuī, apertum**

open square, market place, **forum, -ī,** n.

opinion, **opīniō, -iōnis,** f.; (formally expressed) **sententia, -ae,** f.

opposite to, **adversus; contrā**

or, **aut;** (in questions) **an, vel; sīve, seu**

or not (in questions), **annōn**

origin, **prīncipium, -iī,** n.; **genus, generis,** n.; **orīgō, -iginis,** f.; **stirps, stirpis,** f.

orphan, of an (adj.; there is no equivalent adjective in English), **pupillāris, -is, -e**

orphan, **pupillus, -ī,** m.

other, of two, **alter, -a, -um**

other, another, **alius, - īus**

others, the, **cēterī, -ōrum,** m. pl.

otherwise, **aliās**

ought, I, **mē oportet**

out of, **ē, ex** + abl.

outdo, I, **superō, -āre, -āvī, -ātum**

outermost, **extremus, -a, -um**

outside, **extrā**

oval course for races, **circus, -ī,** m.

over (above), **suprā;** (movement over) **super** + abl.

overcome, I, **superō, -āre, -āvī, -ātum**

own, one's, **proprius, -a, -um**

pace, **passus, -ūs,** m.

pains, take, **operam dō, dāre, dedī, dātum**

part, **pars, partis,** f.

partnership, **cōnsortium, -iī,** n.

past, **praeter**

pattern, **exemplar, exemplāris,** n.

peace, **pāx, pācis,** f.

penalty, **poena, -ae,** f.

people (in the sense of a political community), **populus, -ī,** m.

perceive, **sentiō, -īre, sēnsī, sēnsum**

perform, I, **fungor, fungī, fūnctus sum**

perhaps, **forsitan**

permit, I, **patior, patī, passus sum**

perpetual, **perpetuus, -a, -um**

person represented by an actor, **persōna, -ae,** f.

persuade, I, **persuādeō, -suādēre, -suāsī, -suāsum** + dat.

pig, **sūs, sūis,** c.

pitch camp, I, **castra pōnō, pōnere, posuī**

pity, I, **mē miseret** + gen.

place, **locus, -ī,** m.

place of public business, **forum, -ī,** n.

plan, **cōnsilium, cōnsiliī,** n.

platform, **tribūnal, -ālis,** n.

platform used for public speaking, the Roman forum, **rōstrum, ī,** n.

play, **drāma, drāmatis,** f.

play, I, **lūdō, -ere, lūsī, lūsum**

pleasant, **dulcis, -e**

pleasantness, **grātia, -iae,** f.

pleases, it (impersonal) + dat. of the person being pleased, **libet, libēre, libuit, libitum; placet, placēre, placuit**

pleasing, **grātus, -a, -um**

pluck, **carpō, -pere, -psī, -ptum**

poet, **poeta, -ae,** m.

point out, **dēmōnstrō, -āre, -āvī, -ātum**

point to, **citō, -āre-, āvī, -ātum**

politics, **rēs publicae, rērum publicārum,** pl.

Pompey, **Pompeius, Pompeiī,** m.

poor, **pauper, pauperis**

popular belief or rumour, **vōx populī**

port, **portus, -ūs,** m.

position, **situs, -ūs,** m.; **status, -ūs,** m.

position changed, with, **vice versā**

possession of, I get (+ abl.), **potior, -īrī, potītus sum**

pound-weight of twelve ounces (Roman), **lībra, -ae,** f.

pour, I, **fundō, -ere, fūdī, fūsum**

power (absolute), **imperium, -iī,** n.

powerful, **potēns, -entis**

praise, **laus, laudis,** f.

praise, I, **laudō, -āre, -āvī, -ātum**

pray, I, **precor, -ārī, ātus sum**

prayer, **precem** (no nom. sing.), **precis,** f.

prefer, I, **mālō, mālle, māluī**

prepare, I, **parō, -āre, -āvī, -ātum**

presence of, in the, **coram**

present, I am, **adsum, adesse, adfuī**

press into, press upon, I, **imprimō, -primere, -pressī, -pressum; premō, -ere, pressī, pressum**

priest or priestess, **sacerdōs, sacerdōtis,** c.

print, I, **imprimō, -primere, -pressī, -pressum**

prison, **carcer, carceris,** m.

prisoner, **captīvus, -ī,** m.

produce, I, **creō, -āre, -āvī, -ātum**

profound, **profundus, -a, -um**

project, I, **exsto or extō, -āre, -āvī, -ātum**

promise, I, **polliceor, -ērī, -itus sum; promittō, -mittere, -mīsī, -missum**

promote, **prōmoveō, promovēre, promōvī, promōtum**

proof, **argūmentum, -ī,** n.

prosper, I, **floreō, -ēre, -uī, -itum**

prosperous, **prōsperus, -a, um**

protuberance, **tumor, -ōris,** m.

provided that, **modo, dummodo**

public, belonging to the people, **publicus, -a, -um**

public opinion, **vox populī**

punish, I, **pūniō, -īre, -īvī, -ītum**

punishment, **poena, -ae,** f.; **supplicium, -ī,** n.

purchaser, **emptor, -ōris,** m.

pursue, **prōsequor, -sequī, -secūtus sum**

put in, put on, **impōnō, -pōnere, -posuī, -positum**

queen, **rēgīna, -ae,** f.

question, **quaestiō, - iōnis,** f.

quickly, **celeriter;** as quickly as possible, **quam celerrimē**

race (competitive), **curriculum, ī,** n.

race, family, **gēns, gentis,** f.

race-course, **stadium, stadiī,** n.

rain, **imber, imbris,** m.

rare, **rārus, -a, -um**

read, I, **legō, legere, lēgī, lectum**

real, **vērus, -a, -um**

really, **vērē**

reason, **causa, -ae,** f.; **ratiō, ratiōnis,** f.

receive, I, **accipiō, -accipere, -cēpī, -ceptum**

recently, **nūper**

reckon, **reor, rērī, rātus sum**

reckoned, **rātus, -a, -um** (past participle of **reor**)

recollect, I, **meminī, -isse**

recollection, **memoria, -ae,** f.

red, I am, **rubeō, rubērē**

rejoice, I, **gaudeō, gaudēre, gāvisus sum**

remain, I, **māneō, manēre, mansī, mansum**

remember (imperative of **meminī, -isse**), **memento;** (ability to), **memoria, -ae,** f.

remembrance, time of, **memoria, -ae,** f.

remove, I, **amoveō, amovēre, amōvī, amōtum**

renowned, **nōbilis, -e**

repent (impersonal), **paenitet, paenituit**

repose, I, **requiescō, -quiescere, -quiēvī, -quiētum**

resist, I, **resistō, -sistere, -stitī, -stitum** + dat.

rest, I, **requiescō, -quiescere, -quiēvī, -quiētum**

rest of, remainder, **rēliquus, -a, -um**

rest, the; the others, **cēterī, -ōrum,** m. pl.

restoration, **reductiō, -iōnis,** f.

result, **eventus, -ūs,** m.

retard, I, **retardō, -āre, -āvī, -ātum**

return, I, **redeō, -īre, -īvī** or **-iī, -itum, redeō, -īre, -īvī** or **-iī, -itum** (intrans.)

reveal, uncover, I, **detegō, dētegere, dētēxī, dētēctum**

reward, **praemium, praemiī,** n.

rhetorical figure of speech in which an orator answered his own question, **suggestiō, -iōnis,** f.

rich, **dīves, -itis**

right, set, I, **corrigō, -rigere, -rēxī, -rēctum**

right (law), **iūs, iūris,** n.

rigidity, **rigor, rigōris,** m.

ring, **circus, -ī,** m.

ripe, mature, early, **mātūrus, -a, -um**

river, **flūmen, -minis,** n.

road, **iter, itineris,** n.; **via, -ae,** f.

robber, **lātrō, lātrōnis,** m.

Roman, **rōmānus, -a, -um**

Rome, **Rōma, -ae,** f.

room, **conclāve, -is,** n

root, **stirps, stirpis,** f.; **rādix, rādīcis,** f.

rose, **rosa, -ae,** f.

rout, **fundō, -ere, fūdī, fūsum**

route, **iter, itineris,** n.

rule, **rēgnum, -ī,** n.

rule, I, **regō, regere, rēxī, rēctum**

run, I, **currō, currere, cucurrī, cursum**

running, **curriculum, ī,** n.

rush, I, **vādō, vādere, vāsī**

rush in, attack, I, **irruō, irruere, irruī**

sad, **trīstis, -e**

safety, **salūs, -ūtis,** f.

sail, set, I, **solvō, -ere, solvī, solūtum**

sailor, **nauta, -ae,** m.

salt, **sāl, -is,** m.

same, **īdem, ēadem, idem**

same time, at the, **simul**

sample, **exemplum, -ī,** n.

save, I, **servō, -āre, -āvī, -ātum**

say, I, **dīcō, dīcere, dīxī, dictum; inquam** (irreg.)

scales, pair of (balance), **lībra, -ae,** f.

scarcely, hardly, **vix**

sea, **mare, maris,** n.; **aequor, aequoris,** n.

sea-shore, **lītus, lītoris,** n.

seasickness, **nausea, -eae,** f.

seat, **sella, ae,** f.

second, **secundus, -a, -um**

see, I, **videō, vidēre, vīdī, vīsum**

seem, I (passive of **videō,** to see), **videor, -ērī, vīsus sum**

seer, **augur, -uris,** c.

seize, I, **rapiō, -ere, -uī, raptum; invādō, invādere, invāsī, invāsum**

self, **ipse, -a, -um**

sell, I, **vendō, -dere, -didī, -ditum**

senate, **senātus, -ūs,** m.

senate, meeting-place of senators in Rome, hence court, **cūria, -ae,** f.

senator, **senātor, oris,** m.

send, I, **mittō, mittere, mīsī, missum**

set aside, **dēpōnō, dēpōnere, dēposuī, dēpositum**

set free, I, **līberō, āre, āvī, -ātum**

set out, I, **proficīscor, -ficīscī, -fectus sum**

several, **aliquot**

shameful, **turpis, -e; inhonestus, -a, -um**

shift, I, **mutō, -āre, -āvī, -ātum**

ship, **nāvis, -is,** f.

shore, **lītus, lītoris,** n.

short, **brēvis, -e**

show clearly, **dēmōnstrō, -āre, -āvī, -ātum**

shuddering, **horror, -oris,** m.

shut, I, **claudō, claudere, clausī, clausum**

sick (adjective), **aeger, aegra, aegrum**

sick, I am, **aegrōtō, -āre, -āvī, -ātum**

side of, on this, **cis, citrā**

sight of, in, **palam**

since, **cum, quoniam**

sing, I, **canō, canere, cecinī, cantum; cantō, -āre, -āvī, -ātum**

sister, **soror, -ōris,** f.

sit, I, **sedeō, sedēre, sēdī, sessum**

site, **situs, -ūs,** m.

situation, **situs, -ūs,** m.

skill, **ars, artis,** f.

skill in Latin, **latinitās, -ātis,** f.

slave, **servus, ī,** m.

sleep, I, **dormiō, -īre, -īvī, -ītum**

slender, **gracilis**

sliding fall, **lapsus, -ūs,** m.

slip, **lapsus, -ūs,** m.

slow, **lentus, -a, -um**

small, **parvus, -a, -um**

small joint, **articulus, -ī,** m.

smaller, **minor, -ōris** (comparative of **parvus**)

smallest, **minimus, -a, -um** (superlative of **parvus**)

smallness, **minūtia, -ae,** f.

snows, it, **ningit, ninguit**

so (adv.), **ita**

so (in this way), **sīc**

so (to such an extent), **tam**

so . . . as, **sīc . . . ut; tam . . . quam**

so great, so much, **tantus, -a, -um**

so long as, **dum, dōnec, quoad**

so much, **tantopere**

so that, **ut**

so that not, **ut nōn**

soldier, **mīles, mīlitis,** m.

something, **aliquid**

sometimes, **nōnnumquam**

son, **fīlius, fīliī,** m.

song, **carmen, carminis,** n.

soon, **mox**

soothsayer, **augur, -uris,** c.

sound (healthy), **sānus, -a, -um**

source, ancestor, **orīgō, -īginis,** f.

source, origin (of people), **stirps, stirpis,** f.

space, interval, **spatium, -iī,** n.

spare, I, **parcō, parcere, pepercī, parsum** + dat.

spark, **scintilla, -ae**

speak, I, **loquor, loquī, locūtus sum**

speak against, I, **contrādīcō, -dīcere, -dīxī, -dictum**

speaker, **ōrātor, ōrātōris,** m.

spear, **hasta, -ae,** f.

special, **proprius, -a, -um**

speech, **lingua, -ae,** f.

speed, **celeritās, -ātis,** f.

sports-ground, **stadium, stadiī,** n.

spouse, **coniūnx, coniugis,** c.

spring, **fōns, fontis,** m.

spur, **calcar, -āris,** n.

stand, I, **stō, stāre, stetī, stātum**

stand around, **circumstō, -stāre, -stetī, -statum**

stand out, I, **exstō** or **extō, -āre, -āvī, -ātum**

standing, **status, -ūs,** m.

start up, **citō, -āre-, āvī, -ātum**

state, **cīvitās, -ātis,** f.; **rēspublica, reipublicae,** f.

state (condition), **status, -ūs,** m.

statesmanship, **rēs publicae, rērum publicārum,** pl.

statue, **statua, -ae,** f.

stay, I, **moror, morārī, morātus sum**

stem (of trees or other plants), **stirps, stirpis,** f.

step, pace, **gradus, -ūs,** m.

stern, **torvus, -a, -um**

stiffness, **rigor, rigōris,** m.

stock, **stirps, stirpis,** f.

stone, **lapis, -idis,** m.

stone of a fruit, **nucleus, -ī,** m. (diminutive of **nux, nucis,** f., nut)

stop, **dēsistō, dēsistere, dēstitī, dēstitum**

straight, put, I, **corrigō, -rigere, -rēxī, -rēctum**

stratagem, **māchina, -ae,** f.

stray, I, **errō, -āre, -āvī, -ātum**

street, **via, -ae,** f.

strength, **vīrēs, virium** (gen. pl.)

strong, I am, **valeō, -ere, -uī, valitum** (the post-classical **valui, -ōris,** m. is derived from it)

strong (of men), **fortis, -e;** (of things) **firmus, -a, -um**

successfully, **fēliciter**

suddenly, **subitō**

suffer, I, **patior, patī, passus sum**

suggestion, **suggestiō, -iōnis,** f.

suitable, **idōneus, -a, -um**

summon, I, **citō, -āre-, āvī, -ātum**

sun, **sōl, sōlis,** m.

suppression, dishonest, **suppressiō, -iōnis,** f.

surely . . .? **nōnne**

surely not . . .? **num**

surname, family name, **cognōmen, -nōminis,** n.

swear, I, **iūrō, -āre, -āvī, -ātum**

sweet, **dulcis, -e**

swelling, **tumor, -ōris,** m.
swift, **celer, -eris, -ere; vēlox, -ōcis**
swiftly, **vēlōciter, celeriter**

table, **mēnsa, -ae,** f.
tablet, **cōdex, cōdicis,** m.
take, **capiō, capere, cēpī, captum**
teach, I, **dōceō, -ēre, -uī, doctum**
teacher, **doctor, -ōris,** m.;
    **magister, magistri,** m.
tear (of weeping), **lacrima, -ae,** f.
tell, I, **dīcō, dīcere, dīxī, dictum**
tender, **tener, tenera, tenerum**
terrifying, **horribilis**
territory, **fines, -ium,** m. (pl. of
    **finis**)
than, **quam**
thanks, **grātia, -iae,** f.
that, is, **ea, id; ille, illa, illud**
that not, **quīn; ut nē**
theatrical role, theatrical part,
    **persōna, -ae,** f.
then, **deinde, tum, tunc**
thence, from there, **inde**
there, **ibi**
therefore, **igitur; ergō, itaque**
thin, **rārus, -a, -um**
thing, **rēs, rcī,** f.
think, I, **cogitō, -āre, -āvī, -ātum**
    (reflect, have ideas); **putō, -āre,**
    **-āvī, -ātum** (believe, suppose);
    **arbitror, -ārī, -ātus sum** (hold a
    well-considered opinion); **reor,**
    **rērī, rātus sum** (reckon)
this, **hīc, haec, hōc**
thousand, a, **mille**
thousands, **mīlia, milum,** n. pl.
throat, **iugulum, -ī,** n.
through, **per** + acc.
throw, I, **cōniciō, -icere, -iēcī,**
    **-iectum; iaciō, iacere, iēcī,**
    **iactum**
thrust, **petītiō, -iōnis,** f.
thunder, **tonō, -āre, tonuī**
thus, **sīc, ita**
time, **tempus, -oris,** n.
tired, **fessus, -a, -um**
to, towards, **ad** + acc.
today, **hodiē**
together, **ūnā**

toil, **labor, -ōris,** m.
tomorrow, **crās**
tongue, **lingua, -ae,** f.
tool, **instrūmentum, -ī,** n.
tooth, **dēns, dentis,** m.
top, on . . . of, adj., **summus, -a,**
    **-um**
torture, **supplicium, -ii,** n.
touch, I, **tangō, -ere, tetigī, tāctum**
towards, **ad** + acc.; **versus**
town, **oppidum, -ī,** n.
treasure (a latinised version of the
    Greek word meaning treasure),
    **thesaurus, -ī,** m.
trick, **māchina, -ae,** f.
trouble, take, I, **operam dō, dāre,**
    **dedī, dātum**
troops, forces, **cōpiae, -ārum,** pl.
Troy, **Trōia, -ae,** f.
true, **vērus, -a, -um**
truly, **vērē**
trunk (of tree), **cōdex, cōdicis,** m.
trust, **fides, -eī,** f.
trust, I, **fidō, -ere, fisus sum**
trust (medieval Latin), I, **affidō,**
    **-āre, āvī, -ātum**
truth, **veritās, -ātis,** f.
try, I, **conor, -ārī, -ātus sum**
turn (trans.), **vertō, -ere, vertī,**
    **versum**
twice, **bis**
tying together, **nexus, -ūs,** m.

under, **sub** + acc. or abl.; **subter** +
    acc. or abl.
underneath, **infrā**
understand, I, **intellegō, -legere,**
    **-lēxī, -lēctum**
unfitting, disgraceful, it is, **dēdecet,**
    **-ēre, dēdecuit**
unhappy, **infēlix, infēlīcis**
universe, **mundus, -ī,** m.
unknown to (secretly), **clam**
unless, **nisi, nī**
unlike, **dissimilis, -e**
unlucky, **infēlix, infēlicis** (gen.)
unreasonable, **absurdus, -a, -um**
unwilling, I am, **nōlō, nōlle, nōluī**
up and down, **passim**
upon, **super**

urge, I, **suādeō, -ēre, suāsī, suāsum**
use, I, **ūtor, ūtī, ūsus sum** (+ abl.)
use, **ūsus, -ūs,** m.
useful, **utilis, -e**
useless, **inutilis**

vain, in, **frustrā**
value, **valor, -ōris**
vex (it vexes me), **mē piget, piguit**
  (impersonal verb + gen. of cause)
victory, **victōria, -ae,** f.
virtue, **virtūs, virtūtis,** f.
virtuous, **honestus, -a, -um**
voice, **vōx, vōcis,** f.
voice of the people, **vōx populī**
void, **vacuus, -a, -um**

wage (war), I, **gerō, gerere, gessī,**
  **gestum**
wall, **mūrus, -ī,** m.
wander, **errō, -āre, -āvī, -ātum**
want (wish), I, **volō, velle, vōluī**
war, **bellum, -ī,** n.
warn, I, **moneō, -ēre, -uī, -itum**
waste, I lay, **vastō, -āre-, āvī, -ātum**
water, **aqua, -ae,** f.
way (method), **modus, -ī,** m.
way (road, route), **via, -ae,** f.
weapon, **tēlum, -ī,** n.
wear out, I, **cōnficiō, cōnficere,**
  **cōnfēcī, cōnfectum**

weary (it wearies me), **mē taedet +**
  gen. of cause
weep, I, **fleō, -ēre, flēvī, flētum;**
  **lacrimō, -āre, -āvī -ātum**
well (adv. from **bonus**), **bene**
when?, **quandō?**
when (conjunction); where?
  (interrogative adverb), **ubi**
while (adv.), **dum**
why, wherefore, **quāre**
wide, **lātus, -a, -um**
widely, **lātē**
winter, **hiems, hiemis,** f.
wisdom, **sapientia, -ae,** f.
wise, **sapiēns, -entis**
wish, I, **volō, velle, voluī**
with, **cum** + abl.
without, **sine** + abl.
woe, **vae**
woman, **fēmina, -ae,** f.
word, **verbum, -ī,** n.
worse, **pêior, pêiōris**
worst, **pessimus, -a, -um**
worthy, **dignus, -a, -um**
wound, I, **vulnerō, -āre, -āvī -ātum**
wretched, **miser, misera, miserum**

year, **annus, -ī,** m.
yesterday, **herī**
young man, **iuvenis, -is,** m.
younger, **iūnior, iūnioris**

# LATIN–ENGLISH

**abdūcō, abdūcere, abdūxī,**
  **abductum,** I lead away, abduct
**abeō, abīre, -īvī, -itum,** I go away
**abhinc,** ago
**absentia, -ae,** f., absence
**absurdus, -a, -um,** that which
  offends the ear, unmelodious,
  foolish, unreasonable, absurd
**ac,** and
**accēdō, accēdere, accessī,**
  **accessum,** I approach
**accipiō, accipere, -cēpī, -ceptum,** I
  receive, accept
**ācer, ācris, ācre,** adj. sharp

**aciēs, -ēī,** f., line of battle
**ācriter,** keenly, fiercely
**ad,** + acc., to, towards
**addō, -ere, addidī, additum,** I
  bring to, add
**adeō, adīre, -īvī, -itum,** I
  approach
**adeō,** so far, so, what is more.
**adipiscor, -piscī, adeptus sum,** I
  acquire
**admīror, -ārī, -ātus sum,** I admire,
  wonder at
**adolēscō,-ere, adultus sum,** I
  grow up

adoro

adsum, adesse, adfuī, I am present

adulēscēns, -entis, m., youth

adveniō, -venīre, -vēnī, -ventum, I come to, happen

adversus, against, opposite to

advocātus, -ī, m., one called in to help, especially as adviser in a lawsuit, advocate

aedificō, -āre, -āvī, -ātum, I build

aeger, aegra, aegrum, sick, ill

aegrōtō, -āre, āvī, -ātum, I am ill

Aenēās, -ae, m., Aeneas (the hero of Virgil's *Aeneid*)

aequor, aequoris, n., sea

affīdō, -āre, āvī, -ātum, I trust (medieval Latin)

Africa, -ae, f., Africa

ager, agrī, m., field

agmen, agminis, n., army on the march

agō, āgere, ēgī, actum, I do, drive

agricola, -ae, m., farmer

aiō, I say yes, affirm, assert

alias, at another time, otherwise, elsewhere

alibī, elsewhere

aliquandō, sometimes

aliquid, something

aliquot, some, several

alius, -a, -ud, other

almus, -a, um, nourishing, kind

alter, altera, alterum, one (of two), the other

altus, -a, -um, high, deep

alumnus, -a, -um (adj. used as noun) nursling, foster-child

amīca, -ae, f., friend (female)

amīcus, -ī, m., friend (male)

amō, -āre, -āvī, -ātum, I love

amor, amōris, m., love

amoveō, amovēre, amōvī, amōtum, I remove

an (in questions), or

Anglia, -ae, f., England

animus, -ī, m., soul, spirit

annus, -ī, m., year

ante + acc., before

antequam, before that

aperiō, aperīre, aperuī, apertum, I open

apprehendō, -endere, ensī, -ensum, take hold of

appropinquō, -āre, -āvī, -ātum, I approach

aptus, -a, -um, suitable, fitting, fit for

apud + acc., at the house of, among

aqua, -ae, f., water

arbitror, -ārī, -ātus sum, I think

ardeō, -ēre, arsī, arsum, be on fire

argūmentum, -ī, n., argument, proof

arma, -ōrum, n. pl., arms, armour

ars, artis, f., skill, work of art

articulus, -ī, m., small joint (in the body), moment, crisis

asinus, -ī, m., donkey

assideō, -idēre, -ēdī, -essum, attend, be present at

at, but

atque, and

atquī, but yet

auctōritās, -ātis, f., influence

audeō, audēre, ausus sum, I dare

audiō, -īre, -īvī, -ītum, I hear

augeō, augēre, auxī, auctum, I increase (trans.)

augur, -uris, c., augur, soothsayer, seer

auris, -is, f., ear

aut . . . aut, either . . . or

aut, or

autem, adv., moreover

auxilium, -iī, n., help

avē! (greeting) hail!

avis, -is, f., bird

baccalaureus, -ī, m., a corruption of baccalarius, -ī, m. bachelor (medieval Latin)

barba, -ae, f., beard

barbarus, -ī, m., barbarian

bellum, -ī, n., war

bene (adv. from bonus), well

benedīcō, -dīcere, -dīxī, -dictum, I bless (post-classical Latin)

bis, twice

bonus, -a, -um, good

**brevis, -e,** short
**Britannia, -iae,** f., Britain
**Britannicus, -a, -um,** British
**Britannus, -a, -um,** Briton

**cadō, cadere, cecidī, cāsum,** I fall
**Caesar, Caesaris,** m. Caesar
**calcar, -āris,** n, spur
**camera, -ae,** f., chamber
**canis, -is,** m., dog
**canō, canere, cecinī, cantum,** I
    sing
**cantō, -āre, -āvī, -ātum,** I sing
**capiō, capere, cepī, captum,** I take,
    capture
**captīvus, -ī,** m., prisoner
**caput, capitis,** n., head; a person's
    life, his existence, his status, his
    political or social rights
**carcer, carceris,** m., prison
**carmen, carminis,** n., song
**carpō, -pere, -psī, -ptum,** I pluck
**Carthāginiēnsis, -is,** Carthaginian
**Carthāgō, -inis,** f., Carthage
**cārus, -a, -um,** dear
**castra, -ōrum,** n. pl., camp
**castrum, castrī,** n., fort
**cāsus, -ī,** m., falling, fall, occasion,
    opportunity
**cathedra, -ae,** f., chair, professor's
    chair, official chair
**causa, -ae,** f., cause, reason
**caveō, cavēre, cāvī, cautum,** I am
    on guard against, beware
**cēdō, cēdere, cessī, cessum,** I yield
**celeber, celebris, celebre,** famous
**celebritās, -ātis,** f., crowd,
    multitude, fame, renown
**celer, -eris, -ere,** swift
**celeritās, -ātis,** f., speed
**celeriter,** quickly
**cēnō, -āre, -āvī, -ātum,** dine
**cēnsor, -ōris,** m, censor
**cēterī, -ōrum,** m. pl., the rest, the
    others
**circa, circum,** + acc., around
**circumstō, -stāre, -stetī, -statum,**
    stand around
**circus, -ī,** m., ring, oval course for
    races

**cis, citrā,** on this side of
**citō, -āre-, -āvī, -ātum,** I put into
    violent motion, excite, start up,
    summon, appeal to (authorities),
    point to
**cīvīlis, -e,** civil
**cīvis, -is,** c., citizen
**cīvitās, -ātis,** f., state
**clam,** unknown to
**clāritās, -ātis,** f,. clearness,
    brightness, fame, celebrity,
    renown
**classicus, -a, um,** relating to the
    classes into which Roman
    citizens were divided, especially
    relating to the highest class
    (**classis, is,** f.)
**classis, -is,** f., class (political or
    social), fleet
**claudō, claudere, clausī, clausum,**
    I shut
**cōdex, cōdicis,** m., tree trunk,
    tablet, book, early manuscript
    book
**coepī,** I have begun
**cognōmen, -nōminis,** n., surname,
    family name
**cognōscō, -nōscere, -nōvī,**
    **-nitum,** I learn, discover
**collēga, -ae,** m., colleague
**comes, -itis,** c., companion
**compos, -potis,** having the
    mastery of, in full possession of
    (**mentis,** of mental faculties)
**concilium, -iī,** n., council
**conclāve, -is,** n., room
**concordō, -āre, āvī, ātum,** I agree
**condiciō, -iōnis,** f., condition,
    terms, agreement
**cōnfectus, -a, -um,** worn out
**cōnferō, cōnferre, contulī,**
    **collātum,** I bring together, I
    compare
**cōnfiteor, -fitērī, fessus,** confess
**congredior, -ī, congressus sum,** I
    meet, come together
**cōniciō, -icere, -iēcī, -iectum,** I
    throw
**coniūnx, coniugis,** c., spouse, wife;
    (rarely) husband

**coniūrō, -āre, -āvī, -ātum,** I take an oath together, conspire

**cōnor, -ārī, -ātus sum,** I try

**cōnsentiō, -sentīre, -sēnsī, -sēnsum,** I agree

**cōnsilium, -iī, n.,** advice, plan, intention

**cōnsortium, -iī, n.,** partnership

**cōnstans, -antis,** firm, immovable, constant

**cōnstituō, -uere, -uī, -ūtum,** I decide, determine

**consul, -is, m.,** consul

**contrā, + acc.,** opposite to, against

**contrādīcō, -dīcere, -dīxī, -dictum,** I speak against, contradict

**conveniō, -venīre, -vēnī, -ventum,** I come together, assemble

**cōpia, -ae, f.,** supply, plenty

**cōpiae, -ārum, pl.,** forces, troops

**coram,** in the presence of

**cornū, cornūs, n.,** horn

**corpus, -ōris, n.,** body

**corrigō, -rigere, -rēxī, -rēctum,** I put straight, set right, correct

**crās,** tomorrow

**credō, -dere, -didī, -ditum,** I believe

**creō, -āre, -āvī, -ātum,** I create, make, produce, elect to an office

**crēscō, -ere, crēvī, crētum,** I grow (intrans.)

**crīmen, -inis, n.,** crime, offence

**crūs, crūris, n.,** leg

**cubīle, -is, n.,** couch

**culpa, -ae, f.,** fault, blame

**culpō, -āre, -āvī, -ātum,** I blame

**cum, conj.,** since, whereas, although

**cum, prep. (+ abl.),** with

**cupīdō, -cupīdinis, f.,** desire, longing

**cupidus, -a, -um,** desirous, eager, ardent, passionate

**cupiō, -ere, -īvī or -iī, -ītum,** I desire

**cur,** interrogative adv., why?

**cūra, -ae, f.,** care, concern

**cūria, -ae, f.,** meeting-place of the Senate in Rome, hence court

**cūrō, -āre, -āvī, -ātum,** I care for, bother about

**curriculum, ī, n.,** running, race, course

**currō, currere, cūcurrī, cursum,** I run

**currus, -ūs, m.,** chariot

**dē, + abl.,** about, concerning

**dēa, -ae, f.,** goddess

**dēbeō, -ēre, -uī, -itum,** I owe, must

**decet, -ēre, decuit,** it is fitting

**dēdecet, -ēre, dēdecuit,** it is unfitting, disgraceful

**dēfendō, -fendere, -fendī, -fensum,** I defend

**dēferrō, dēferre, dētulī, dēlātum,** I bring down, offer

**deinde,** then

**dēlectō, -āre,** I delight

**dēleō, -ēre, -ēvī, -ētum,** I destroy

**dēlictum, -ī, n.,** crime

**dēlīrium, -iī, n.,** hallucinations, frenzied excitement (post-classical)

**dēlīrō, -āre,** go astray, be insane

**dēminuō, -uere, -uī, -ūtum** (transitive, taking acc.) diminish; (intransitive, taking gen. or abl.) suffer the loss of

**dēminūtiō, -iōnis, f.,** lessening, loss of (see **dēminuo**)

**dēmōnstrō, -āre, -āvī, -ātum,** I point out, show clearly

**dēnique,** finally

**dēns, dentis, m.,** tooth

**dēnuō,** again, anew

**dēpōnō, dēpōnere, dēposuī, dēpositum,** set aside, entrust

**dēsistō, dēsistere, dēstitī, dēstitum,** stop, leave off

**dēspērō, -āre, -āvī, -ātum** (both transitive and intransitive), I am without hope, despair

**detegō, dētegere, dētēxī, dētēctum,** uncover, reveal

**deus, -eī** (irregular), **m.,** god

**diabolus, -ī, m.,** devil

**dīcō, dīcere, dīxī, dictum,** I say

**diēs, diēī, m.,** day

**difficilis, -e,** difficult
**difficultās, -ātis,** f., difficulty
**diffugiō, -ugere, -ūgī,** disperse
**dignitās, -ātis,** worth, merit,
   dignity
**dīligēns, -entis,** diligent
**discessus, -ūs,** m., departure
**discō, discere, didicī,** I learn
**dissimilis, -e,** unlike
**diū** (adv.), for a long time
**dīves, -itis,** rich
**dīvidō, -videre, -vīsī, -vīsum,** I
   divide
**dō, dare, dedī, datum,** I give
**doceō, -ēre, -uī, doctum,** I teach
**doctor, -ōris,** m., teacher
**dominus, -ī,** m., lord, master
**domus, -ūs** (irregular), f., house,
   home
**dōnec,** while, so long as
**dōnum, -ī,** n., gift
**dormiō, -īre, -īvī, -ītum,** I sleep
**drāma, drāmatis,** f., drama, play
**dūcō, dūcere, dūxī, ductum,** I lead
**dulcis, -e,** sweet, pleasant,
   delightful
**dum,** while, so long as
**dummodo,** only, provided that
**dūrus, -a, -um,** hard
**dux, ducis,** m., leader, commander,
   general

**ē, ex,** + abl., out of
**ebur, eboris,** n., ivory
**edō, edere** or **ēsse, ēdī, ēsum,** I eat
**efficiō, -ere, -fēcī, -fectum,** I
   accomplish, bring about
**egeō, -ēre, -uī,** I lack, I need
**egō,** I
**ēgredior, -gredī, -gressus sum,** I
   go out
**ēheu,** alas
**emō, emere, ēmī, emptum,** I buy
**emptor, -ōris,** m., buyer, purchaser
**en,** behold, look
**enim** (conjunction), for
**eō, īre, īvī** or **iī, itum,** I go
**epistola** or **epistula, -ae,** f., letter
**equus, -ī,** m., horse
**ergō,** therefore

**errō, -āre, -āvī, -atum,** I wander,
   stray, err, be in error, be mistaken
**et,** and
**et ... et,** both ... and
**etenim,** for
**etiam,** also
**etiamsī,** even if, although
**etsī,** even if, although
**ēveniō, ēvenīre, ēvēnī, ēventum,**
   to happen
**eventus, -ūs,** m., consequence,
   issue, result, event, occurrence
**ex** (see **ē**)
**exemplar, exemplāris,** n., pattern
**exemplum, -ī,** n., sample, example
**exeō, exīre, -iī, -ītum,** I go out
**exercitus, -ūs,** m., army
**expōnō, -pōnere, -posuī,**
   **-positum,** I explain,
**exsequor, -sequī, -secūtus sum,**
   I follow a corpse to the grave,
   follow to the end, carry out,
   accomplish, execute
**exsistō, -ere, -stitī** (irregular), I
   exist, I am, appear to be
**exstō** or **extō, -āre, -āvī, -ātum,**
   I stand out, project, am still in
   esistence
**extrā,** outside
**extrēmus, -a, -um** (superlative of
   **exter**), outermost, extreme

**faciēs, iēī,** f. appearance
**facile,** easily
**facilis, -e,** easy
**faciō, facere, fēcī, factum,** I do,
   make
**factum, -ī,** n., deed, act
**facundus, -a, -um,** eloquent
**falsus, -a, -um,** false
**fames, famis,** f., hunger
**familia, -ae,** f., household of slaves,
   household
**fātum, -ī,** n., divine utterance, fate
**faveō, favēre, fāvī, fautum,** I
   favour
**fēlēs, -is,** f., cat
**fēlīciter,** happily, successfully
**fēlīx** (gen. **fēlīcis**), happy, fortunate
**fēmina, -ae,** f., woman

**ferē,** almost, nearly

**ferō, ferre, tulī, lātum,** I carry, bring

**ferōciter,** fiercely

**ferox, ferōcis,** fierce

**ferreus, -a, -um,** of iron

**fessus, -a, -um,** tired

**festīnō, -āre, -āvī, -ātum,** I hurry

**fidēs, -ēī,** f., trust, faith

**fidō, -ere, fisus sum,** I trust

**filia, -ae,** f., daughter

**filius, -iī,** m., son

**finis, -is,** m., end; (pl.) territory

**finitimus, -a, -um,** neighbouring

**fiō, fierī, factus sum,** I am done, be made, become

**firmus, -a, -um,** strong

**flagrō, -āre, -āvī, -ātum,** I blaze, burn, blow

**fleō, -ēre, flēvī, flētum,** I weep

**floreō, -ēre, -uī, -itum,** I prosper, flourish

**flōs, flōris,** m., flower

**flūmen, -minis,** n., river

**fōns, fontis,** m., spring, fountain

**forma, -ae,** f., form, figure; plan, design

**fors, forte** (only in nom. and abl. sing.), chance, luck

**forsitan,** perhaps

**forte** see **fors**

**fortis, -e,** brave, strong

**fortiter** (adv.), bravely

**fortitūdō, -inis,** f., fortitude, strength

**forum, -ī,** n., open square market place, place of public business

**francus, -a, -um** (a renaissance word). **Lingua franca** was a mixed language, mainly Italian but incorporating several other languages, used as the language of commerce and industry throughout the Mediterranean.

**frangō, frangere, frēgī, fractum,** I break

**frāter, frātris,** m., brother

**frōns, frontis,** f., forehead

**fructus, fructūs,** m., fruit

**fruor, fruī, frūctus sum or fruitus**

**sum** (direct object in the abl.), I enjoy

**frustrā,** in vain

**fugiō, fugere, fūgī,** I flee

**fulgurō, -āre,** to lighten

**fundō, -ere, fūdī, fūsum,** I pour, rout

**fungor, fungī, functus sum,** I perform

**Gallī, -ōrum,** Gauls, the

**Gallia, -ae,** f., Gaul

**gaudeō, gaudēre, gāvīsus sum,** I rejoice, enjoy

**gēns, gentis,** f., race, family

**genū, genūs,** n., knee

**genus, generis,** n., birth, descent, origin; (of living beings) class, kind

**gerō, gerere, gessī, gestum,** I carry on, wage

**gracilis,** slender

**gradus, -ūs,** m., step, pace

**graecus, -a, -um,** Greek

**grānum, ī,** n., grain

**grātia, -ae,** f., pleasantness, favour, thanks

**grātus, -a, -um,** pleasing, welcome

**gravis, -is,** heavy, serious

**hābeō, -ēre, -uī, -itum,** I have, hold

**habitō, -āre, -āvī, -ātum,** live, dwell

**hasta, -ae,** f., spear

**herī,** tomorrow

**hērōs, -ōis,** m., hero

**heu,** alas

**hīc,** here

**hīc, haec, hōc,** this

**hiems, hiemis,** f., winter

**hinc,** from there

**hōdiē,** today

**homō, hominis,** m., man

**honestus, -a, -um,** virtuous

**honōrārius, -a, -um,** done as an honour, given as an honour

**honōs, -ōris,** m., honour

**hōra, -ae,** f., hour

**horribilis,** terrifying

**horror, -ōris,** m., shuddering, dread, fright, object of dread

**hortor, -ārī, -ātus sum,** I encourage

**hortus, -ī,** m., garden

**hostis, -is,** c., enemy

**hūc,** to this place, hither

**humilis,** humble

**humus, -ī,** f., earth, ground

**hypothesis, -is,** f., hypothesis

**iaciō, iacere, iēcī, iactum,** I throw

**iam,** already, by now

**ianua, -ae,** f., door

**ibi,** there

**īdem, ēadem, idem,** the same

**idōneus, -a, -um,** adj., suitable

**Īdūs, īduum,** f. pl., Ides (date)

**igitur,** therefore

**ignāvus, -a, -um,** idle, cowardly

**ignis, -is,** m., fire

**ignōrō, -āre, -āvī, -ātum,** I am ignorant of, not to know

**īlicō,** instantly

**ille, illa, illud,** that

**imber, imbris,** m., rain

**immemor, -ōris,** forgetful, unmindful of

**impedīmentum, -ī,** n., hindrance, obstruction, impediment, baggage (especially of an army)

**impediō, -īre, -īvī, -ītum,** I hinder

**imperātor, -is,** m., general

**imperium, -iī,** n., command (for instance of an army), dominion, absolute power, empire

**imperō, -āre, -āvī, -ātum** (+dat.), command

**impetrō, -āre, -āvī, -ātum,** I accomplish, obtain request

**impōnō, -pōnere, -posuī, -positum,** put in, put on

**impossibilis, -ile,** impossible (medieval Latin, though classical Latin had **possibilis,** derived from **possum**)

**imprimō, -primere, -pressī, -pressum,** I press into, press upon, imprint, print

**improbus, -a, -um,** dishonest

**in,** +acc., into; +abl., in

**incautus, -a, -um,** careless

**incendō, -dere, -dī, -sum,** I burn (trans.)

**incipiō, incipere, incēpī, inceptum,** begin

**incolō, -ere, -uī,** I inhabit

**incredibilis, -e,** incredible

**inde,** thence, from there

**index, -dicis,** m., one that informs or indicates, guiding principle, forefinger

**ineō, inīre, iniī, initum,** I enter

**infēlīx, infēlicis,** unhappy, unlucky

**infinītus, -a, -um,** infinite

**infrā,** below, underneath, lower down or further on

**ingēns, -tis,** huge

**ingredior, -gredī, -gressus sum,** I step into, enter

**inhonestus, -a, -um,** shameful

**initium, initiī,** n., beginning

**inops, inopis,** destitute, in need

**inquam** (irreg.), I say

**īnsidiae, -ārum,** f. pl., ambush

**īnsignis, -e,** distinguished, notable

**instrūmentum, -ī,** n., tool, implement

**intellegō, -legere, -lēxī, -lēctum,** I realise

**inter,** + acc., among, between

**intereā,** meanwhile

**interest,** it concerns

**interficiō, -ficere, fēcī, fectum,** kill

**interim,** meanwhile

**interrēgnum, -ī,** n., period between two reigns, interregnum

**interrogō, -āre, -āvī, -ātum,** I inquire, question, interrogate

**intersum,** I lie between

**intrā,** within, inside

**intrōdūcō, -dūcere, -duxī, -ductum,** I introduce

**inutilis, -e,** useless

**invādō, invādere, invāsī, invāsum,** I enter, assault, seize

**inveniō, -venīre, -vēnī, -ventum,** I find

**invidia, -ae,** f., envy

**invincibilis, -e,** invincible

ipse, -a, -um, self
īra, -ae, f., anger
irruō, irruere, irruī, I rush in, attack
is, ea, id, that
ita . . . ut, so . . . that
ita, thus, so
Ītalia, -ae, f., Italy
itaque, therefore
iter, itineris, n., journey, route
iterum, again
iūdex, -icis, c., judge
iugulum, -ī, n., throat
iungō, -ere, iūnxi, iūnctum, I join
together
iūnior, iūnioris, younger
Iuppiter, Iovis, m., Jupiter
iūrō, -āre, -āvī, -ātum, I swear,
take an oath
iūs, iūris, n., right, law
iūsiūrandum, -ī, oath
iustus, -a, -um, just
iuvenis, -is, m., young man
iuvō, -āre, iūvī, iūtum, I help
iuxtā, next to, beside

labor, -ōris, m., toil
labōrō, -āre, -āvī, -ātum, I labour
lacrima,-ae, f., tear (of weeping)
lacrimō, -āre, -āvī, -ātum, I weep
lacūna, -ae, f., cavity, hollow, gap,
deficiency, loss
laedō, laedere, laesī, laesum, I
hurt, I injure
lapis, -idis, m., stone
lapsus, -ūs, m., gradual movement
downwards, sliding, fall, error
lātē, widely
latinitās, ātis, f., skill at Latin;
good command of Latin
latīnus, -a, -um, Latin
Latine, in Latin
lātrō, latrōnis, m., robber
lātus, -a, -um, adj., wide
laudō, -āre, -āvī, -ātum, I praise
laus, laudis, f., praise
lāvīnius, -a, -um, Lavinian
legātus, -ī, m., ambassador, officer
legō, legere, lēgī, lectum, I read
lēgō, -āre, -āvī, -ātum, charge,
appoint, bequeath

lentus, -a, -um, slow
leō, leōnis, m., lion
lepidus, -a, -um, elegant
levis, -is, light
lēx, lēgis, f., law
līber, lībera, līberum, adj., free
liber, librī, m., book
līberī, -ōrum, m. pl., children
līberō, -āre, -āvī, -ātum, I set free
lībērtās, -ātis, f., freedom
libet, libēre, libuit, libitum
(impersonal + dat. of the person
being pleased), it pleases
lībra, -ae, f., balance, pair of scales,
the Roman pound-weight of
twelve ounces
licet (as a conjunction), granting
that, although
licet, licēre, licuit or licitum est, it
is lawful, it is allowed, one can,
one may (+ dat. of person)
lingua, -ae, f., tongue, speech,
language
linter, lintris, f., boat
littera, -ae, f., a letter of the
alphabet; (pl.) writing, literature,
document
lītus, lītoris, n., sea-shore, shore
locus, -ī, m., place
Londinium, Londiniī, n., London
longus, -a, -um, long
loquor, loquī, locūtus sum, I speak
lūcēscō, -ere, become light
lūdō, -ere, lūsī, lūsum, I play
lūna, -ae, f., moon
lūx, lūcis, f., light

māchina, -ae, f., machine, device,
stratagem, trick
magis, more
magister, magistrī, m., master,
teacher
magnopere, greatly
magnus, -a, -um, great
mālō, malle, māluī, I prefer
mālum, - ī, n., apple
mālus, - ī, m., ship mast, apple tree
malus, -a, -um, bad
māneō, -manēre, mansī, mansum,
I remain

**manus, -ūs,** f., hand

**mare, maris,** n., sea

**martius, -a, -um,** of the month of March

**māter, mātris,** f., mother

**mātūrus, -a, -um,** ripe, mature, early

**maxime** (adv., from superlative of **magnus**), most highly

**medicīna, -ae,** f., art of healing, means of healing

**medius, -a, -um,** middle

**melius,** better (adv.)

**mementō,** imperative of **meminī,** I remember

**meminī, -isse,** I remember, recollect, mention

**memor, -ōris,** mindful

**memoria, -ae,** f., memory, ability to remember, time of remembrance, recollection

**memoriae mandō, -āre, -āvī, -ātum,** I commit to memory

**mēns, mentis,** m., mind, mental faculties

**mēnsa, -ae,** f., table

**mēnsis, -is,** m., month

**meō, meāre,** go

**mereor, meruī, meritus sum,** I earn, deserve

**merīdiēs, -diēī,** m., midday, noon

**meus, -a, -um,** my

**mīles, mīlitis,** c., soldier

**mīlia, mīlium,** n. pl., thousands

**mille,** a thousand; **mille passuūs,** a mile

**minimus, -a, -um** (superlative of **parvus**), smallest, least

**minor, -ōris** (comparative of **parvus**), smaller, lesser

**minūtia, -ae,** f., smallness, littleness

**mīrābilis, -e,** wonderful

**mīror, -ārī, ātus sum,** I admire, wonder at

**miser, misera, miserum,** unhappy

**miseret** (impersonal verb: **mē miseret**) (+gen.), I pity

**mittō, mittere, mīsī, missum,** I send

**modo,** only, provided that

**modus, -ī,** m., measure, limit, boundary, manner, way, method

**moneō, -ēre, -uī, -itum,** I advise

**mōns, montis,** m., mountain

**morior, morī, mortuus sum,** I die (future participle, **moriturus)**

**mora, -ae,** f., delay

**moror, morārī, morātus sum,** I delay, stay

**mors, mortis,** f., death

**moveō, movēre, mōvī, mōtum,** I move (trans.)

**mox,** adv., soon

**mulier, mulieris,** f., woman

**multiplex, -icis,** manifold

**multus, -a, -um,** much, many

**mundus, -ī,** m., the universe, the world

**mūrus, -ī,** m., wall

**mūtō, -āre, -āvī, -ātum,** I shift, change, alter

**nam,** for

**nascor, nascī, nātus sum,** I am born

**nausea, -eae,** f., seasickness

**nauta, -ae,** m., sailor

**nāvis, -is,** f., ship

**nē,** lest

**nec ... nec,** neither ... nor

**necō, -āre, -āvī, -ātum,** I kill

**negō, -āre, -āvī, -ātum,** I deny

**nēmō, nēminis,** c., no one

**neque, nec,** conj., neither

**neque ... neque,** neither ... nor

**nesciō, nescīre, nescīvī, -ītum,** I do not know

**neu,** and that not

**nēve,** and that not

**nēve ... nēve,** neither ... nor

**nexus, -ūs,** m., binding, tying together, connecting

**nī,** unless

**niger, nigra, nigrum,** black

**nihil,** n., nothing

**nil,** n., nothing

**ningit, ninguit,** it snows

**nisi,** if not, unless

**nōbilis, -e,** renowned, noble

**noceō, -ēre, uī, -itum** (+dat.), I hurt

**noctū,** adv., by night

**nōlō, nolle, nōluī,** I am unwilling

**nōmen, nōminis,** n., name

**nōn,** negative, not

**nōndum,** not yet

**nōnne,** surely . . .?

**nōnnumquam,** sometimes

**nōscō, nōscere, nōvī, notum,** I get to know

**noster, nostra, nostrum,** adj., our

**notō, -āre, -āvī, -ātum,** I mark, distinguish, mark out, observe

**nūbēs, nūbis,** f., cloud

**nūbō, nūbere, nūpsī, nūptum,** I marry (of woman)

**nucleus, -iī,** m. (diminutive of **nux, nucis,** f., nut), kernel of a nut, stone in a fruit

**nullus, -a, -um,** no

**num,** surely not . . .?

**numquam,** adv., never

**nunc,** adv., now

**nuntiō, -āre, -āvī, -ātum,** I announce

**nūper,** lately, recently

**nux, nucis,** f., nut

**ob** (+ acc.), on account of

**obeō, -īre, -iī, itum,** I go to, go against, go over, enter upon, engage in; (with **diem** or **mortem,** at least understood) die

**obiter,** by the way, in passing, incidentally

**occīdō, occidere, -cīdī, cīsum,** I kill

**ōdī, ōdisse,** I hate

**odium, -iī,** n., hatred

**officium, -iī,** n., dutiful action, deference, official employment

**ōlim,** formerly, once upon a time

**omnis, -e,** all

**onus, oneris,** n., burden

**opera, -ae,** f., pains, trouble, exertion

**operam dō, dāre, dedī, dātum,** I pay attention, take pains, take trouble

**operor, operārī, operātus sum,** I labour, am busy, am occupied

**oportet** (impersonal verb: **mē oportet**), I ought

**oppidum, -ī,** n., town

**oppugnō, -āre, -āvī, -ātum,** I attack

**opus, operis,** n., work

**ōrātor, ōrātōris,** m., speaker

**ordō, -inis,** m., rank

**orīgō, orīginis,** f., origin, source, beginning

**orior, orīrī, ortus sum,** I arise

**ōrō, -āre, -āvī, -ātum,** I beg

**ōsculum, -ī,** n., kiss

**paene,** adv., almost

**paenitet, paenituit** (impersonal), repent

**palam,** in sight of

**par, paris,** equal

**parcō, parcere, pepercī, parsum** (+ dat.), I spare

**pareō, -ēre, -uī, -itum** (+dat.), I obey

**parō, -āre, -āvī, -ātum,** I prepare

**pars, partis,** f., part

**parvus, -a, -um,** small

**passim,** here and there, up and down, far and wide, indiscriminately

**passus, -ūs,** m., pace, yard

**pater, patris,** m., father

**paterfamiliās, patrisfamiliās,** head of the family

**patior, patī, passus sum,** I suffer, permit, allow

**patria, -ae,** f., fatherland

**paucus, -a, -um,** few

**paulus, -a, -um,** a little

**pauper, -is,** adj., poor

**pāx, pācis,** f., peace

**pecūnia, -ae,** f., money

**pēior, pēiōris,** worse

**per** (+ acc.), through

**perītus, -a, -um,** experienced, expert

**perpetuus, -a, -um,** perpetual

**persōna, -ae,** f., theatrical role, theatrical part, character or person represented by an actor

**persuādeō, -suādere, -suāsī, -suāsum** (+ dat.), I persuade

**perveniō, -venīre, -vēnī, -ventum,** I arrive

**pēs, pedis,** m., foot

**pessimus, -a, -um,** worst

**petītiō, -iōnis,** f., attack, thrust, attack in words

**piget, piguit** (impersonal), be vexed (by)

**placet, placēre, placuit,** it pleases

**plēnus, -a, -um,** full

**plūs, plūris** (comparative of **multus**), more

**poena, -ae,** f., fine, punishment, penalty

**poeta, -ae,** m., poet

**polliceor, -ērī, -itus sum,** I promise

**Pompeius, Pompeiī,** m., Pompey

**pōne,** behind

**pōnō, pōnere, posuī, positum,** I place

**populus, -ī,** m., people (in the sense of a political community), nation

**possum, posse, potuī,** I am able

**post** (+ acc.), after

**postea,** afterwards

**posterior, posterius** (comparative of **posterus** and **poster**), following after, next, later

**postquam,** after (conj.)

**potēns, -entis,** powerful

**potior, -īrī, potītus sum,** I get possession of (+ abl.)

**prae,** before, in front of

**praebeō, -ēre, -uī, -itum, mē** (reflexive verb) (+ adj.), to show or prove oneself (valiant, wise, or whatever)

**praeclarus, -a, -um,** honourable

**praedicō, -āre, -āvī, -ātum,** declare, proclaim

**praemium, -iī,** n., reward

**praestantia, -ae,** f., excellence

**praesum, -esse, -fuī,** be chief person in, be in command of

**praeter,** beside, past

**precem** (no nom. sing.), **precis,** f., entreaty, prayer

**precor, -ārī, ātus sum,** I pray

**premō, -ere, pressī, pressum,** I press

**prīmō,** adv., first, at first

**prīmum,** adv., first, at first

**prīmus, -a, -um,** adj., first (superlative of **priscus**, ancient)

**prīnceps, -cipis,** m., chief

**prīncipium, -iī,** n., beginning, origin, foundation, first element, first principle

**prior, prius,** gen. **priōris,** former (comparative of **priscus,** ancient)

**priusquam,** before that

**prō** (+ abl.), for, on behalf of

**procul,** far (adverb)

**proelium, -iī,** n., battle

**proficīscor, -ficīscī, -fectus sum,** I set out

**profundus, -a, -um,** deep, profound

**prōgredior, -gredī, -gressus sum,** I advance

**prohibeō,- ēre, -uī, -itum,** I prohibit, forbid

**promittō, -mittere, -mīsī, -missum,** I promise

**prōmoveō, -movēre, -mōvī, -mōtum,** promote

**prope** (+acc.), near (prep.)

**proprius, -a, -um,** one's own, special

**propter** (+ acc.), near, on account of, by reason of, because of

**prōsequor, -sequī, -secūtus sum,** I follow, accompany, attack, pursue

**prōsperus, -a, -um,** prosperous (adj.)

**proximus, -a, -um** (adj.), next

**pūblicus, -a, -um,** belonging to the people, public

**pudet, puduit** (impersonal), be ashamed

**pudīcus, -a, -um,** modest, chaste, virtuous

**puella, -ae,** f., girl

**puer, puerī,** m., boy

**pugna, -ae,** f., fight

**pugnō, -āre, -āvī, -ātum,** I fight
**pulcher, pulchra, pulchrum,** beautiful
**pulchritūdō, -inis,** f., beauty
**pūniō, -īre, -īvī, -ītum,** I punish
**pupillāris, -is,** m. (from **pupillus,** orphan, ward), of an orphan, of a ward
**putō, -āre, -āvī, -ātum,** I think

**quaestiō, -iōnis,** f., question
**quam** (interrogative adv. used with another adv.), how, than, as
**quam,** than (comparative conjunction), as . . . as possible (used as an adv. with the superlative)
**quamvis,** although, however much
**quandō,** when?
**quantum,** how much?
**quantus, -a, -um,** how great?
**quāre,** why? wherefore?
**quasi,** as if, just as, as it were
**-que,** and
**-que . . . et,** both . . . and
**-que . . . -que,** both . . . and
**quemadmodum,** as, how
**quī, quae, quod,** who, which (relative pronoun)
**quia,** because
**quīdam, quaedam, quoddam,** a certain
**quidem,** indeed.
**quīn,** that not
**quis, quis, quid,** who? what? (interrogative pronoun)
**quō,** where . . . to?
**quoad,** while, so long as
**quod,** because
**quōmodo,** how? in what manner?
**quondam,** formerly, once
**quoniam,** since
**quoque,** also
**quotiēns,** as often as

**rādix, rādīcis,** f., root
**rapiō, -ere, -uī, raptum,** I seize
**rārus, -a, -um,** loose, thin, rare, infrequent
**ratiō, -iōnis,** f., reason

**rātus, -a, -um** (past participle of **reor**), reckoned, fixed, determined (**pro rata parte,** according to a fixed proportion, in proportion)
**reddō, -ere, reddidī, redditum,** give back
**redeō, -īre, -iī, -itum,** I return (intrans.)
**reductiō, iōnis,** f., a bringing back, restoration
**referō, referre, rettulī, relātum,** I bring back, carry back, submit for consideration
**rēgīna, -ae,** f., queen
**rēgnum, -ī,** n., kingdom, rule
**regō, regere, rēxī, rēctum,** I rule
**relinquō, -linquere, -līquī, -lictum,** I leave
**reliquus, -a, -um,** remaining
**removeō, -movēre, -mōvī, -mōtum,** I withdraw
**reor, rērī, rātus sum,** I reckon, think, judge
**repetītiō, -iōnis,** f., beginning
**requiescō, -quiescere, -quiēvī, quiētum,** I rest, repose
**rēs, reī,** f., thing, matter
**rēs publicae, rērum publicārum,** pl., politics, statesmanship
**resistō, -sistere, -stitī** (+ dat.), I resist
**rēspūblica, rēipūblicae,** f., state; (in pl.) politics, statesmanship
**retardō, -āre, -āvī, -ātum,** retard, delay
**retineō, -ēre, -uī, -entum,** I keep, detain.
**revertor, -ī, reversus sum,** I go back, return
**rēx, rēgis,** m., king
**rīdeō, rīdēre, rīsī, rīsum,** I laugh
**rigor, rigōris,** m., stiffness, rigidity, hardness
**rigor mortis,** stiffness of death, stiffening of the body after death
**rogō, -āre, -āvī, -ātum,** I ask
**Rōma, -ae,** f., Rome
**rōmanus, -a, -um,** adj., Roman

**rosa, -ae,** f., rose
**rōstrum, -ī,** n., that which gnaws,
(in birds) beak, platform for
public speaking*
**rubeō, rubērē,** I am red
**rūrsus,** again
**rūs, rūris,** n., country (as opposed
to town)

**sacerdōs, sacerdōtis,** c., priest or
priestess
**saepe,** often
**sagitta, -ae,** f., arrow
**sāl, -is,** m., salt
**salūs, -ūtis,** f., safety
**salvē!** hail! hello!
**sanguineus, -a, -um,** bloody
**sanguis, sanguinis,** m., blood
**sānus, -a, -um,** sound, healthy
**sapiēns, -ientis,** wise
**sapientia, -iae,** f., wisdom
**satis,** enough
**scintilla, -ae,** f., spark, glimmer,
faint trace
**sciō, scīre, scīvī, scītum,** I know
**scrībō, scrībere, scrīpsī, scrīptum,**
I write
**sē** (reflexive pronoun), himself,
herself, itself, themselves
**secundum,** next, along, according
to
**secundus, -a, -um,** second,
favourable
**sed** (conj.), but
**sedeō, sedēre, sēdī, sessum,** I sit
**sedīle, sedīlis,** n., chair
**seges, segetis,** f., corn
**sella, ae,** f., seat
**semel,** once
**semper,** always
**senator, -oris,** m., senator
**senātus, -ūs,** m., senate
**senectūs, -ūtis,** f., old age

**senex, senis,** m., old man
**sententia, -ae,** f., opinion (formally
expressed), motto
**sentiō, -īre, sēnsī, sēnsum,** I feel,
perceive
**sequor, sequī, secūtus sum,** I
follow
**servō, -āre, -āvī, -ātum,** I save
**servus, -ī,** m., slave
**seu,** whether, or
**seu ... seu,** whether ... or
**sī,** if
**sī modō,** if only
**sī nōn,** if not
**sīc ... ut,** so ... as
**sīcut,** as
**similis, -e,** like
**simul,** at the same time
**sine** (+ abl.), without
**siquidem,** in as much as
**situs, -ūs,** m., layout, site, position,
situation
**sīve,** whether, or
**sīve ... sīve,** whether ... or
**sōl, sōlis,** m., sun
**soleō, solēre, solitus sum,** I am
accustomed
**sōlus, -a, -um,** only, alone
**solvō, -ere, solvī, solūtum,** I loose,
loosen, set sail
**soror, -ōris,** f., sister
**spatium, -iī,** n., space, interval
**speciēs, speciem** (no gen.), f.,
appearance, form
**speculum, -ī,** n., mirror
**spērō, -āre, āvī, -ātum,** I hope
**spēs, spēī,** f., hope
**stadium, -ī,** n., classical Greek
measurement of about 202
yards; race-course, chariot-
course, sports-ground
**statim,** immediately
**statua, -ae,** f., statue
**status, -ūs,** m., standing, position,
condition, state
**stirps, stirpis,** f. (of trees or other
plant) stock, stem; (of people)
source, origin, root, foundation
**stō, stāre, stetī, statum,** I stand
**studeō, -ēre, uī,** be eager, take pains

---

* In its secondary sense, it was
originally the speaker's platform in
the Roman Forum, where it was
adorned with 'beaks' of captured galleys; thence: pulpit, office that enables
someone to gain the public ear.

**suādeō, -ēre, suāsī, suāsum,** I urge

**sub,** under, underneath

**subitō,** suddenly

**subter,** under (motion)

**suggestiō -iōnis,** f., a rhetorical figure of speech in which an orator answered his own question

**sum, esse, fuī,** I am

**summus, -a, -um,** highest, top, very great

**super,** over, upon (+acc. or abl.)

**superō, -āre, āvī, ātum,** I surpass, overcome, outdo

**supplicium, -iī,** n., punishment, torture

**suppressiō, -iōnis,** f., embezzlement, dishonest suppression

**suprā,** above, over

**sūs, sūis,** c., pig, swine, sow

**suus, -a, -um,** his, her, its, their (possessive reflexive adjective - see **sē**)

**tabula, -ae,** f., board, writing-tablet, document

**taedet** (impersonal verb: **mē taedet**) I am weary (+ gen.)

**tam,** so

**tamen,** however

**tametsī,** although

**tamquam,** as though

**tandem,** at length

**tangō, tangere, tetigī, tāctum,** I touch

**tantopere,** so much, so greatly

**tantum,** only

**tantus, -a, -um,** so great

**tegō, tegere, tēxī, tēctum,** I cover

**tēlum, -ī,** n., weapon, javelin

**tempus, temporis,** n., time

**teneō, tenēre, tenuī, tentum,** I hold

**tener, tenera, tenerum,** adj., tender

**tergum, -ī,** n., back

**terra, -ae,** f., land, earth

**terreō, -ēre, -uī, -itum,** I frighten

**thesaurus, -ī,** m., treasure (a Latinised version of the Greek word meaning treasure)

**timeō, -ēre, -uī,** I fear

**timor, -ōris,** m. fear

**tondeō, -ēre, totondī, tōnsum,** I shave

**tonō, -āre, tonuī,** thunder

**tōnsor, -ōris,** m., barber

**torvus, -a, -um,** stern, grim

**tōtus, -a, -um,** whole

**trāiectus, -ūs,** m., crossing

**trāns** (prep.) (+ acc.), across

**trānseō, -īre, īvī, ītum,** I cross

**trānsferō, -ferre, -tulī, -lātum,** I carry across

**tremō, -ere, uī,** I tremble, shake, quake

**tribūnal, -ālis,** n., platform, judgement-seat

**trīstis, -e** (adj.), sad

**Trōia, -ae,** f., Troy

**tū,** you

**tum,** then

**tumor, -ōris,** m., swelling, protuberance

**tunc,** then

**turpis, -e,** disgraceful, shameful

**tuus, -a, -um,** your

**ubi,** when (conjunction), where? (interrogative adv.)

**ultimus, -a, -um,** most distant, furthest, extreme, last

**ultrā,** beyond

**umquam** (adv.), ever

**ūnā,** together

**ūnus, -a, -um** (number) one

**urbs, urbis,** f., city

**ūsus, -ūs,** m., use

**ut,** so that, as

**ut ... ita,** as ... so

**ut nē,** that not, lest

**ut nōn,** so that not

**ut sī,** as if

**uter, utra, utrum,** which (of two)

**uterus, -ī,** m., womb

**utī,** as

**utilis, -e,** useful

**ūtor, ūtī, ūsus sum** (+ abl.), I use

**utrum ... an** (*or* annon), whether ... or ..., whether ... or not? (asking a question)

**utut,** however, although
**uxor, -ōris,** f., wife

**vacuus, -a, -um,** empty, void
**vādō, vādere, vāsī,** I go, hasten, rush
**vae!** woe! alas!
**valē!** farewell! goodbye!
**valeō, -ēre, -uī, valitum,** I am strong, to be worth (the later **valor, -ōris** is derived from it)
**valor, -ōris,** value
**vastō, -āre-, -āvī, -ātum,** I lay waste
**vehementer,** vehemently, violently, strongly, powerfully, exceedingly
**vel,** or, either
**vel … vel,** either … or
**vēlōciter,** swiftly
**vēlox, -ōcis,** swift
**velut,** as
**velut sī,** as if
**velutī,** as
**vendō, -dere, -didī, -ditum,** I sell
**veniō, venīre, vēnī, ventum,** I come
**vēnor, vēnārī, vēnātus,** I hunt, chase
**ventus, -ī,** m., wind
**verbātim,** word for word (a medieval Latin word derived from the Latin **verbum**)
**verbum, - ī,** n., word
**vērē,** truly, really, indeed
**vereor, -ērī, -itus sum,** I fear
**vēritās, -ātis,** f., truth
**vērō,** but, moreover, in fact
**versus,** towards, in that direction, against
**vertō, -ere, vertī, versum,** I turn (trans.)
**vērum,** but, moreover

**vērus, -a, -um,** true, real, genuine
**vester, vestra, vestrum,** your
**vetō, -āre, uī, -itum,** I forbid, prohibit
**vetus, veteris,** old
**vexō, -āre, -āvī, -ātum,** I annoy
**via, -ae,** f., street, way
**vice versa,** with position changed
**victōria, -ae, f.,** victory
**videō, -ēre, vīdī, vīsum,** I see
**videor, -ērī, vīsus sum,** I seem
**vincō, vincere, vīcī, victum,** I conquer, defeat
**vīnum, -ī,** n., wine
**vir, -ī,** m., man
**vīrēs** see plural of **vīs**
**virgō, -inis,** maiden
**virīlis, virīle,** manly
**vīrium,** strength
**virtūs, virtūtis,** f., courage
**vīs** (in sing. only, acc. **vim** and abl. **vī**), f., force; (in pl. all cases) **vīrēs**
**vīsum,** seen
**vīta, -ae,** f., life
**vītō, -āre, -āvī, -ātum,** I avoid
**vitrum, -ī,** n., glass
**vīvō, vīvere, vīxī, victum,** I live
**vīvus, -a, -um,** alive, living, of a living person
**vix,** scarcely
**vocō, -āre, -āvī -ātum,** I call
**volō, velle, voluī,** I wish, am willing
**vōx populī,** the voice of the people, public opinion, the general verdict, popular belief or rumour
**vōx, vōcis,** f., voice
**vulnerō, -āre, -āvī -ātum,** I wound
**vulnus, -eris,** n., wound
**vultus, -ūs,** m., expression (on face), look

# The Latin Used in Everyday English

ALL THE FOLLOWING idioms can be found untranslated – in other words, as part of the English language – in most standard English dictionaries. In the case of each one, I follow it immediately with a completely literal translation. Where this does not make complete sense, perhaps because of the extraordinary conciseness of the Latin, I then give a more remote translation which does clearly show its practical meaning. Very occasionally I give the context in which it is ordinarily used and/or examples to make its use clearer.

Readers who have reached this part of the book should normally not need help in parsing the Latin, and I therefore give this help only when the parsing is especially difficult. I am, however, hoping that they will take it upon themselves to make sure that they understand the Latin construction of any idiom as fully as they understand its ordinary meaning in English, so that going through this appendix is mind-sharpening for them as well as usefully adding to their English vocabulary.

**Ab initio.** From the beginning. From the outset.

**Ab origine.** From the source. From the beginning. 'Aboriginal', referring to the original inhabitants of a country, comes directly from this idiom.

**Addenda.** Things to be added *or* which ought to be added.

**Ad hoc** (used both as an adjectival and as an adverbial phrase). To this thing *or* for this thing. For this purpose. Arranged for this special purpose.

**Ad hominem.** To the man *or* to the person. Personal. (Especially used as a technical term in logic and rhetoric, to describe an argument which attacks the *person* making the argument rather than the *argument itself*.) *See also* **Ad rem.**

**Ad idem.** To the same (thing). 'We are *ad idem* on this matter' means 'We are at one … '.

**Ad infinitum.** Towards infinity. Without limit.

**Ad libitum, ad lib.** Until that (point) which gives pleasure. As much as you like. To pleasure *or* at pleasure. To any extent. Off the cuff. (Normally used as an adverb phrase. As a verb – as in 'he adlibbed' – it means to invent or extemporise. *See* **Ex tempore. Libitum** is probably a past participle, but could conceivably be a supine.)

**Ad nauseam.** To seasickness. On and on to a sickening extent. Endlessly.

**Ad rem.** To the thing. Dealing with an issue.

**Adsum.** I am present. I am here.

**Ad valorem.** According to value (as opposed to volume). In proportion to the estimated value – for instance of goods.

**Advocatus diaboli.** Devil's Advocate. (In its primary meaning, it is the person officially appointed by the Catholic Church to make sure that every possible objection to a canonisation of a saint has been considered before it takes place.)

**Aegrotat**. He, *or* she, is ill. A certificate indicating that a student is ill and unable to take his exams.

**Affidavit** (from medieval Latin). He has stated on oath.

**A fortiori**. From the stronger thing. With stronger reason *or* force. More conclusively.

**Agenda**. Things to be done *or* things that ought to be done. Things to be acted upon.

**Alias**. Otherwise. At another time. (Used as either an adverb or a noun to indicate an adopted name by which someone is called 'on other occasion'.)

**Alibi**. Elsewhere. In a legal situation, the plea that one was elsewhere when an alleged act took place.

**Aliquot**. *Either* 'some' *or* 'so many'. Mathematical term, meaning 'integral factor'.

**Alma mater**. Nourishing mother. Metaphorically, a person's school or university.

**Alter ego**. The other I. One's other self. Hence, an intimate friend.

**Alumnus** or **alumna**. Foster child. Metaphorically, a graduate of a school or university.

**Amicus curiae**. Friend of the court. Disinterested observer. Someone not a party to particular court proceedings but allowed to take part in them to help the court with research or advice.

**Animus**. Soul. Spirit. Animating spirit. Hence animosity.

**Anno Domini** or **A.D.** In the year of the Lord. (There is no zero A.D.)

**Annus mirabilis**. Wonderful year, used for a special year in which more than one memorable thing has happened.

**Ante meridiem** *or* **a.m.** Before midday *or* before noon.

**A posteriori**. From after. From what comes after. From what follows. (In logic) working out from the effect back to the cause. Inductive. Gained from experience. *See* **A priori**.

**A priori**. From (what comes) before. Reasoning from cause to effect (opposite of '**a posteriori**' reasoning).

**Aqua vitae**. Water of life. (In relation to drink) ardent spirit.

**Artium Baccalaureus**. A.B., now B.A. Bachelor of Arts, a degree conferred by a university. *See* **Magister Artium**.

**Audi alteram partem**. Hear the other side (an important principle in both law and reasoning).

**Augur**. A person, among the ancient Romans, who tried to divine the future from the flight and cries of birds.

**Ave**. Hail. Welcome *or* farewell.

**Ave atque vale**. Hail and farewell.

**Benedictus benedicat**. May the Blessed One bless. (A standard grace at the start of a meal.)

**Bona fide**. In good faith. Genuine or genuinely. Without deception.

**Bona fides**. Good faith. Genuineness.

**Casus belli**. Occasion of war. Action justifying war. An excuse for war.

**Carpe diem** (Horace). Pluck the day. Seize the day. Enjoy the moment. Make the most of life.

**Cave!** 'Watch out!' (imperative); once used in most boys' preparatory schools.

**Caveat**. Let him beware. (A **caveat** means a warning.)

**Caveat emptor**. Let the buyer beware. (Until fairly recently, the legal Common Law position.)

**Ceteris paribus**. Other things (being) equal.

**Cf.** Short for the Latin **confer**. Compare (with something else in a list, in a book, etc.).

**Circa**. Around *or* about: used for dates and large quantities. Often abbreviated to **c.** or **ca.**

**Circus**. A ring. A rounded, or oval, area lined with tiers and seats. A travelling show of horses, riders and other acts traditionally performed in circuses.

**Codex**. Tree-trunk. Block of wood. Tablet. Book. Manuscript book. (Today, used to describe early manuscripts, for instance of the Bible, in book form rather than in the form of a parchment roll.)

**Cognomen**. The name coming after the name of a collection of families connected by common descent (as in Marcus Tullius *Cicero*). Nickname.

**Compos mentis**. Having command of the mind, *or* having full possession of the mind. Of sound mind. Sane.

**Consensus**. Having been agreed. An agreement of opinion or of testimony.

**Consortium**. Partnership. Temporary co-operation of several large interests in order to affect some common purpose.

**Contra**. Against *or* opposite of. (Pros and cons – abbreviation of pros and contras – means arguments for and against.)

**Contra mundum**. Against the world. Defying everyone. Against all comers.

**Corpus**. Body (literal or metaphorical). Body of writings *or* collection of writings.

**Corpus Christi**. Body of Christ. Festival of the Body of Christ (Thursday after Trinity Sunday).

**Corpus delicti**. The body of the crime. The corpse of someone murdered. Metaphorically, the factual evidence, at least apparent, of a crime.

**Corpus juris**. Body of law. The collected laws of a country.

**Corrigendum**. That which ought to be, *or* needs to be, corrected (most usually used in connection with errors in a printed book).

**Cui bono?** To whom good? Who stands to benefit? (Typically asked when looking for a motive for a crime.)

**Cum grano (salis)**. With a grain of salt. With caution *or* reserve.

**Curriculum vitae**, commonly shortened to **CV**. Course of life. Main events of a person's life (especially as relevant in a job application).

**Datum** *and* **data**. Given thing(s). A thing/things known to be granted. In logic or law, an assumption or premise from which to draw inferences.

**De facto**. From *or* by the fact. A *de facto* government is one that is in power irrespective of how it arrived there.

**Dei gratia**. By God's grace.

**De jure**. From *or* by the law. A *de jure* government has the legal and constitutional right to be in office whether or not it *is* in office.

**Delirium tremens**. Sometimes abbreviated to **DTs**. **Deliro** means 'I plough a furrow askew', 'I go off the rails'. Hence **delirium**: a disordered state of mind resulting in incoherent speech; hallucinations; frenzied excitement. **Tremo** means I am shaking or quaking. Therefore **delirium tremens** is an extreme form of delirium, with terrifying delusions, to which heavy drinkers are particularly liable.

**De minimis non curat lex**. The law does not concern itself with the smallest things *or* with trivial matters *or* with trifles.

**De mortuis nihil** (or **nil**) **nisi bonum**. Concerning the dead, nothing unless good. Do not speak ill of the dead.

**Deo volente**. God willing. If nothing happens to prevent it.

**De profundis**. From the depths. Out of the depths (of sorrow). (Psalm 129:1 in Catholic Bibles, 130:1 in Protestant Bibles.)

**Deus ex machina**. God out of a machine. (First used to represent a Greek theatrical convention, where a god would swing onto the stage, high up in a machine, solving humanly insoluble problems and thus resolving the action of a play. It now refers to a wholly outside person who puts matters right, a providential interposition, a power or event that comes in the nick of time to solve a difficulty.)

**Dramatis personae**. People of a drama. The characters in, or cast of, a play.

**e.g.** Short for **exempli gratia**. *See below*.

**Eiusdem generis**. Of the same kind. (In law a rule of construction and interpretation applying to documents and statutes.) *See also* **Sui generis**.

**E libris** *or* **ex libris**. Out of the books of (the person who puts his or her name under these words). A book belonging to the library or collection of books of such a person.

**Emeritus**. Earned. Well-earned. Honorary. (Hence) honourably discharged from service.

**Ergo**. Therefore (often used jocularly). *See also* **Post hoc ergo propter hoc**.

**Erratum** and **errat**. **Erro** means I wander, or I stray, and thence I waver, and thence I err, I am in error, I am mistaken. **Erratum** (the perfect participle): a thing which has been got wrong; a fault or error. A mistake made in printing or writing.

**Et al**. Short for **et alii**. Abbreviation used in bibliographies when citing multiple editorship or authorship, to avoid having to write out all the names.

**Et cetera**, usually abbreviated to **etc**. And the remaining things. And the rest. And so on.

**Ex ante**. Before the event.

**Ex cathedra**. From the chair of office. Authoritatively by virtue of one's office. Applied especially when a Pope is speaking officially.

**Exeat**. He may *or* let him go out (subjunctive). (Used in schools and university colleges to indicate permission for temporary absence.)

**Executor**. The Latin **exsequor** means to follow a corpse from the grave. Hence the noun: one who carries out something; someone appointed by a testator to execute his will.

**Exempli gratia**, usually shortened to **e.g.** By the favour of example. By the help of example. For example.

**Exeunt** (plural of **exit**). They go away. They leave (usually the stage in a theatrical production).

**Ex-libris**. *See* **E libris**.

**Ex officio**. Out of the office. By virtue of one's office.

**Ex gratia**. Out of grace. As an act of grace. Not under any compulsion.

**Ex hypothesi**. From the hypothesis (a term used in logic).

**Exit**. He goes out. Departure of an actor from the stage. Death. A passage by which to leave (as in a railway station).

**Ex parte**. From *or* for one side only.

**Ex post facto**. After the fact. Retrospectively.

**Extant**. They stand out; are still in existence. (Especially applies to documents.)

**Ex tempore**. Out of time *or* from time. On the spur of the moment. Off the cuff. Without preparation. Extempore.

**Facsimile** (**fac** and **simile**). (A command) 'Make a like *or* similar thing.' Made up of.

**Factotum** (**Fac totum**!). 'Make the whole'. Man or woman of all work. Servant who manages the affairs of his master or mistress.

**Floruit**. He flourished. Period during which a person alive if the exact dates of birth and death are not known.

**Fons et origo**. The spring *or* fountain and the origin. The source and the origin (of something).

**Forum**. (In ancient Rome) a public place for judicial and other business. A place for public discussion. A book, periodical or other publication giving opportunity to debate a subject.

**Genus**. A kind. A class (of things). (In logic) a kind of thing which includes further, subsidiary kinds. (In zoology) a group of different animals or plants which have structural characteristics in common that are distinct from those of all other groups. (Thus cats and tigers belong to the *cat* genus.) *See* **Species**.

**Gratis** (short for **gratiis**, from **gratia**, a favour). With favours. Gratuitous or gratuitously. (Given) for nothing, without charge, free.

**Habeas corpus**. You are to have (i.e. to produce) a body. A writ to bring a person before a court, to ensure that the person's imprisonment is not illegal.

**Homo sapiens**. Wise member of mankind. Man distinguished from other animals by his ability to reason.

**Honorarium**. A thing done *or* given as an honour. A voluntary fee.

**Horror vacui**. Fear of empty space. Compulsion to make marks in every space.

**Ibid., ibidem**. In the same place. Used in footnotes: a quotation comes from the same source.

**Idem**. The same. In a work by the same author. The same word.

**i.e.** Short for: **id est**, meaning 'that is'. That is to say (when explaining something immediately before those words).

**Ignoramus.** We do not know. (In law) we take no notice (of something). An ignorant person.

**Impedimenta**. Hindrances, obstructions, baggage, especially of an army.

**Imperium.** Command, for instance of an army. Dominion. Absolute power. Empire.

**Imprimatur**. Let it be printed. (An official licence to print.)

**In absentia**. In the absence. In one's absence. (In law, one can be convicted *in absentia* if one is not in attendance at one's trial.)

**In articulo mortis**. In the moment of time of death. At the instant of death.

**In camera**. In a (private) room. Not in public.

**Index**. Forefinger (as in 'index finger'). One that informs or indicates. Guiding principle. Alphabetical list, usually at the end of a book. List of books forbidden by the Catholic Church to be read by Catholics.

**In extremis**. In extreme things. In extremity. At the point of death. (Colloquially) near to the point of death.

**In flagrante delicto**, sometimes abbreviated to **in flagrante**. In the blazing crime. While the crime is ablaze. In the act of committing a crime. Caught red-handed.

**Infra**. Below. Lower down *or* further on (especially in a book).

**Infra dig**. Abbreviation of **Infra dignitatem**. Beneath one's dignity. Unbecoming.

**In memoriam**. In memory of.

**In loco**. In the place of.

**In loco parentis**. In the place of a parent.

**In medias res**. Into middle things. Into mid-most things. Into the thick of it.

**In propria persona**. In one's own person (when speaking or writing on one's own behalf.

**In re**. In the matter of.

**In situ**. In (its) original place.

**In statu pupillari**. In the standing or position of an orphan or ward. Under guardianship.

**Inter alia**. Amongst other things.

**Inter alios**. Amongst other people.

**Interregnum**. Between the reign. (When a country has no ruler between the end of one reign and the accession of a successor.)

**In toto**. In the whole thing. Completely.

**Intra vires**. Within the permitted powers (of someone). *See* **Ultra vires**.

**In utero**. In the womb.

**In vino veritas**. In wine, truth (truth coming out after too much drink).

**In vitro**. In glass. In a test-tube (for instance, in a laboratory).

**Ipso facto**. In the fact itself. By that very fact.

**Lacuna** (derived from **lacus**, lake, basin or hollow). A cavity. A hollow. A hiatus. A missing portion, for instance in an ancient document.

**Lapsus linguae**. A slip of the tongue.

**Libido**. Desire. Emotional craving promoting any human activity. Lust.

**Libra**. The Roman pound-weight of twelve ounces. (The abbreviation lb. is now used to indicate pound-weight, as in 10 lb, and the abbreviation £ to indicate the pound sterling.)

**Lingua franca**. A common tongue or language. Mixed language used as the language of commerce and industry throughout the Mediterranean.

**Locus**. Place. The exact locality of something. (Used technically in mathematics.)

**Locus classicus**. Place of the first class. The best-known and most authoritative passage on a particular subject.

**Locum tenens**. Holding the place. Acting deputy or substitute, especially for a member of the clergy or for a doctor.

**Loc. cit.** Short for **loco citato**. In the place cited. (Used in footnotes to mean that the source of the reference or quotation has already been given.)

**Magister Artium**, usually shortened to **M.A.** Master of Arts (university degree superior to Bachelor of Arts). *See* **Artium Baccalaureus**.

**Magnum opus.** Great work. Great literary or other artistic undertaking. The most important production of a writer or other artist. Masterpiece.

**M.D.**, short for **Medicinae Doctor** . Teacher of the Art of Healing (a title incorrectly given to those members of the medical profession who, although qualified to practice, have not attained doctorate status).

**Mea culpa.** My fault *or* by my fault.

**Medicinae Doctor**. *See* **M.D.**

**Memento mori.** Remember that you are to die. A reminder of death, such as a skull.

**Mens sana in corpore sano.** Sound *or* healthy mind in sound *or* healthy body.

**Minor.** Lesser.

**Minutiae.** Smallnesses. Precise details. Trivial details.

**Mirabile dictu** (Virgil). Wonderful in the saying. Wonderful to relate.

**Modus operandi.** Method of working. The way in which a person sets about working. The way in which a thing operates.

**Modus vivendi.** Way of living. Arrangement between people who have agreed to differ and/or to compromise.

**Mutatis mutandis.** The things that ought to be changed having been changed. After making the necessary changes.

**N.B.** *See* **Nota bene**.

**Nem. con.** (short for **nemine contradicente**). No one against. Unanimously.

**Ne plus ultra.** No more further. Much the best.

**Nexus** (from **necto**, I bind). A link. A connection.

**Nihil** or **nil**. Nothing. No number or result (especially in games).

**Nil desperandum** (Horace). Nothing meet for the despairing of. Nothing worthy of despair. Do not give up.

**Nolle prosequi.** Not to wish to pursue (for instance, a matter). Not to wish to proceed. (A prosecution is stopped by entry of a *nolle prosequi* when the court official judges that there is not enough evidence to justify proceeding.)

**Non compos mentis** (negative of **compos mentis** – *see entry*). Not in one's right mind.

**Non omnis moriar** (Horace). The whole of me will not die.

**Non sequitur.** It does not follow. An inference or conclusion that does not follow from its premises in the work quoted. A claim that is illogical.

**Nota bene** or **N.B.** Note well. Observe what follows. Take notice.

**Nucleus** (diminutive of **nux**, nut). (In astronomy) the condensed part of the head of a comet. The central part of the seed of a plant or, figuratively, of a story, of a community, of an empire, etc.

**Obiit** (followed by the date of death). He died. ('Obituary' comes from the same source.)

**Obiter.** By the way. On the journey. In passing. (**Obiter dictum** and **obiter dicta** refer to what is said by a judge to reinforce his judgement, though not essential to his decision.)

**Odium.** Hatred. Widespread dislike either incurred by people or relating to an action.

**Op. cit.**, from **opere citato**. In the work cited. (Similar to **loc. cit.** – *see entry*.)

**Pace**. In peace. (In announcing a contrary opinion) with due respect to. In all deference to.

**Pari passu**. With equal pace. At the same pace. On the same terms. At an equal rate of progress. Simultaneously.

**Passim**. Here and there. Far and wide. In every part. Indiscriminately. (Used in indexes to indicate too many instances scattered throughout to enumerate each one.)

**Paterfamilias** (strangely, not the more obviously grammatical **Paterfamiliae**). The father of the family. Head of the family (often used jocularly).

**Pax**. Peace. 'Truce!' (called out urgently).

**Pax Britannica** (derived from the original **Pax Romana** - *see below*). British peace. Peace imposed by British rule. (In both cases) peace imposed widely over the world by a powerful nation.

**Pax Romana**. Roman peace. Peace imposed by Roman rule.

**Per**. Through. By. By means of. Because of. **Per annum**: by the year *or* yearly. **Per caput** (*not* the illiterate **per capita**): a head, per head, each; **per diem**: by the day. **Per pro**, or **p.p.**, originally **per procurationem**: by the agency of *or* on behalf of (someone who is not himself or herself signing a document). **Per se**: by itself, *or* in itself, *or* intrinsically, *or* for its own sake.

**Per impossibile**. Through the impossible thing. (Hypothetically) even though it is impossible (as in: 'Assume, *per impossibile*, that…').

**Per pro**. *See* **per** *above*.

**Per se**. *See* **per** *above*.

**Persona non grata**. Person not in favour, unacceptable.

**Per stirpes**. Through stocks *or* stems (of trees or other plants). (In human beings) sources *or* origins. (Used by lawyers when distributing an inheritance among families.)

**Petitio principio**. Request on the principle. Begging the question. Assuming, as part of one's argument, the truth, in the matter under dispute. (*Not* provoking the question, or giving rise to the question – the illiterate usage all too common today.)

**Post eventum**. After the event.

**Post hoc ergo propter hoc**. *After* this therefore *because of* this. (Used fallaciously in argument to show supposedly that, because something *comes after* something, it can be inferred that the first thing *caused* the second thing.)

**Post mortem**. After death. A clinical examination of a dead body. A discussion of something after it is over (for instance in a card game such as bridge).

**Post scriptum** (usually shortened to **P. S.**) After the thing that has been written. Thing written afterwards. Addition usually at the end of the letter after the signature.

**PP**. *See* **Per pro**.

**Prima facie**. At first sight. Apparently.

**Primus inter pares**. First among equals. The senior member of a group of colleagues, *or* their spokesman.

**Pro**. On behalf of. In favour of (as in people who are pro Latin).

**Pro bono publico**. For the public good. (Used for lawyers, or for their work, when they on occasion undertake work without payment.)

**Pro forma**. For the sake of form. (A term applied to practices or documents done as a pure formality, perfunctorily, or seek to satisfy the minimum requirements.)

**Promoveatur ut amoveatur**. Let him be promoted so that he may be removed. (The process by which an unwanted person is 'kicked upstairs' to a post with more dignity but less influence.)

**Pro rata**. According to the rate. Divided in proportion.

**Pro tem., pro tempore**. For the time. For the time being.

**P.S.** *See* **Post scriptum**.

**Proximo**, often abbreviated to **prox**. **Mense** is understood after it. In, *or* of, the next month, as in 'on the 3rd prox.'

**Qua** (short for **qua via** or **qua parte** meaning 'by which way' and 'by which part' respectively). By whom *or* by which. As. In the capacity of.

**Quantum**. How much? An amount. As much as is wanted. As much as is necessary. As much as is allowed. (Quantum theory is the hypothesis according to which the atom is stable, and also according to which, in radiation, energy of electrons is discharged, but continuously and uniformly although in separate amounts or quanta.)

**Quasi**. As if. That is to say. As it were. (When hyphenated with a noun or adjective as in 'quasi-intelligently) not really.

**Quid pro quo**. What for what. Something for something (*or* one thing for another). Something in return. An equivalent

**Quod erat demonstrandum** (often shortened to **Q.E.D.**) Which was meet to be proved. The thing which is to be proved. (By implication) the thing that now has been proved.

**Quod vide**, abbreviated to **q.v.** Which thing see *or* see that thing (imperative). See (telling the reader to look for the word just mentioned, perhaps in the glossary of a book).

**Quondam**. Once. Formerly. (Referring to something that once had a specific character, but no longer has it) sometime *or* former.

**Quorum**. Of whom (in the context of: out of whom it is our will let you be [whatever]). A fixed number of members of an assembly, society or board of directors that must be present in order to make the proceedings valid.

**Quo vadis**. Where are you going to *or* hastening to?

**q.v.** *See* **Quod vide**.

**Rara avis**. A rare bird. A kind of person or thing rarely encountered. A rarity.

**Re**. In the matter of. With regard to. Concerning.

**Reductio ad absurdum**. Reduction to the absurd. The reduction to absurdity. Proof of the falsity of (for instance, of a principle, the proof being that the principle leads to a logical result that is absurd and therefore impossible).

**Referendum**. That which ought to be laid before (originally, laid before the Senate). A referring of certain political questions to the electorate for a direct decision by a general vote on a single question.

**Regina**. Queen. The reigning queen (for instance, used in official signatures to public proclamations).

**Repetitio mater memoriae**. Repetition is the mother of memory *or* of the ability to remember. (Author's comment: may those words ring in your ears, gentle reader, as you work your way through this book.)

**Requiescat in pace**. May he *or* she rest in peace. (An expression wishing eternal rest and peace to someone who has died, typically appearing on headstones.)

**Res ipsa loquitur**. The thing itself speaks. The thing speaks for itself. (Used in court-rooms to imply something to be so obvious that it does not need proof.)

**R.I.P.** *See* **Requiescat in pace**.

**Rigor mortis.** Stiffness of death. Stiffening of the body after death.

**Rostrum**. That which gnaws. (In birds) a beak. The platform for public speaking, originally in the Roman Forum, which was adorned with 'beaks' of captured galleys. Pulpit. Office that enables someone to gain the public ear.

**Scintilla**. A spark. A glimmer. A faint trace (as in 'not a scintilla of evidence').

**Sequentes** *or* **sequentia**, usually shortened to **Seq**. The following words *or* lines. What follows.

**Sic**. Thus; used in brackets in quotations in order to show that the writer has made a mistake – as in. '*Gwynn's* (sic) *Latin* is a wonderful book.'

**Sine die**. Without day. Without (setting) a date (of business indefinitely adjourned).

**Sine qua non**. Without which not. Anything indispensable, and without which another thing cannot exist. An indispensable condition or qualification.

**Species**. Appearance. Idea. Kind *or* species *or* division of a genus. *See* **Genus**.

**Stadium**. A classical Greek measurement of about 202 yards. A course for a foot-race or a chariot-race. A modern athletics or sports-ground.

**Status quo ante**, usually shortened to **status quo**. The state in which before. The same state as before (as in 'maintaining the *status quo*').

**Stet**. Let it stand. Do not delete. This instruction cancels an alteration in proofreading.

**Sub judice**. Under the judge. What is to remain under judgement *or* consideration. Still before the courts. Not yet decided.

**Subpoena**. Under penalty. A writ commanding that a person attend a court of justice, under the penalty of the punishment if he or she does not.

**Sub rosa**. Under the rose. Privately or furtively.

**Suggestio falsi**. Suggestion of (something) false. (In law) a positive misrepresentation, which does not go as far as a lie, but is a conscious concealment of truth. *See also* **Suppressio veri**.

**Sui generis**. Of its own kind. Unique. *See also* **Eiusdem generis**.

**Supra**. Above. Previously (typically used in a book to refer to something that has gone before).

**Suppressio veri**. Suppression of something true. A misrepresentation by concealment of one or more facts that ought to be made known in the interest of justice.

**Tabula rasa**. A erased tablet. An empty slate. (Metaphorically) an empty page. (Figuratively) the human mind at birth, when it has no inborn impressions of any kind.

**Tempus fugit**. Time flees. Time flies.

**Terra firma**. Firm land. Dry land.

**Thesaurus** (Latiniscd Greek word) Treasure. An elaborate dictionary, commonly giving the closest alternatives to each individual word.

**Tumor**. Swelling. Protuberance.

**Ultimatum** (late Latin, from verb **ultimo**). A thing which has come to an end. A final proposal or statement of terms, the rejection of which by the other party may lead to a rupture or, in the case of two countries in opposition, a declaration of war.

**Ultimo**. In the last (applying to months) – opposite of **proximo**, *see entry*.

**Ultra vires**. Beyond powers. Beyond (one's) legal powers.

**Vade mecum**. Go with me. (Metaphorically) a little book or something carried about on the person.

**Velis nolis** (origin of 'willy-nilly'). May you wish, may you not wish. Whether you like it or not.

**Verbatim** (derived from the Latin **verbum** in medieval Latin). Word-for-word (as in 'It was copied *verbatim*').

**Versus**, often shortened to **vs.** and **v.** Against (used in legal cases and games, as in 'Regina vs. Smith' and 'England v. Australia').

**Veto**. I forbid. The constitutional right of a sovereign or other head of state to reject a legislative enactment. A prohibition.

**Via**. Way. Road. (Used in the ablative as a preposition) by way of; through.

**Vice versa**. The change having been turned. The other way round.

**Vide** (imperative). See. (Often used in books with reference to what is else-where – for instance, **Vide supra**, See above, *and* **Vide infra**, See below.)

**Viva voce**. With the living voice. Oral (as in 'oral examination').

**Vae victis** (Roman expression). Woe to the conquered!

**Viz** (shortened **videlicet**, itself shortened from **videre licet**). It is lawful to see. It is permitted to see. One may see. That is to say. To wit. Namely.

**Vox populi**. The voice of the people. Public opinion. The general verdict. Popular belief or rumour.

# Further Reading

I expect for the first time in the entire history of literature, biblio-graphical pride of place goes, not to a book, but to a bookshop devoted exclusively to the classics, The Hellenic Book Service (89, Fortess Road, London, NW5 1AG). It was founded in 1966 just when the abandon-ment of Latin in education was starting, and its continuing existence in our present era is surely verging on the miraculous. To be found there is everything in print and, most valuable of all, a large collection of sec-ond-hand books in the basement, which between them have contributed greatly to my decisions on how best to put this book together. **Vivat semper** the shop, and **vivat quam diutissime** its co-founder and present owner, Mrs. Frederick (Monica) Williams.

Pride of equal second place unquestionably goes to the three grammar books by Dr. Benjamin Hall Kennedy: *Kennedy's Public School Latin Grammar*, published in 1871; *Kennedy's Revised Latin Primer*; and *Kennedy's Shorter Latin Primer*, published later in the nineteenth century. (The last two were very satisfactorily revised by Sir Henry Mountford in 1930 and 1931 respectively.) One or other of the Kennedy's were used in almost all schools in England for about a century, and indeed they are genuine clas-sics of English Literature – until recently, the word 'Kennedy's' was sufficient to identify them even in ordinary conversation.

Magnificent also is *Gildersleeve's Latin Grammar*, 1867. It has, however, the disadvantage that it was published too early to take advantage of Dr. ~Kennedy's brilliant innovation in the case-order of nouns, adjectives and pronouns. Up until Kennedy's time the order worldwide had always been nom., gen., dat., acc., voc., abl., or abl., voc. From Kennedy's time onwards all Latin textbooks in England (including of course this book) have followed his example, though none have done so in America or almost anywhere outside the former British Empire, English-speaking or otherwise.

For a long time (until the 1960s), considered indispensable for use with 'Kennedy's', were *Latin Prose Composition* by M. A. North and the Rev. A. E. Hillard, first published in the late nineteenth century, and two books introductory to it *Elementary Latin Exercises* (for practising English into Latin) and *Elementary Latin Translation* (for Latin into English) both of them by the Rev. A. E. Hillard and C. G. Botting and both published in the early part of the twentieth century by Rivingtons. Their purpose was to provide sufficient exercises for all the Latin learnt in the Kennedy books to ensure the ability to understand and use effort-lessly each element of grammar learnt. (They actually refer to relevant places in Kennedy's books for each set of exercises.) Mastery of the con-tents of the Kennedy, Hillard and Botting and North and Hillard books will produce an excellent Latinist.

Perhaps surprisingly, given how opposed are modern education-theories to the traditional manner in which the books just mentioned teach, all of them are at present in print.

The following books are all of them completely sound and useful. Most of them are not now in print. I have given them in date-order of publication, with the exception of the first two on the list, which I consider to be of exceptional usefulness. As to the first of the two, if I were asked to choose one book to add to the ones so far mentioned, I should choose *Foundations for Latin Prose Composition* by L. W. P. Lewis and E. H. Goddard (Heinemann, 1931). The second of my choices highlighted here is *Latin at Eleven* by G. M. Singleton (Macmillan, 1962), valuable not least because – but by no means only because – its contents amount to completely authentic evidence in confirmation of what stage of Latin was, until recently, reached by children of the most ordinary intelligence by the age of eleven. The other books:

*A First Latin Course* by Dr. Sir William Smith (John Murray, 1860)

*Sermo Latinus – A Short Guide to Latin Prose Composition* by J. P. Postgate, despite its age as useful as any of them (n.p. 1902).

*Latin Prose Composition* by E. C. Marchant and G. Watson (Bell, 1929).

*The Latin Sentence – an Outline of the Essential Constructions in Latin Syntax* by M. Toyne and P. H. Sykes, a booklet of only thirty pages but very useful (Evans Bros., 1933).

*Civis Romanus – A Reader for the First Two Years of Latin* by J. M. Cobban and R. Colebourn (Methuen, 1936).

*Mentor – An Exercise Book and Companion to "Civis Romanus"* by R. Colebourn (Methuen, 1938).

*'Bradley's Arnold' Latin Prose Composition* Revised by Sir James Mountford (Longmans, 1938).

*Facilitas – An Introduction to Latin Prose Composition* by O. N. Jones (Blackie, 1951).

*The Latin Way* by K. D. Robinson and R. L. Chambers (Christopher's, 1947).

*Latin Sentence and Idiom* by R. Colebourn (Methuen, 1948).

*Via Vertendi – A Latin Unseen Course* by B. W. M. Young (Longmans, Green & Co., 1952). Full of useful advice on translating from Latin.

*The Approach to Latin Writing* by James Paterson and Edwin Macnaughton (Oliver and Boyd, 1953).

*A New Latin Composition* by Max I. Machin (Harrap & Co., 1960).

*A Basic Latin Grammar* by C. W. E. Peckett and A. R. Munday (Rivingtons, 1966).

Of the modern Latin textbooks, there is not one that I can safely recommend. Apart from anything else, even of the best ones all are actually *deficient* in one or other respects. For instance, many of them do what was never done before recently: omitting the vocative case other than in footnotes. There is no adequate reason for leaving out a case at all, let alone one that is quite often used, as the vocative is. It does not even make learning the words by heart easier. Other modern books even leave out completely an entire tense, the future perfect tense. And so on.

Typically useful dictionaries, all in print, are, in descending order of size:

*A Latin Dictionary* by Charlton Lewis and Charles Short.

*Cassell's New Latin–English English–Latin* Dictionary.

*Collins Gem Latin Dictionary – Latin–English English–Latin.*

Of several books on the correct pronunciation of classical Latin, *Vox Latina – A Guide to the Pronunciation of Classical Latin* by W. Sydney Allen (Cambridge University Press, 1965) is sufficiently comprehensive and well-argued to stand on its own.

For more general classical knowledge, The Everyman's Library *A Smaller Classical Dictionary* (Dent, 1952) is a treasure of information on the people and places of classical antiquity up till the time of the early Christian Fathers.

# Acknowledgements

Most of all, we – you, my readers, and I – owe this book to the publishing team at Ebury Press. My experience with Ebury has been consistently – and all the more so by contrast with experiences with their publishers of other authors of my acquaintance – a joy: professional, efficient, encouraging, calm when difficulties have arisen, unfailingly courteous whatever the pressure. I am going therefore to name them all. Mr. Jake Lingwood, whose team it is. Miss Elen Jones, editor, who was specifically responsible for the detailed handling of the project in every respect. Mr. Anthony Heller, in charge of production. Mrs. Claire Scott, who at the time of writing this has scarcely featured yet, but with whom, judging from my experience with my previous book published by Ebury, I shall be having a most enjoyable and valuable immediately-post-publication relationship.

The following were employed by Ebury on a freelance basis: Mrs. Mary Chamberlain, copyeditor, who I have been told is the best in her field and who certainly supported this assessment with the brilliance – I do not exaggerate – of her work on this book. Mrs. Belinda Baker, the proofreader. Sarah Newton, Latin consultant. Mr. Edward Pickford, the typesetter, who I have also been told is the best in his field.

Outside the Ebury team, the following have helped me, most of them on a purely voluntary basis, with their only motive that of making the book a better one than it otherwise would have been.

Much the greatest contributor was Mr. John Daly, a highly competent Latinist who became involved at quite a late stage, drastically reorganised the parts of the book, and also made significant additions to the text and many equally significant corrections. Also very valuable in the help they gave were his two children, Mlle. Thérèse, aged sixteen, and M. Patrick, aged fourteen, who took on the demanding responsibility of checking the text, and in particular the vocabularies, for accuracy in the tiniest details, which included extensive verification of the macrons. Professor Colin Leach, formerly of Oxford University, and by far the most accomplished of the Latinists whom I consulted, was kind enough to go through a fairly late draft, and picked up a number of errors as well as offering valuable suggestions which I was grateful to accept. As remarkable as any, in the help he gave me, was a former Latin student of mine (via Skype), Mr. Khush James. Early on when I was putting this book together, he offered me his help in an editing capacity. I submitted to him a draft, confident, from my knowledge of him, that he would make a useful contribution even though he was just turning eighteen, and, to my astonishment, his many comments were genuinely of a professional standard, and I was pleased to adopt most of them. My wife Frederica, with much else on her plate, undertook the labour of painstakingly going through the typeset proof to try to eliminate any tiny errors that the rest of us may have missed. Finally, I consider myself fortunate to have had Miss Cat Ledger, my agent, once again by my side.

My deep gratitude to all.

# Index